American Journalism and "Fake News"

Recent Titles in Contemporary Debates

AMERICAN JOURNALISM AND "FAKE NEWS"

Examining the Facts

Seth Ashley, Jessica Roberts, and Adam Maksl

Contemporary Debates

An Imprint of ABC-CLIO, LLC
Santa Barbara, California • Denver, Colorado

Library of Congress Cataloging-in-Publication Data

Names: Ashley, Seth, author. | Roberts, Jessica (Jessica Stewart), author. |
  Maksl, Adam, author.
Title: American journalism and "fake news" : examining the facts /
  Seth Ashley, Jessica Roberts, and Adam Maksl.
Description: Santa Barbara, Caifornia : ABC-CLIO, 2018. | Series: Contemporary
  debates | Includes bibliographical references and index.
Identifiers: LCCN 2018035231 (print) | LCCN 2018047013 (ebook) |
  ISBN 9781440861840 (ebook) | ISBN 9781440861833 (alk. paper)
Subjects: LCSH: Journalism—United States—History—21st century. |
  Journalism—Objectivity—United States.
Classification: LCC PN4867.2 (ebook) | LCC PN4867.2 .A84 2018 (print) |
  DDC 071/.309051—dc23
LC record available at https://lccn.loc.gov/2018035231

ISBN: 978-1-4408-6183-3 (print)
       978-1-4408-6184-0 (ebook)

23 22 21 20 19   1 2 3 4 5

This book is also available as an eBook.

ABC-CLIO
An Imprint of ABC-CLIO, LLC

ABC-CLIO, LLC
130 Cremona Drive, P.O. Box 1911
Santa Barbara, California 93116-1911
www.abc-clio.com

This book is printed on acid-free paper ∞

Manufactured in the United States of America

Contents

How to Use This Book

American Journalism and "Fake News": Examining the Facts is part of ABC-CLIO's Contemporary Debates reference series. Each title in this series, which is intended for use by high school and undergraduate students as well as members of the general public, examines the veracity of controversial claims or beliefs surrounding a major political/cultural issue in the United States. The purpose of this series is to give readers a clear and unbiased understanding of current issues by informing them about falsehoods, half-truths, and misconceptions—and confirming the factual validity of other assertions—that have gained traction in America's political and cultural discourse. Ultimately, this series has been crafted to give readers the tools for a fuller understanding of controversial issues, policies, and laws that occupy center stage in American life and politics.

Each volume in this series identifies 30–40 questions swirling about the larger topic under discussion. These questions are examined in individualized entries, which are in turn arranged in broad subject chapters that cover certain aspects of the issue being examined, for example, history of concern about the issue, potential economic or social impact, or findings of the latest scholarly research.

Each chapter features 4–10 individual entries. Each entry begins by stating an important and/or well-known **Question** about the issue being studied—for example, "Do traditional newspapers still play a role in modern journalism?" or "Does President Trump use the term 'fake news' to try to discredit any reporting that is critical of him or his administration?"

The entry then provides a concise and objective one- or two-paragraph **Answer** to the featured question, followed by a more comprehensive, detailed explanation of **The Facts**. This latter portion of each entry uses quantifiable, evidence-based information from respected sources to fully address each question and provide readers with the information they need to be informed citizens. Importantly, entries will also acknowledge instances in which conflicting data exist or data are incomplete. Finally, each entry concludes with a **Further Reading** section, providing users with information on other important and/or influential resources.

The ultimate purpose of every book in the Contemporary Debates series is to reject "false equivalence," in which demonstrably false beliefs or statements are given the same exposure and credence as the facts; to puncture myths that diminish our understanding of important policies and positions; to provide needed context for misleading statements and claims; and to confirm the factual accuracy of other assertions. In other words, volumes in this series are being crafted to clear the air surrounding some of the most contentious and misunderstood issues of our time—not just add another layer of obfuscation and uncertainty to the debate.

❖

Introduction: Journalism's Role in Democratic Society

Journalism is the process of representing reality in a way that aims to inform and empower citizens with a truthful account of important issues and events. At its best, journalism can serve as the cornerstone of democracy by facilitating informed self-government and supporting a shared civic life. At its worst, journalism can distort, mislead, and distract. Good journalism can be identified by its commitment to the ideals of verification, independence, transparency, and accountability.

It's no secret that journalism is an embattled component of American life. Journalism is frequently accused of being biased, polarizing, sensational, and "fake." These days, it's rare that people even discuss "journalism." Instead, we hear about "the news" or "news media" or simply "the media." But journalism is a unique form of communication with specific responsibilities and goals. While there is no one way to define or practice journalism, many people who work in the field and who study it agree that good journalism delivers accurate and impartial news and information based on the ideals of accuracy and fairness. By uncovering previously unknown information and putting facts in context, journalism generally aims to serve some larger public service related to the needs of democratic society. It helps citizens make informed decisions about their lives and communities by serving as a monitor to power and by providing a public forum. It can be entertaining as well as informative, it can be aimed at large mass audiences or smaller niche groups, and its focus can range from local to global. It can be delivered through a range of media formats, including newspapers, magazines, radio, television, the Internet, and mobile devices. Whatever form it takes, journalism continues to play a significant role in American life as its best practitioners aspire to provide a truthful account of important issues and events.

It hasn't always been this way, and it's impossible to define journalism today without considering its storied past. Modern journalism, with its orientation toward ideals such as objectivity and fairness, is a 20th-century invention, but something like it has been around as long as human civilization. For most of human history, information and knowledge were shared through word of mouth by poets and storytellers. As written language developed, the few monks and scribes who could read and write were commissioned to record religious texts and philosophical tracts. Ancient Romans were perhaps the first to post bulletins on public message boards more than 2,000 years ago. But it was the arrival of the printing press—essentially the world's first Xerox machine—in 1456 that made mass communication possible as printers and publishers gained the ability to reach an increasingly literate audience. The world's first newspaper was printed in Germany in 1605, and the first newspaper in the American colonies appeared in 1690 in Boston. Colonial newspapers reflected the interests of their readership, comprised mostly of small numbers of wealthy and educated men involved in local politics and commerce. But this era coincided with emerging concepts of individual liberty and freedom from government censorship. The famous John Peter Zenger trial of 1735 established the idea that a democratic press should be free to criticize public officials, which set the stage for the First Amendment to the Constitution, adopted in 1791. The First Amendment enshrined the concept of press freedom and its importance to democratic self-governance.

In the early- to mid-1800s, printers (those who owned printing presses) gained unprecedented political freedom but remained aligned with the political organizations that funded them, and the content generated by this "partisan press" advocated for their parties' interests. Despite their political freedom, printers also were heavily subsidized by government through printing contracts and postal subsidies. They did not operate for profit, and they stressed news and politics over entertainment and gossip. Spurred by the Industrial Revolution and the rise of capitalism, the commercial press emerged in the mid-1800s as publishers realized they could make a profit by making content more objective and less partisan. This shift allowed them to reach a wider audience and sell space to a greater variety of advertisers. "Penny papers" made news available to an emerging middle class that clamored for political and business coverage as well as scandal and human-interest stories. The latter trend grew in the late 1800s as "yellow journalism" emphasized a mix of sensational stories about crime and celebrities along with the earliest investigative reporting, exposing corruption in government and business. As newspapers began to attract more readers, commercial pressures led editors to strive for impartiality—or "objectivity"—in their content in order to secure broad appeal. Objective journalism became the norm only in the 20th century as reporting slowly became a reputable profession.

Modern journalism reflects these contradictory origins. Some news outlets look increasingly like the early partisan press, while others continue to strive for independence and impartiality. Virtually all news outlets are subject to commercial and market-based financial pressures, which can have both positive and negative effects on news content. The high watermark of modern journalism is often thought to be coverage of the Watergate scandal, which ultimately ended the Nixon presidency in the 1970s. Another celebrated era of news coverage was the 1960s civil rights movement, when journalists' reporting on racist oppression helped dismantle Jim Crow elements of the American South and generate public support for federal civil rights legislation. Newspapers were praised for revealing government deceptions about the Vietnam War when they published the secret "Pentagon Papers" in 1971. In these cases, news organizations served the public's need for truth and transparency in democratic life.

Other examples, however, show a different trend. Some critics believe that news coverage of the 2003 Iraq War was notoriously one-sided in favor of a U.S. invasion. Journalists continue to struggle to cover acts of terrorism in proper proportion to other important topics. In addition, squeezed news budgets over the past decade generally have led to less original and investigative reporting overall as the field of journalism struggles to find its way forward.

This complex history is reflected in long-standing debates over journalism and its role in society. Despite its lofty ideals, journalism has never been perfect. One of the field's most famous practitioners and critics, Walter Lippmann (1889–1974), highlighted journalism's shortcomings in his 1922 book *Public Opinion*. Lippmann wrote about "the world outside and the pictures in our heads" to note the difference between reality as it is represented through the news media (pictures in our heads) and reality as it actually exists (the world outside). Journalists are constantly constructing our perceived reality when they decide what to cover and how to cover it (and what *not* to cover). That doesn't mean journalists have some nefarious agenda aimed at subverting truth and dominating discourse.

To the contrary, journalists are more likely to be diligent gatherers of information doing their best to digest and present mostly mundane facts in a coherent manner as accurately and transparently as possible, even as they contend with a range of challenges and pressures. In producing journalism, it is impossible to completely close the inevitable gap between representation and reality. But many practitioners believe that the goal should be to make it as narrow as possible.

John Dewey (1859–1952), a prominent educator and one of Lippmann's contemporaries, agreed with many of Lippmann's concerns about the potential for journalism to serve as a vehicle for creating an informed society. Dewey called Lippmann's work "perhaps the most effective indictment of democracy as currently conceived ever penned" (Dewey 1922, 286). Dewey agreed that news is forced to focus too narrowly on decontextualized events rather than describing the more abstract conditions and forces that regulate the flow of society. But Dewey thought news could do a better job of "treating news events in the light of a continuing study and record of underlying conditions" (Dewey 1922, 288). Dewey rejected Lippmann's proposal to turn governance over to an army of experts who would effectively manage public affairs. Instead, he argued for a greater commitment to the education of both citizens and journalists and for "continuous reporting of the news as the truth, events signalized to be sure, but signals of hidden facts, of facts set in relation to one another, a picture of situations on which men can act intelligently" (Dewey 1922, 288). Dewey believed in the potential of journalism to accurately inform and educate the public in a way that could facilitate effective self-governance.

Lippmann and Dewey had different views on how to handle the challenges posed by the needs of democracy, but both agreed that creating an informed citizenry is no easy task considering the limitations of journalists and citizens alike. How we come to know the world around us is a fundamental dilemma, and it is not a new one. Going back at least as far as the ancient Greeks, the philosopher Plato outlined the same problem in his allegory of the cave, in which prisoners who could see only shadows on a cave wall could not know the difference between objects being represented and the objects themselves. The gap between representation and reality is central to the question of how we acquire knowledge (philosophers call this "epistemology"), and it has captivated thinkers ever since. Such philosophical questions might seem a far cry from journalism, but in defining and examining the field, it is useful to consider the fundamental problem of how we know our world.

In a more modern and practical context, journalism is often taken for granted as a practice or product that plays some undefined but central role in our shared civic and political lives. For those of us who consume news at all (many simply don't), we often scan headlines and read articles in newspapers and news feeds, snacking on bits of information that seem relevant to us in our quest to know the world around us and to make decisions that will yield positive outcomes. We consume television and radio broadcasts, often passively accepting what journalists and their bosses have deemed to be the most important news of the day. We have a sense that news is not supposed to be biased, so we are on the lookout for spin and propaganda. But beyond this, most people are not asked to think much about the role of journalism in their lives, and few know much about the processes involved in "making" the news. A range of forces and influences—from advertisers to nonprofit groups to simple time constraints—dictate at least to some degree how news is reported. Journalism today faces incredible pressures and threats due to the changing economic and technological environments in which news is produced, distributed, and consumed. And to further complicate matters, news today can be produced by anyone with access to a computer or smartphone. On one hand, this remarkable innovation helps remove barriers to access that citizens once faced, allowing a greater multitude of voices to share their perspectives and participate in public conversations. On the other hand, this development has opened the information floodgates, making it harder than ever to sort through all that is available to us and separate the wheat from the chaff. Meanwhile, the modern media environment makes it easier than ever to retreat into homogenous spheres where people can luxuriate exclusively in the ideas and opinions that are most aligned with their own (sometimes referred to as "echo chambers" or "filter bubbles").

Thus, journalism today faces many challenges—so much so that questions have been raised about its usefulness and even its capacity for survival. To some, journalism has been subsumed by the larger realm of digital communications, where everything online appears to be an equally valid piece of "content." Broadly, the effects have been a steady decline in how much citizens trust news media as well as a diminishment in the size and influence of the journalistic product. As some traditional news outlets go out of business and close up shop, others are being consolidated under ever-larger corporate owners, many of which have no real interest in producing high-quality journalism. Shrinking budgets lead to job cuts, which means fewer journalists working in the industry today. Those who remain have fewer resources to do their work, and they are forced to produce a greater volume of work across a variety of platforms. It's no longer enough to report and write an article; today many journalists also take photographs, shoot videos, create graphics, post on social media, respond to online commenters, create podcasts, and so on. For most working journalists, it is harder today than any time in recent history to do good work.

But the picture is not entirely bleak. A few news outlets have bucked the trend and actually invested resources in their staffs and their products. "New media" start-ups continue to pop up on the web all the time, and some have become well established and respected outlets alongside their traditional brethren. Many of these digital-only outlets, ranging from ProPublica to Politico to Vice to BuzzFeed, have produced important work that once was the province of daily metropolitan newspapers, where most original reporting has historically originated. The United States has a modest public media presence compared to other developed nations, but PBS (television's Public Broadcasting Service) and NPR (National Public Radio) continue to thrive among niche audiences. Cable television news is as profitable and popular as ever, although this format has come to favor commentary and regurgitation of partisan talking points over original reporting. Most Americans continue to get news from local television stations, which provide some valuable journalism but are dominated by sports, weather, commercials, and lighthearted features about the community. In the digital realm, search engines such as Google and social media platforms such as Facebook and Twitter dominate the web, especially for younger Americans. Web users often turn to these platforms for news, but of course, they produce no original journalism of their own. Instead, they collect, or "aggregate," content from all types of sources, which might or might not include journalism depending on the user's profile. Even if a news feed includes journalism, that doesn't mean any revenue is making it back to the original content creator. Meanwhile, social media valuations skyrocket not because they have created any content of their own but because of the immense amounts of data they can collect about their vast audiences.

In this context, journalists and news organizations continue to seek new business models and new methods for reaching audiences and for informing and engaging citizens in various ways. Ultimately, journalism today exists at a crossroads, and ongoing changes in technology, economics, politics, and culture will influence the path forward.

FURTHER READING

Alterman, Eric. 2008. "Out of Print." *The New Yorker*, March 24. https://www.newyorker.com/magazine/2008/03/31/out-of-print.

Benkler, Yochai. 2006. *The Wealth of Networks: How Social Production Transforms Markets and Freedom*. New Haven, CT; London: Yale University Press.

Christians, Clifford G., Theodore L. Glasser, Denis McQuail, Kaarle Nordenstreng, and Robert A. White. 2009. *Normative Theories of the Media: Journalism in Democratic Societies*. Urbana: University of Illinois Press.

Dewey, John. 1922. "'Public Opinion' (Review)." *New Republic*, 286–288. http://www.unz.org/Pub/NewRepublic-1922may03-00286.

Kovach, Bill, and Tom Rosenstiel. 2014. *The Elements of Journalism: What Newspeople Should Know and the Public Should Expect*. Revised and updated 3rd ed. New York: Three Rivers Press.

Lippmann, Walter. 1922. *Public Opinion*. New York: Harcourt.

McChesney, Robert, and John Nichols. 2010. *The Death and Life of American Journalism: The Media Revolution That Will Begin the World Again*. 1st Nation Books. Philadelphia, PA: Nation Books.

McChesney, Robert W. 2013. *Digital Disconnect: How Capitalism Is Turning the Internet against Democracy*. New York: The New Press.

McChesney, Robert Waterman, and Victor W. Pickard, eds. 2011. *Will the Last Reporter Please Turn Out the Lights: The Collapse of Journalism and What Can Be Done to Fix It*. New York: The New Press. Distributed by Perseus Distribution.

Schudson, Michael. 2008. *Why Democracies Need an Unlovable Press*. Cambridge, UK; Malden, MA: Polity.

Schudson, Michael. 2012. *The Sociology of News*. 2nd ed. Contemporary Societies. New York: W. W. Norton & Company.

Shoemaker, Pamela J., and Stephen D. Reese. 2014. *Mediating the Message in the 21st Century: A Media Sociology Perspective*. 3rd ed. New York: Routledge/Taylor & Francis Group.

Starr, Paul. 2009. "Goodbye to the Age of Newspapers (Hello to a New Era of Corruption)." *New Republic*, March 3. https://newrepublic.com/article/64252/goodbye-the-age-newspapers-hello-new-era-corruption.

1

Journalists: What They Do and Whom They Work For

Journalists are often thought to have a significant amount of autonomy to tell stories that are newsworthy and of substantial interest to the public. But journalists work within cultural and professional contexts that affect the work they produce. Though many say they follow professional norms, journalists work within organizations and social structures that indirectly influence content. As it has become easier and less expensive to produce and distribute mass messages in the era of digital media, understanding who journalists are and the contexts in which they work is essential to being media literate. If today's technological resources and tools allow anyone to publish, how do we identify the work of journalists, and what, if anything, sets it apart from other forms of media? Exploring individual journalists, the work they do, and the organizations in which they do it shows the complex system in which journalism is produced.

Q1. ARE JOURNALISTS REPRESENTATIVE OF THE POPULATION THEY SERVE?

Answer: Generally speaking, no. The digital age has made determining who is a journalist an increasingly difficult task, particularly considering the rise of bloggers and citizen journalists. Therefore, developing descriptive profiles of the demographics of journalists in the 21st century is increasingly difficult. That said, scholars have attempted to do just that among journalists who work for mainstream or established news and media organizations, particularly newspapers and broadcast stations. In general, professional journalists in the United States are not representative of the overall population they aim to serve. They are more likely to be white, male, and middle-aged, though television stations tend to be more diverse in these areas. Additionally, journalists tend to have higher educational attainment and make slightly higher salaries compared to the general U.S. population. Finally, while Democrats generally outnumber Republicans in newsrooms, the majority of journalists consider themselves to be politically independent.

The Facts: Journalists have been traditionally defined by where they worked; if someone worked for a newspaper or broadcast station and they engaged in work that helped produce or publish journalism, then they were a journalist. In fact, where there are legal definitions of journalist, such as in state shield laws that allow reporters to keep sources confidential, there is almost always a reference to specific media channels like newspapers or television or requirements that one must be employed and receive income as a journalist to be considered one. However, as the barriers to entry into mass communication practices have been lowered, questions have arisen as to whether those who engage in communications practices aimed at reaching the public are in fact journalists. Should bloggers, those with popular YouTube channels, or others who engage in information collection and dissemination about current events be considered journalists? It is an ongoing debate that has both legal and ethical implications, especially in the United States where generally there has been a hesitancy to define journalist and journalism for fear that such a definition might lead to increased control, especially from the government, which could lead to First Amendment challenges.

Despite the challenges of defining who is and is not a journalist in broader society, most Americans still get most of their news through professional news outlets. According to the Pew Research Center (Mitchell et al. 2016), 57 percent of Americans get news often from television and 38 percent often get news from online sources. Among online news consumers, 76 percent responded that they sometimes or often get that information from professional news outlets. Therefore, it's useful and important to understand the nature of journalists working in those professional news organizations.

However, even within professional news organizations, defining who is a journalist has become nearly as difficult as defining journalists in broader society. The American Society of News Editors (ASNE), formerly the American Society of Newspaper Editors, has conducted a survey every year since 1978 in which it has counted the numbers of journalists working in newsrooms. For most of the history, the organization included specific jobs in newsrooms that it considered journalistic, such as reporters, editors, photojournalists, designers, video producers, and the like. But as newsrooms have expanded to include job titles like content coach, social media manager, and audience engagement analyst, for example, the organization has likewise expanded its definition to include all those who contribute in some way to journalism being created. The Radio and Television Digital News Association (RTDNA), formerly the Radio and Television News Directors Association (RTNDA), likewise conducts a yearly survey of TV and radio newsrooms, and its results have shown growth in positions that were rare or nonexistent in past eras of TV news, including multimedia journalists (MMJs, also known as backpack journalists), who go out in the field on their own without camera operators or field producers, and increased numbers of staff devoted solely to content development for the web and social media. There are multiple occupations reported to the Bureau of Labor Statistics (BLS) that would likely include journalists, most notably the categories for "Reporters, Correspondents, and Broadcast News Analysts" and "Editors," though it's difficult to determine where new positions focused on social media or technology within newsrooms fit within the BLS data.

These changing definitions and criteria make it difficult to develop demographic, geographic, or psychographic profiles of journalists. That said, there have been many attempts to do so over the past few decades. For example, organizations such as ASNE have been surveying newspapers (and, in the past decade, online-only organizations) since 1974, and RTDNA/RTNDA has been surveying television and broadcast stations since 1994. Additionally, scholars have been developing profiles of the journalistic profession since the early 1970s, when University of Chicago researchers published the first comprehensive national study of journalists (Johnstone, Slawski, and Bowman 1976). Scholars from Indiana University have published findings from additional national surveys every decade since in their American Journalist series (Weaver and Wilhoit 1986, 1996; Weaver et al. 2007; Willnat, Weaver, and Wilhoit 2017).

Demographically, journalists tend to be older and whiter and are more likely to be male than the overall U.S. population. They are much more likely to have a bachelor's degree than the overall population and are slightly more highly paid than the average U.S. worker. They are also more likely than the average American to be politically independent.

According to the most recent study by the Indiana University researchers (Willnat, Weaver, and Wilhoit 2017), in the survey conducted in 2013, the median age of journalists was 47 years, compared to 37 years in 1971, 32 years in 1982, 36 years in 1992, and 41 years in 2002.

Women make up slightly more than one-third of overall newsrooms, with the percentage of women in TV news at 44 percent in 2017 per RTDNA (Papper 2017), and the percentage of women in daily newspapers at 39 percent per ASNE (American Society of News Editors 2017). While those figures have increased slightly in recent years, Willnat, Weaver, and Wilhoit (2017) show only slight increases in the number of women journalists in newsrooms since 1982, hovering around 33–34 percent in 1982, 1992, and 2002 and reaching 37.5 percent in 2013. Though the authors say that 49 percent of all full-time U.S. journalists hired between 2009 and 2013 were women, the slight increase in women's presence likely reflects the fact that newsrooms have generally been hiring fewer journalists than in years past. For comparison, women make up about 47 percent of the overall U.S. labor force in 2010, according to the U.S. Census Bureau.

Journalists employed in professional newsrooms have been getting more racially and ethnically diverse since wide-scale surveys began in the 1970s, but there is still not parity with overall demographics of the U.S. population. According to the 2017 ASNE survey of daily newspapers and daily news websites, about 17 percent of journalists were racial or ethnic minorities. In RTDNA's 2017 survey, minorities made up about 24 percent of the television news workforce. Both findings show the largest percentage of minorities employed in newsrooms in the history of the surveys, but they still lag behind the minority population in the United States in general, which in 2016 was 38.7 percent, according to the Census Bureau.

The race and gender disparities in professional journalism are especially interesting considering that the demographics of students pursuing degrees in journalism and mass communication (JMC) are far more diverse. In 2015, about 31 percent of undergraduate degrees in JMC were granted to minority students, and about 66 percent of all undergraduate JMC degrees were granted to women (Gotlieb, McLaughlin, and Cummins 2017). Those findings about gender especially have been remarkably consistent over the past few decades. In other words, women make up two-thirds of JMC graduates but only one-third of the journalism workforce. One potential explanation for this gap could be that women JMC graduates tend to be more likely than men to pursue jobs in public relations and advertising, according to a 2013 survey of JMC graduates conducted by University of Georgia researchers (Becker, Vlad, and Simpson 2014). BLS data, for example, show that more than 60 percent of public relations specialists are women. Men in JMC programs are more likely to pursue jobs in newspapers, radio, and television. Women who enter the profession may also be more likely to leave journalism sooner than their male colleagues. For example, of those who have up to four years of experience, there are just about as many female journalists as male journalists (Willnat, Weaver, and Wilhoit 2017). But among those with 20 or more years of experience, only about one-third are women.

Professional journalists tend to be college educated, with 92 percent of journalists in the 2013 "American Journalist" survey saying they were college graduates. That's compared to 58 percent who were college graduates in 1971. Of those in 2013 who went to college, 51 percent majored in journalism or broadcasting. The level of educational attainment among journalists is much higher than the 33 percent of the U.S. population with bachelor's degrees. The survey also noted that the median salary for U.S. journalists was $50,028 in 2013, compared to the average salary of those in the civilian workforce in 2012 of $45,535. However, there tends to be a very large gender pay gap, with women journalists earning significantly less than men (an average $44,342 compared to $53,600).

Politically, though journalists who identify as Democrats outnumber Republicans (28.1 percent versus 7.1 percent), the majority of journalists identify as independents (50.2 percent), according to the 2013 "American Journalist" survey. The proportion of Democrats closely matches the proportion in the overall population (30 percent), though the proportion of Republicans is far less than the overall population (24 percent). The proportion of independents is about 10 percentage points higher than the overall population (44 percent).

Though there is an intense interest in charting the diversity in newsrooms and working to increase the degree to which newsrooms are representative of the public they serve, there is still a large gap. There have been some increases in racial diversity in newsrooms, but gender diversity has remained stagnant. Further, as journalism has become a more professionalized field, with journalists more educated and slightly better paid than the average citizen, there is increasing social distance between journalists and the communities they cover. Finally, though journalists tend to be more politically independent than partisan, with both the percentage of Democrats and Republicans decreasing over time, there is still a disparity between Democrats and Republicans in some newsrooms that may contribute to some feelings of disproportionate representation among more politically conservative Americans.

FURTHER READING

American Society of News Editors. 2017. "ASNE, Google News Lab Release 2017 Diversity Survey Results with Interactive Website." Newsroom Diversity Survey. Last modified October 10, 2017. http://asne.org/diversity-survey-2017.

Becker, Lee B., Tudor Vlad, and Holly A. Simpson. 2014. "2013 Annual Survey of Journalism & Mass Communication Graduates." Last modified August 6, 2014. http://www.grady.uga.edu/annualsurveys/Graduate_Survey/Graduate_2013/Grad_Report_2013_Combined.pdf.

Gotlieb, Melissa R., Bryan McLaughlin, and R. Glenn Cummins. 2017. "2015 Survey of Journalism and Mass Communication Enrollments: Challenges and Opportunities for a Changing and Diversifying Field." *Journalism & Mass Communication Educator* 72 (2): 139–153. https://doi.org/10.1177/1077695817698612.

Johnstone, John W.C., Edward J. Slawski, and William W. Bowman. 1976. *The News People: A Sociological Portrait of American Journalists and Their Work.* Chicago: University of Illinois Press.

Mitchell, Amy, Jeffrey Gottfried, Michael Barthel, and Elisa Shearer. 2016. "The Modern News Consumer: News Attitudes and Practices in the Digital Age." Pew Research Center. July 7. http://www.journalism.org/2016/07/07/the-modern-news-consumer/.

Papper, Bob. 2017. "RTDNA Research: Women and Minorities in Newsrooms." RTDNA Research. Last modified July 3. https://www.rtdna.org/article/rtdna_research_women_and_minorities_in_newsrooms_2017.

Weaver, David H., and G. Cleveland Wilhoit. 1986. *The American Journalist: A Portrait of U.S. Newspeople and Their Work* (Vol. 1). Bloomington: Indiana University Press.

Weaver, David H., and G. Cleveland Wilhoit. 1996. *The American Journalist in the 1990s: U.S. Newspeople at the End of an Era.* Bloomington: Indiana University Press.

Weaver, David H., Randal A. Beam, Bonnie J. Brownlee, Paul S. Voakes, and G. Cleveland Wilhoit. 2007. *The American Journalist in the 21st Century: U.S. News People at the Dawn of a New Millennium.* Bloomington: Indiana University Press.

Willnat, Lars, David H. Weaver, and G. Cleveland Wilhoit. 2017. *The American Journalist in the Digital Age: A Half-Century Perspective.* New York: Peter Lang Publishing.

Q2. CAN ANYONE BE A JOURNALIST?

Answer: Essentially, yes. In the United States, there is no professional licensing board for journalists as there are licensing authorities for other professionals, such as doctors, nurses, lawyers, and teachers. However, there are some legal definitions of "journalist" that are used to provide some narrow special protections for those professionals practicing the craft. Nonetheless, because of the lack of licensing, anyone can perform "acts of journalism" in the sense that anyone can gather news and disseminate it to the public. In fact, digital technologies have lowered the financial and technological bar to do so. That also means that anyone can claim to be a journalist, and with the rise of the Internet and popularity of cable news networks' opinion programming, it's increasingly difficult to tell the difference between a journalist gathering and disseminating the news and those offering analysis and opinion tied to political factions or ideologies.

The Facts: The United States doesn't license journalists, though that is not a universal norm. In an analysis of about 100 developed and developing countries from the Center for International Media Assistance (Strasser 2010), at least one in four have some sort of rules stipulating who may work as a journalist. Those restrictions vary from age or education requirements to the issuance of press credentials that require towing the government line. Sometimes those requirements are advanced by journalists themselves, who use the exclusivity as bargaining power with publishers and others.

Modern moves around the world to license the press stemmed in large part from a desire to make the press a supporting agent in developing democracies, especially as new nations developed in Africa and Asia after the end of World War II. Countries saw licensing journalists as a way to improve the overall professionalism of journalism, creating a type of quality control for an institution vital to democratic society. In the 1960s and 1970s, some international organizations, including a program under the United Nations Educational, Scientific and Cultural Organization (UNESCO), encouraged the development of media watchdog councils to guide the practice around the globe. In many Western countries, this potential mechanism of control was seen almost as another element of the Cold War, and even today, the practice of licensing journalists is prevalent in countries that were former colonies, such as areas of Africa, or that still have some form of communist-based government, such as China and North Korea. That said, controlling journalists' voices to serve as propaganda is not the only reason countries control who may or may not be called "journalists." In some parts of Latin America and Europe, for example, the purpose of licensing is to allow journalism to be a more exclusive profession and therefore gives those who are allowed to practice journalism a stronger voice against the government. Journalism licenses are limited and exclusive, so journalists are able to yield power against their own publishers too.

The idea of licensing journalists has been floated by U.S. lawmakers in states including Michigan and Indiana over the years, but the moves have often been symbolic, and they've had virtually no chance of either becoming law or passing constitutional scrutiny. That's in part because of the social and historical foundations on which the U.S. Constitution's protections are based. For example, one of the historical antecedents of the founding of the United States was a history in England of controlling the press through licensing. Up until the 1720s in the American colonies, presses were still licensed and government censors previewed publications. Though there is some disagreement as to the complete motivations for the inclusion of freedom of the press in the U.S. Constitution's Bill of Rights, the desire to rid the young country of prior restraint—the censoring of content prior to publication—was widely desired by the founders. The U.S. Supreme Court has repeatedly affirmed this interpretation. For example, in 1938, it ruled unconstitutional a city ordinance in Griffin, Georgia, requiring publications distributed within the city to be licensed. The Court's majority opinion stated whatever the motivation for passing the ordinance, its "character is such that it strikes at the very foundation of the freedom of the press by subjecting it to license and censorship" (*Lovell v. City of Griffin*, 303 U.S. 444 (1938)).

Though journalists are not licensed in the United States, those who are part of the traditional or institutional press are sometimes afforded special legal privileges. For example, many states protect journalists' ability to withhold from disclosure in court information or the source of information they use in putting together their investigative reports. These so-called shield laws vary widely in who is able to claim such a privilege. In some states, the protection exists only for those who work for an established media outlet, such as a newspaper, television station, or news wire service, or those who receive an income for the work of collecting and disseminating the news. There is no federal shield law, in part because of the definitional problems that are compounded by an era in which virtually anyone can be a publisher online, and indeed courts and legislators around the world are confronted with this problem (Johnston and Wallace 2017). Some states and at least one federal appeals court have extended protections to those who are practicing journalism no matter their organizational affiliation. In 1998, the federal Third Circuit Court of Appeals developed the *Madden* test, which allows individuals to claim protection if they are engaged in investigative journalism, are gathering news, and at the beginning of the newsgathering process intended to disseminate the information to the public (*In re Madden*, 151 F.3d 125 (1998)). A few other places in the law may define journalists, such as the federal Freedom of Information Act and some state open records laws, which sometimes direct government agencies to waive or reduce fees for journalists to access or copy documents. For example, federal regulations state that "any person or entity that gathers information of potential interest to a segment of the public, uses its editorial skills to turn the raw materials into a distinct work, and distributes that work to an audience" can be considered a member of the news media and is thus exempt from having to pay search and review fees for records.

Though journalists are rarely defined in law, and the First Amendment effectively prohibits the licensing of journalists, government agencies and private individuals and organizations can and often do restrict access to information, individuals, or events to only those affiliated with traditional or institutional press organizations. For example, though anyone can write about the White House, only those credentialed by it can access the building and attend briefings. While imperfect, legal protections can be helpful when they attempt to provide some definition of journalists. Without clearly established guidelines, many government organizations and private entities that provide press credentials lack open standards about who does and does not get credentialed. A 2014 survey of journalists found that nearly one in five who have requested credentials from at least one organization report having been denied at least once (Hermes et al. 2014). Freelance journalists were more likely to have been denied credentials than those who were employed by publications. For example, 20 percent of freelancers were denied credentials to cover Congress, whereas only 4 percent of employees were denied. About a quarter of freelancers were denied access to state and municipal government offices, whereas only 2–4 percent of employees were denied. Nearly half of freelancers were denied credentials from fire departments and other emergency services agencies, whereas no employees were denied. About a quarter of freelancers were denied access to private venues, whereas only 11 percent of employees were denied.

There is a definite advantage to being a full-time, employed member of the institutional press, whether that benefit is legal protection or simply access. But some scholars find the lack of access and legal protections to those not in that traditional space to be problematic, especially as some traditional newsrooms increasingly rely on freelancers and "citizen journalists" for production of the news they publish or broadcast. "When employed journalists are not available to cover important events (particularly at a local level), denying credentials to freelancers and other independent newsgatherers can significantly limit public access to information," stated the authors of the 2014 survey.

Though there remain barriers to entry into the world of newsgathering, particularly in terms of who can access sources and information and who can claim legal protections, the fact is that most barriers to publish information have been significantly lowered. Today, anyone with a cell phone and an Internet connection can publish for the world to see. Additionally, as traditional media organizations are pushed to compete with blogs and social media publishers for public attention, the more those organizations rely on persons who offer partisan opinion and analysis rather than verified facts. That's especially true of cable TV news. In fact, the Pew Research Center's 2013 "State of the News Media" report found that about two-thirds of cable TV news programming was opinion or commentary versus one-third that focused more on "hard-news." Media organizations today employ workers who might be called commentators, contributors, or columnists in addition to the more traditional journalists and reporters, and it's increasingly difficult to understand how the characteristics and expectations for each role intersect or differ from one another.

For example, a pair of scholars examined the coverage surrounding NPR's 2010 dismissal of its senior news analyst Juan Williams for opinionated comments he had made about terrorism on Fox News, on which he often appeared as a commentator (Thomas and Hindman 2015). For NPR leadership, his role as a "news analyst" prohibited him from offering opinions on controversial issues. In response, some journalists suggested that the role of "analyst" means that opinions may be offered. Others suggested that this was a result of the blurring lines between so-called objective reporting and opinion journalism. Others suggested that problems exist in part because the roles and expectations of media workers differ across news organizations, and there is no industry-wide agreement on what each role means.

Though this study focused on just one incident, it showed significant confusion among journalists, who presumably have a fairly in-depth understanding of the media landscape. "If members of the journalistic community have difficulty making sense of the differences among 'analysts,' 'commentators,' and 'columnists' (and how they are distinguished from 'reporters' and how all of this coheres under the banner of 'journalism'), we must pause to consider if members of the public, possessing

varying degrees of media literacy, are able to navigate such slippery definitions," the authors note (Thomas and Hindman 2015, 480). However,
little is known about the degree to which members of the public indeed
distinguish among the different roles now present in news organizations.

FURTHER READING

Hermes, Jeffrey, John Wihbey, Reynol Junco, and Osman T. Aricak.
2014. *Who Gets a Press Pass? Media Credentialing Practices in the United
States.* Cambridge, MA: Berkman Center for Internet and Society.
https://journalistsresource.org/wp-content/uploads/2014/06/Berkman
Shorenstein_WhoGetsPressPass.pdf.

Johnston, Jane, and Anne Wallace. 2017. "Who Is a Journalist?" *Digital
Journalism* 5 (7): 850–867.

Peters, Jonathan, and Edson C. Tandoc Jr. 2013. "'People Who Aren't
Really Reporters at All, Who Have No Professional Qualifications':
Defining a Journalist and Deciding Who May Claim a Privilege." *NYU
Journal of Legislation and Public Policy Quorum*: 34–63.

Strasser, Steven. 2010. *Registering Reporters: How Licensing of Journalists
Threatens Independent News Media.* Washington, DC: Center for International Media Assistance. https://www.cima.ned.org/wp-content/
uploads/2015/02/CIMA-Licensing_of_Journalists.pdf.

Thomas, Ryan J., and Elizabeth B. Hindman. 2015. "Confusing Roles,
Uncertain Responsibilities: Journalistic Discourse on Juan Williams,
NPR, and Fox News." *Journalism & Mass Communication Quarterly* 92
(2): 468–486.

Q3. DO INDIVIDUAL JOURNALISTS HAVE THE POWER TO DECIDE WHAT IS PUBLISHED OR AIRED?

Answer: Generally, no, although there are some exceptions. For example,
some news organizations give particularly prominent or popular figures
the authority to publish news directly to both organizational and individual platforms (including social media) without much editing or other
oversight. In addition, more veteran journalists tend to have more autonomy than less experienced ones. However, in most organizations, there
is some hierarchy in which editors and producers can exert power over
what is ultimately published or aired. The steps in these hierarchies can
be thought of as "gates" that information must pass through to advance
beyond that level. The larger the news organization, the more gates exist

before something becomes news. In the digital age, when most journalists are expected to use social media to disseminate news or to publish stories quickly to websites, fewer gates may be used for certain types of stories. Even in this era, more journalists than in the past say their stories are getting reviewed by others prior to publication.

The Facts: Though journalists filter information and decide what to share with their audiences, the influence of individual journalists on what is ultimately published or aired is often only one step in a much more complex and multipart series of decisions. One dominant line of research in media sociology in the past half-century or so has been in the area of gatekeeping—the way in which information passes through a variety of checkpoints as it is constructed for dissemination to the public. Those checkpoints or gates either constrain or facilitate the flow of information from one step to the next (Shoemaker and Vos 2009).

Though the idea of gatekeeping was originally applied to the progression of food from store and garden to an individual's plate, the first application to journalism came with David Manning White's (1950) study of how one newspaper wire editor decided which news items to publish in his newspaper's pages and which to disregard. White's study focused on the individual decisions of one journalist, which he said were "subjective" and "based on the 'gate keeper's' own set of experiences, attitudes, and expectations" (White 1950, 390). White argued that even though the study focused on just one person, that individual level was the most important because each paper has its own "Mr. Gates" making those subjective decisions. Critics said White's study was too focused on a journalist's individual decisions, forgetting the broader cultures in which the journalist was socialized. For example, classic studies of newsrooms (e.g., Gans 1979; Tuchman 1978) found that journalists often share certain values to determine what is chosen as news. Moreover, their values are embedded in the work they do throughout the reporting process and not just at the tail end, when an editor decides which finished news stories to publish and emphasize (e.g., by placing it on the front page rather than somewhere in the interior of the newspaper).

Gatekeeping scholars identify five levels or types of influence that can be used to analyze how content is produced (Shoemaker and Reese 2014; Shoemaker and Vos 2009). The first is the individual level. This level can include individual characteristics, like background, experience, and demographics as sources of influence, and also looks at how those characteristics interact with personal and professional roles to influence content. For example, an individual journalist growing up in an economically advantaged household might be predisposed to believe strongly in capitalism, a belief that may influence the lens with which he or she views the world, which could affect the content he or she produces. Another example could be that the experience of journalists with journalism degrees would likely increase their belief in and adherence to professional codes of ethics, which could have an effect on content through decisions on whether to engage in controversial reporting practices.

The second level of gatekeeping looks at communication routines of journalists and news workers. Many scholars consider this level to exert the most influence on content. This level has to do with the day-to-day normal work of journalists, focusing on how tasks are completed. Routines come from different places or people, and they can include sources, media organizations, and audiences. For example, when journalists decide what to cover, they're often trying to consider the audience and what might bring readers or viewers to their story. Many scholars have shown that journalists tend to share preexisting definitions of news. Those "elements of newsworthiness" include factors like timeliness, or how recently the news happened; prominence, or the fame, importance, or influence of the people involved in the story; and proximity, or how physically close to the audience or journalist the event took place. For example, a story about the mayor of a small town delivering a major speech is likely to be more newsworthy and therefore chosen for coverage by the small town's newspaper than a story about a regular citizen from another town across the country.

Routines and structures of a media organization can also influence content. For example, media organizations have traditionally been limited by the space they have to publish news in a newspaper or magazine or the time allotted for a story on TV. The Internet and cable news allow for more space to publish, but organizations are limited by the time constraints on the journalists, who, in a digital age, are expected to complete more stories and engage with audiences via social media, often with fewer resources and less time to do so. The amount of work organizations require of journalists, therefore, has an effect on the content they produce. Additionally, media organizations often dispatch their reporters to cover certain topics, called "beats," where news normally happens. For example, local government or "crimes and courts" beats are assigned to reporters who are expected to "find news" in those places, thereby limiting where they're looking for newsworthy information. In fact, these beats are fairly common across media organizations, which has the further effect of leading reporters to often travel in "packs," which further limits the news items that might eventually be communicated to audiences.

The routines or socialized norms of journalists' sources can have an effect on content as well. For example, if a reporter's access to a source is limited by public relations professionals, the content will be affected. In addition, because of increased work expectations of journalists, the best source may simply be the one that is available. For example, if an expert source is needed and a reporter calls three people, then the one who gets back in contact with the reporter first may be the one who ends up in the story, even if that expert might not be the best one. These routines can be seen as a simple means to get the job done or necessary tasks to complete a story. But as those tasks become institutionalized and influence the way journalists do their jobs, journalists can come to rely too heavily on them. That overreliance then can be manipulated by nonjournalists wishing to influence content. For example, public relations practitioners can proactively make their experts and officials available for interviews if they know a journalist may be working on a particular story, making that part of the reporting process easier and more expedient for an overextended journalist.

Gatekeeping theory's third level of influence is the news organization itself. Such influences can be the organizational structure, including what roles individuals play in the organization, what the lines of authority are in the organization, and what policies dictate the work done in the organization. Overarching organizational goals also play a major part in influencing content, especially the degree to which profit making is a primary purpose of the organization. In fact, profitability tends to be the primary goal of most organizations in the United States, which has a media system largely made up of for-profit entities. Since the 1980s, as ownership of most major media has become concentrated in only a half dozen or so corporations, the influence of the profit goals of the larger organizations can create additional constraints that ultimately influence content. The economic influences are often not direct in the sense that journalists are forced or even encouraged to cover advertisers favorably, for example; rather, they are indirect. For example, stories that bring in more viewers or readers are more likely to make more money in an online environment in which ad revenues are dependent on how many people see and interact with the ad, and, therefore, those stories are more likely to be covered. In fact, many newsrooms now closely track which stories are most popular, using statistics such as how many people read an article online or interact with it on social media. That information is then shared with journalists, who make decisions on what to cover based in part on what will get the most clicks or likes or shares. Even when the business and news sides of an organization are separate and there is no direct dictate to cover one thing or not cover another, journalists at lower levels perceive organizational goals, and those goals may implicitly affect news work, especially if the success or even existence of the news organization may be perceived to be in peril.

The fourth level of gatekeeping looks at the influence of social institutions that exert influence over journalists and their work. For example, these outsider influences might include advertisers, public relations practitioners, governments, investors, and even the audience itself. Interest groups and public relations practitioners can anticipate routines of journalists and thus more easily disseminate their messages. Additionally, other news organizations often influence each other, sometimes implicitly pushing each other to cover the same stories, contributing to "pack journalism" discussed earlier. For example, many smaller organizations look to national news companies like *The New York Times* to set a broader national news agenda. In breaking news reporting, news organizations might use one another as sources, creating a kind of echo chamber that can amplify mistakes in reporting. Because most news organizations are commercial entities and media consumption is spread across many channels, organizations are increasingly trying to tailor their content to appeal to niche audiences, which advertisers find appealing. That means that though the advertisers aren't dictating content, organizations are looking to the kinds of audiences advertisers want and tailoring content to stories that would interest those audiences. Governments, through mechanisms like regulation of broadcast media or control of public documents, influence content as well.

Technology and the structures created by tech companies influence content. For example, Facebook is a primary source through which audiences are referred to news organizations, so it has a tremendous influence over the routines of journalists and the environment in which they produce content, which ultimately influences the content itself. Technology and social media companies represent a major gate in an era when large numbers of people access news through those channels.

Finally, the fifth level of gatekeeping deals with the broader social systems in which news is created and consumed. The overarching ideological characteristics of a culture can fundamentally frame media content as media organizations perpetuate those dominant ideologies. For example, the United States has a capitalist economic system that promotes private ownership and free markets, and it has a democratic political system that promotes self-government, individual rationality, and autonomy. Stories from U.S. journalists thus frequently emphasize related ideals. For example, a story about a new business might focus on the individual business owner and the qualities that contributed to his or her success rather than broader social structures that might have been integral to that success.

Processes at lower levels of influence operate within these broader cultural norms. After all, social institutions, news organizations, and individuals exist within this culture, and routines are developed and solidified within that culture.

Though technology has facilitated faster-paced reporting and publishing environments where individual journalists can report news without other journalists' involvement, such as through websites or social media, fewer journalists publish their work without it first being edited by others. One study, for example, found that whereas 29 percent of journalists in 1982 said their stories were not edited by others, the percentage dropped to 14 percent in 2013 (Willnat, Weaver, and Wilhoit 2017). That means that more journalists perceived their work to be edited now than in the past. Additionally, fewer journalists have said in recent decades that "they almost always can get a subject covered that they think should be covered," with 59 percent agreeing with the statement in 1982 compared to 34 in 2013, according to that same survey. Journalists in supervisory roles or those covering a specific topic area or beat tend to perceive greater freedom. Though the decreasing autonomy of journalists can be problematic for the professionalization of the field, these figures support the theory that individual journalists exert relatively little control over content compared to the multiple levels of factors discussed here. Indeed, journalists perceive the greatest constraints on their decision-making authority coming from commercial imperatives.

FURTHER READING

Gans, Herbert J. 1979. *Deciding What's News: A Study of CBS Evening News, NBC Nightly News, Newsweek, and Time*. New York: Random House.

Shoemaker, Pamela J., and Stephen D. Reese. 2014. *Mediating the Message in the 21st Century*. New York: Routledge.

Shoemaker, Pamela J., and Timothy Vos. 2009. *Gatekeeping Theory*. New York: Routledge.

Tuchman, Gaye. 1978. *Making News: A Study in the Construction of Reality*. New York: Free Press.

White, David M. 1950. "The 'Gate Keeper': A Case Study in the Selection of News." *Journalism Quarterly* 27: 383–390.

Willnat, Lars, David H. Weaver, and G. Cleveland Wilhoit. 2017. *The American Journalist in the Digital Age: A Half-Century Perspective*. New York: Peter Lang Publishing.

Q4. ARE JOURNALISTS OBJECTIVE?

Answer: No, but their methods can be, which means their work still can be fair, accurate, and complete. Everyone—including journalists—makes decisions about where to focus their attention. Journalists make subjective judgments about what to cover and how to cover the news, and journalistic conventions dictate that certain issues and events will be covered and in certain ways. But that doesn't mean journalists try to subvert truth or peddle an agenda. Professional journalists typically operate according to news values such as timeliness, relevance, proximity, and prominence. They seek out different points of view, and they verify assertions. While some news outlets and commentators today do embrace a particular political ideology, most working journalists still do their best to follow an objective method of reporting to minimize the influence of their own subjectivity. Different observers have different points of view regarding their success. And journalists can fall prey to the same social and cultural biases as other members of society.

The Facts: Objectivity is a widely known and widely misunderstood journalistic ideal, sometimes even by journalists themselves (Kovach and Rosenstiel 2014; Schudson 1978). Of course, no human—including journalists—is objective; everyone has a unique background that gives him or her a perspective on the world. It's particularly hard to imagine that someone who develops expertise on a topic—such as the inner workings of government—would not have a personal opinion about it. That doesn't stop good journalists from striving for complete independence from faction—total objectivity. For example, some journalists are so fiercely dedicated to this understanding of objectivity that they abstain from voting in elections. In this line of thinking, even casting a private vote forces them to take sides in their minds, which could detract from their neutrality. Not voting is also an outward demonstration to other journalists and the public of one's commitment to objectivity. Other journalists consider voting a private, civic duty that they can participate in without losing their independence. (This has become slightly more complicated as some state parties move to closed primaries, where participation becomes a matter of public record and the act is no longer private.)

The idea of not voting comes from a good place—the desire to be neutral and impartial, both in reality and in perception. But most scholars and journalists agree that this is not really what objectivity is about. Most journalists do follow codes of ethics that recommend avoidance of overt political activity. For example, journalists typically do not contribute money to candidates; campaign on behalf of candidates; attend rallies as

private citizens; or display yard signs or bumper stickers of political candidates, parties, or organizations. When journalists do have an unavoid-
able conflict of interest, such as writing about a civic organization they
belong to, they typically are transparent about this in their writing or via
a disclaimer.

Still other journalists see the ideal of objectivity as a total sham. In
this view, no journalist should even pretend to be impartial or suggest to
the public that they are somehow immune from having a point of view.
Champions of this viewpoint believe journalists should be open and honest about their allegiances so the public can see where they are coming
from. These journalists typically work as freelancers and for organizations
that do not aim to convey a perception of objectivity. They are generally
happy to provide their take on the news via analysis and commentary.
Journalists themselves are not solely responsible for this development.
The public has expressed a preference for "voice," or opinion, in news
content, especially when that "voice" aligns with their own.

Thus, the ideal of objectivity is interpreted differently by journalists
and the public alike. But regardless of where one falls on this spectrum,
journalists are not meant to be objective themselves. Rather, journalists
are trained and typically practice a *method* of objective reporting, which is
meant to minimize the influence of a reporter's own perspective. Historically, this practice is informed by the emergence of the scientific method,
which makes claims and develops theories based on observation and evidence (Schudson 1978). In journalism, the practice is accomplished by
omitting the reporter's opinion and instead ensuring that all stakeholders
on a topic get a fair chance to participate in a story and give their perspective. This is how objectivity has become associated with concepts of
"fairness" and "balance," which can be useful. In political coverage, it is
common to provide a point of view from "both sides." For example, in the
debate over health care in the United States, Republicans and Democrats
often have legitimate opposing views about the proper role of the federal
government in ensuring access to health care, and it is useful for Americans to hear these different perspectives.

This is where it gets tricky. Some believe that reporting what both sides
have to say is sufficient. As long as both sides get their say, the reporting
is neutral and complete. However, others suggest this approach reduces
the journalist's role to that of a court stenographer, who simply records
what people say—even if those statements are demonstrably false. Critics of the "both sides" approach say reporters must go further by seeking
to verify the claims being made and examining the relevant evidence.
They should be skeptical of the information provided by sources, and

their reporting should include an evenhanded assessment of the facts so that citizens can know whose point of view most closely aligns with the truth (Craft and Davis 2013; Kovach and Rosenstiel 2014). This sort of arbitration—where reporters might appear to be "taking sides"—can be a valuable form of public affairs journalism, but it also can lead to accusations of bias, especially from people or organizations whose claims are accurately identified as untruthful or misleading.

Where do journalists fall on this spectrum of approaches? According to a 2013 survey (Willnat, Weaver, and Wilhoit 2017), journalists say investigating government claims and analyzing complex problems have become their most important professional roles. This suggests a penchant for verification and analysis that goes beyond the stenographer approach. On the other hand, a study of journalists' use of Twitter in the 2012 U.S. presidential election showed that journalists were far more likely to take a stenographic approach and simply pass along the claims of candidates rather than engage in fact-checking or examining evidence (Coddington, Molyneux, and Lawrence 2014). Similarly, many news outlets during the 2016 election did not provide nuanced and factual information that would benefit citizens. Instead, they focused heavily on polling and other aspects of the presidential "horse race" (e.g., its overwhelming negative tone) rather than substantive discussion of issues and the candidates' proposals for addressing them (Shorenstein 2016). News outlets, including the "big three" cable news channels of Fox News, CNN, and MSNBC, provided endless airtime to candidates, especially Donald Trump, to speak directly to the television audience without examining or challenging many of their claims through original reporting. Newspapers did a better job of examining relevant evidence and explaining the policy implications of the major candidates and parties, but overall, the amount of coverage of actual policy issues was almost nonexistent compared to the amount of horse-race coverage of who was ahead in the polls on a given day or the unconventional rhetoric used during the campaign. Finally, journalists' keen interest in being seen as objective and impartial made many of them dubious about making comments that would open them to attacks that they were "taking sides."

While simply presenting "both sides" can be useful for avoiding accusations of bias and letting news audiences make up their own minds on a topic, it can also create problems. For starters, there are often more than two sides to a story. American politics is dominated by two political parties, but that doesn't mean other worthwhile perspectives don't exist. Also, presenting a two-sided debate between public officials might leave out the lived experience of ordinary citizens affected by their policy making.

Furthermore, the "both sides" approach can lead to the problem of "false equivalency," where an apparent sense of 50/50 balance masks a critical reality. For example, years of "both sides" reporting on the issue of global warming have given many citizens the impression that there remains a legitimate scientific debate about whether the earth is getting hotter due to human activity. In reality, the science has been settled on this for quite some time, and "balanced" reporting has misled the public, thereby making it harder to consider and implement effective public actions to mitigate the problem.

Should journalists be in the position of evaluating claims like this, or is it better for a journalist to simply report "both sides" on a topic? In terms of remaining "objective," it is certainly safer and easier to simply report both sides and avoid the sticky problem of "truth." On the other hand, if journalists want to provide a valuable public service, it is important that they avoid drawing attention to invalid claims without highlighting their inaccuracy. Taken to its extreme, the idea of balance becomes absurd. For example, a few conspiracy-minded folks still embrace the idea of a "flat Earth." Should reporters qualify any reference to planet Earth by highlighting the ongoing "debate" about its roundness? Most would say no. Ultimately, it is important for journalists to present a diversity of viewpoints, but it is also their job to make some attempt to sort fact from fiction even if they run the risk of being branded as "biased" by parties who disagree or have ulterior motives for keeping the facts of an issue or event in dispute.

More subtly, journalists are subject to the same cultural and social influences and biases that pervade the population at large. Even when they do attempt to follow objective methods of reporting, journalists can still fail to treat different populations equally. Women and minorities often do not receive the same treatment as their white male counterparts in news coverage. For example, female politicians often are asked about their families and their ability to be caretakers while pursuing political office, a line of questioning that male politicians rarely encounter. News coverage of Sarah Palin, the Republican vice presidential candidate in 2008, and of Hillary Clinton, as she campaigned to be president in 2008 and 2016, often obsessed over their appearance and mannerisms rather than their positions on issues or their fitness for office. "Implicit biases" are the stereotypes all humans hold based on their personal experience and their socialization to the world around them. Research on implicit bias has found that most humans hold at least some stereotypes regarding race, religion, gender, age, and other social factors (Payne, Niemi, and Doris 2018). Good journalists (and good humans) work to develop an awareness of their own biases and blind spots. If journalists truly aspire to make their reporting neutral and objective, they should reject stereotypes of all kinds even when—perhaps especially when—this flies in the face of pervasive cultural norms.

We can learn more about objectivity by considering its origins. Many forces contributed to the rise of objectivity, which didn't take hold in the profession until the 1920s (Schudson 1978). In fact, journalism wasn't even considered a "profession" until around then. Before that, journalists weren't expected to have any training or follow any set of professional norms or ethics. Many aimed primarily to tell a good story, and they had no reason to examine the subjectivity of perception. It was only in the early 1900s that journalism schools were created, and the job became the purview of a different class of citizens in the context of an expanding market economy. Journalists around this time also became increasingly skeptical in the face of the emerging public relations industry and propaganda efforts surrounding World War I.

Before this time, there was no such thing as objectivity. In early colonial America all the way up to the Civil War, newspapers were expected to have partisan viewpoints depending on their affiliation with a political party or organization. Some scholars point to two factors—one technological, one economic—that led to changes in the late 1800s and early 1900s. First, the invention of the telegraph in 1844 led early wire services (mainly the Associated Press, established in 1846) to minimize partisanship and standardize their work in order to make their reporting accessible to as many subscribing news outlets as possible. Second, the invention of advertising gave rise to new market opportunities. As advertising became the main source of revenue for a newspaper, publishers realized they could become more appealing to advertisers by reaching larger audiences, especially those with the means to consume the goods and services being advertised. Objectivity—rather than partisanship—became regarded as the surest pathway to larger audiences and thus more money. Regardless of whatever mixture of factors led to the rise of objectivity, it is very much a 20th-century invention.

Ultimately, instead of asking, "Are journalists objective?" or even "Is this story objective?" the better questions are: Is this journalist acting independently or are they acting on someone else's behalf? Is the story complete? Is it accurate? Is the information verified by independent experts or by lived experience? How do you know? Ask if the reporter has abided by the old journalistic mantra that demands skepticism and verification for every piece of information: If your mother tells you she loves you, check it out.

FURTHER READING

Coddington, Mark, Logan Molyneux, and Regina G. Lawrence. 2014. "Fact Checking the Campaign: How Political Reporters Use Twitter to Set the Record Straight (or Not)." *International Journal of Press/Politics* 19 (4): 391–409. https://doi.org/10.1177/1940161214540942.

Craft, Stephanie, and Charles N. Davis. 2013. *Principles of American Journalism: An Introduction.* New York: Routledge.

Kovach, Bill, and Tom Rosenstiel. 2014. *The Elements of Journalism: What Newspeople Should Know and the Public Should Expect.* Revised and updated 3rd ed. New York: Three Rivers Press.

Payne, Keith, Laura Niemi, and John M. Doris. 2018. "How to Think about 'Implicit Bias.'" *Scientific American.* Accessed June 8, 2018. https://www.scientificamerican.com/article/how-to-think-about-implicit-bias/.

Schudson, Michael. 1978. *Discovering the News: A Social History of American Newspapers.* New York: Basic Books.

Shorenstein Center. 2016. "Research: Media Coverage of the 2016 Election." Harvard University Kennedy School of Government. https://shorensteincenter.org/research-media-coverage-2016-election/.

Willnat, Lars, and David H. Weaver. 2014. "The American Journalist in the Digital Age." Bloomington: Indiana University School of Journalism. Accessed February 15, 2018. http://archive.news.indiana.edu/releases/iu/2014/05/2013-american-journalist-key-findings.pdf.

Willnat, Lars, David H. Weaver, and G. Cleveland Wilhoit. 2017. "The American Journalist in the Digital Age: How Journalists and the Public Think about Journalism in the United States." *Journalism Studies,* October, 1–19. https://doi.org/10.1080/1461670X.2017.1387071.

Q5. ARE JOURNALISTS EXPECTED TO FOLLOW ANY FORMAL ETHICAL GUIDELINES IN THEIR WORK?

Answer: Yes, ethical training is part of standard journalism education, and most journalists say they follow institutional codes of ethics prescribed by employers and professional associations. American journalists tend to say they follow those codes unwaveringly, with the overwhelming majority of journalists saying journalists should always follow codes, even when extraordinary measures would require putting those codes aside. American journalists also indicate that they disapprove of aggressive reporting tactics, such as paying for information or claiming to be someone else.

Most journalists describe such methods as disreputable violations of journalistic integrity.

The Facts: Professional organizations for journalists, such as the Society of Professional Journalists and the Radio and Television Digital News Association, maintain formal, published codes of ethics. Additionally, many individual news organizations have their own published ethics guides, including organizations like The Washington Post, ProPublica, and National Public Radio. Many of these ethics codes frame the obligations of journalists around the duties they have to various stakeholders.

The Society of Professional Journalists' Code of Ethics refers to obligations to "seek truth and report it," "minimize harm," "act independently," and "be accountable and transparent." It charges journalists to verify claims, use original sources whenever possible, provide context, and function as watchdogs of powerful people and institutions. But it also states that journalists should balance that obligation to report truth with another obligation to minimize potential harm, to show compassion for subjects of news and those affected by it, and to "avoid pandering to lurid curiosity" even if the information is truthful. It also expects journalists to avoid conflicts of interest, such as reporting on social organizations to which they belong or using friends or family as sources. The code also expects journalists to be open whenever possible about reporting practices, explaining ethical decisions, and responding to errors. Most professional associations and news organizations have similar principles and goals.

The earliest such "codes" came about in the early 20th century when organizations like the American Society of Newspaper Editors and Sigma Delta Chi (which would later become the Society of Professional Journalists) created them (in 1923 and 1926, respectively). These codes often stressed ideas about objectivity. For example, the 1926 Sigma Delta Chi code listed its first two principles as "Truth is our ultimate goal" and "Objectivity in reporting the news is another goal, which serves as a mark of an experienced professional" (Ward 2015).

Though scholars suggest that the precursors to the norm of journalistic "objectivity," such as impartiality and factuality, existed since the early days of the English and American periodical press in the 17th and 18th centuries, it was only widespread by the 1930s and was dominant through several decades in the middle of the 20th century. This norm put more focus on the distinctions between news versus opinion and led to less use of interpretation or perspective, with editors enforcing rules questioning many adjectives and verbs in reports, for example. "To 'editorialize' was the reporter's mortal sin," according to ethicist Stephen J. A. Ward (2015, 239). This new norm, in part, helped journalists define themselves as "professionals."

Journalists then were professionals who followed strict guidelines. For some, the role was almost akin to a religious calling. Walter Williams, founding dean of the University of Missouri School of Journalism, the nation's first journalism school, even created a "creed" for journalists in 1914. This "Journalist's Creed" outlined "beliefs" that journalism should function in the public interest, that news should never be suppressed, that accuracy and fairness are essential to journalism, and that journalists should operate independently and unmoved by pride or power, among several others.

The rise of objectivity as an ethical norm was also an extension of a broader societal embrace of searching for truth using an objective scientific method. People were also increasingly comfortable and trusting of institutions that used objective procedures to function. Such procedures were seen as necessary in an increasingly interconnected and complex world. For many editors and newspaper leaders, it was also a response to the so-called yellow journalism era of the late 19th century, during which newspaper publishers like Joseph Pulitzer and William Randolph Hearst used sensationalism and exaggeration to compete for readers.

Though objectivity was a dominant professional norm during the middle of the 20th century, it had its limits. Some were concerned that citizens aren't always rational when consuming information, and while a journalistic account may be measured, calm, and report "just the facts," not all information in the marketplace of ideas is presented so. Responses in the mid-20th century moved to incorporate analysis and interpretation into the objective norm. In later decades, journalists further incorporated more "storytelling" techniques into their reporting, experimenting with "inventive 'leads' and [writing] gripping narratives that 'took' readers to the scene" (Ward 2015, 258).

The end of the 20th and beginning of the 21st centuries, and more specifically the invention and widespread use of digital media technologies, brought about a shift in journalism ethics. "The once cozy world of journalism ethics—a somewhat sleepy domain of agreed-on codes of ethics too often presumed to be invariant—is already a faint memory," wrote Ward (2015, 342). According to Ward, few previously ironclad principles, like objectivity or even verification before publication, go unchallenged in this era. Whereas predigital journalism ethics were very structured and crafted specifically for professionals, the ongoing development of new digital media ethics is "untidy" and is for everyone. Today, barriers to entry into the media market are very low, and virtually anyone can be a "citizen journalist" and publisher. This is a significant contrast to the development of objectivity in the late 19th century, when mass media companies could be somewhat monopolistic. Our media today are far more global as well, and digital technologies have made communication around the globe fast and easy. Though audiences still get the majority of their news from just a handful of companies, increased competition from some new outlets, audience's significant use of social media for news, and the lightning speed and global reach of new digital platforms make establishing a more universal or widely accepted ethics code difficult.

These changes force questions about the very nature of journalism ethics, such as identity (e.g., who is a journalist?), scope (e.g., if anyone can publish online, do we expect journalism ethics to apply to all, trained professionals and "citizen-journalists" alike?), content (e.g., what principles, such as objectivity, should guide us?), and community engagement and impact (e.g., what community standards should guide us, especially in a global media community?). Digital journalism ethics are still emerging, and Ward hopes for a day when journalism ethics are really a part of communication or media ethics, relevant to citizens and journalists alike and taught as a core part of public education. It would be considered "an evolving cross-cultural discourse, not a settled doctrine within boundaries" (Ward 2015, 371).

Indeed, some professional organizations have moved to develop such process-oriented ethical guidelines. In 2015, the Online News Association (ONA), an influential professional journalism organization focused solely on digital news, started its Build Your Own Ethics Code project (Online News Association n.d.). The project is a website that takes users through more than 40 ethical issues relevant to digital media journalism, including topics such as user-generated content, social media, data journalism, metrics, click-bait, and privacy. Users are provided with a variety of choices for each topic. At the beginning of the interactive project, users are asked to explain "the nature" of their journalism, focusing primarily on issues of reporting versus analysis (e.g., whether journalists should express opinions in their work) and independence (e.g., whether journalists should avoid community involvement or how closely they work with the business/advertising side of the organization). Though there is significant flexibility in how users can tailor a code to their news organization, ONA expects an acceptance of fundamentals relating to telling the truth, avoiding conflicts of interest, respecting audiences, and acting professionally with various stakeholders. In this way, the ONA project is a sort of middle ground between the rule-driven journalism ethics of the 20th century and the emergent and ever-evolving digital media ethics for which Ward advocates.

Though journalism ethics are in some level of flux in the present digital age, professional journalists still overwhelmingly ascribe to fairly conservative and universal notions of ethical journalism practice. The overwhelming majority of full-time professional journalists working for traditional media organizations in the United States (93.2 percent) agreed or strongly agreed that journalists should always adhere to those codes, regardless of circumstance (Vos and Craft 2016). Just 14.8 percent agreed or strongly agreed that "it is acceptable to set aside moral standards if extraordinary circumstances require it," and just 10.1 percent agreed or strongly agreed that what's ethical in journalism is "a matter of personal judgement."

More relevant to the question of whether journalists act ethically is the acceptability of more controversial or aggressive reporting practices. Scholars from Indiana University have surveyed journalists about their acceptance of various reporting practices for several decades. They've found that journalists' willingness to use such tactics has generally dropped over the four-decade period. For example, the percentage of journalists who accept paying for information as a legitimate method of newsgathering, a practice often called "checkbook journalism," dropped from 27 percent in 1982 to 17 percent in 2002 to just 5 percent in 2013. In 1982, 20 percent of journalists said it was acceptable to claim to be someone else while reporting, whereas only 7 percent agreed with that tactic in 2013. In 1982, two-thirds of journalists said "getting employed to gain inside information" was acceptable reporting behavior, while only one-quarter agreed with the tactic in 2013. Vos and Craft (2016) asked similar questions of American journalists as part of the multinational Worlds of Journalism project. Just 1 percent of journalists surveyed said it is "always justified" to pay people for confidential information, with an additional 11.7 percent saying it's "justified on occasion." Just 2.2 percent said it's "always justified" to claim to be another person, with an additional 9.4 percent saying it's sometimes justifiable. Virtually all journalists rejected "altering or fabricating" quotes, with just 2.7 percent saying it's "always justified" and 1.2 percent saying it's "justified on occasion." Journalists also reject publishing without verification (2.4 percent "always justified," 8 percent "justified on occasion"), accepting money from sources (2.4 percent "always justified," 1 percent "justified on occasion"), and altering photographs (2.4 percent "always justified," 7.7 percent "justified on occasion"), for example.

By contrast, some of these practices are more accepted in other countries around the world, including some with similar free media systems (Worlds of Journalism Study 2016). For example:

- Paying people for confidential information (United States, 1 percent always, 11.7 percent on occasion; Australia, 1.5 percent always, 26.9 percent on occasion; Canada, 0.9 percent always, 33.3 percent on occasion; China, 31.4 percent always, 50.5 percent on occasion; Germany, 6.1 percent always, 50 percent on occasion; Mexico, 3.5 percent always, 25.6 percent on occasion; and the United Kingdom, 1.5 percent always, 51.4 percent on occasion)
- Claiming to be someone else (United States, 2.2 percent always, 9.4 percent on occasion; Australia, 0.7 percent always, 12.7 percent on occasion; Canada, 2.3 percent always, 36.4 percent on occasion; China, 20.7 percent always, 65.6 percent on occasion; Germany, 6.2 percent always, 43.7 percent on occasion; Mexico, 8.2 percent always, 33.2 percent on occasion; and the United Kingdom, 0.1 percent always, 46.3 percent on occasion)
- Publishing stories with unverified content (United States, 2.4 percent always, 8 percent on occasion; Australia, 1.3 percent always, 34.3 percent on occasion; Canada, 0.6 percent always, 15.5 percent on occasion; China, 2.3 percent always, 15.4 percent on occasion; Germany, 3.7 percent always, 33.8 percent on occasion; Mexico, 3.7 percent always, 4.2 percent on occasion; and the United Kingdom, 1.3 percent always, 23.8 percent on occasion)

Journalism ethics are influenced by how journalists see themselves and their roles within society. Research by Willnat, Weaver, and Wilhoit (2017) shows that the majority of journalists (62.2 percent) rate the interpretative/watchdog role of the press as very important. About 18.3 percent of journalists said that the role to simply disseminate the news is very important, about 20.6 percent said that the press should be adversarial in its relationship to the government, and about 25.3 percent indicated that journalists should be encouraging political involvement and setting the political agenda. However, actual analyses of journalistic work product reveal that the majority (60 percent) of content shows primarily a disseminator role and only one-third shows any evidence that it included interpretative/watchdog elements. This may suggest that although journalists may say that journalism ethics and role conceptions drive their day-to-day decision making, the fact is that the more traditional objective disseminator role of journalists is prevalent in practice, at least for the time being.

FURTHER READING

Online News Association. n.d. "Build Your Own Ethics Code." Accessed February 10, 2018. https://journalists.org/resources/build-your-own-ethics-code/.

Radio and Television Digital News Association. 2015. "RTDNA Code of Ethics." Last modified June 11. https://www.rtdna.org/content/rtdna_code_of_ethics.

Society of Professional Journalists. 2014. "SPJ Code of Ethics." Last modified September 6, 2016. https://www.spj.org/ethicscode.asp.

Vos, Tim P., and Stephanie Craft. 2016. "Country Report: Journalists in the United States." In Worlds of Journalism Study. https://epub.ub.uni-muenchen.de/34878/1/Country_report_US.pdf.

Ward, Stephen J. A. 2015. *The Invention of Journalism Ethics: The Path to Objectivity and Beyond.* 2nd ed. Montreal, Canada: McGill-Queen's University Press.

Weaver, David H., and G. Cleveland Wilhoit. 1986. *The American Journalist: A Portrait of U.S. Newspeople and Their Work.* Vol. 1. Bloomington: Indiana University Press.

Weaver, David H., and G. Cleveland Wilhoit. 1996. *The American Journalist in the 1990s: U.S. Newspeople at the End of an Era.* Bloomington: Indiana University Press.

Weaver, David H., Randal A. Beam, Bonnie J. Brownlee, Paul S. Voakes, and G. Cleveland Wilhoit. 2007. *The American Journalist in the 21st Century: U.S. News People at the Dawn of a New Millennium.* Bloomington: Indiana University Press.

Worlds of Journalism Study. 2016. "Aggregated Tables for Key Variables (2012–2016)." Accessed February 10, 2018. http://www.worldsofjournalism.org/research/2012-2016-study/data-and-key-tables/.

Q6. DO TRADITIONAL NEWSPAPERS STILL PLAY A ROLE IN MODERN JOURNALISM?

Answer: Yes. Despite the proliferation of new online media and the success of cable television news, the bulk of original news reporting—information that has not previously appeared elsewhere and is based in fact rather than opinion—still comes from journalists who work at traditional national and regional newspapers, even as much of the print news business continues to struggle and decline. Some original reporting also comes from emerging digital-only news outlets, new nonprofit outlets, and local and national network television outlets. Despite their financial success, cable television news outlets produce little original reporting; instead, they primarily offer commentary based on the reporting of others.

The Facts: The greatest asset of any news organization is its reporting staff. Skilled journalists who can gather and report original news are responsible for producing the information citizens need to be self-governing. Experienced journalists know how to develop lasting relationships with sources, how to analyze data and documents, how to find answers to questions, and how to present information in clear, compelling formats. Even today, most of these journalists still tend to work for so-called traditional or legacy print news outlets, which tend to be large organizations with a history of original reporting and the financial and technological resources to hire large staffs (Anderson, Downie, and Schudson 2016). The salaries paid to the reporting staff at a newspaper tend to be the largest ongoing expense, so it is not surprising that many news outlets have cut their reporting staffs in order to save money as revenues have declined (Alterman 2008).

Historically, newspapers have enjoyed local and national monopolies in the news industry because of the high barriers to entry into the field. Before the Internet, a news outlet needed access to a printing press, which costs millions of dollars to own and operate. (This led one famous publisher to remark that "freedom of the press belongs to the man who owns one.") Today, even though they continue to produce most original reporting, print news outlets have struggled to remain financially viable due to technological changes and competition from other kinds of news sources. As news has moved online, a newspaper's traditional revenue sources—advertising, classifieds, and subscriptions—have all declined. Meanwhile, the Internet has given rise to countless "aggregators," which collect and curate the work produced by others and repackage it without producing any financial benefit for the original source. At the same time, a handful of new online-only news outlets have succeeded in finding new business models that allow for the hiring of skilled journalists.

Since the emergence of digital media, industry observers have debated whether newspapers will survive and whether they still serve a purpose in American life. Thousands of journalism jobs have disappeared in the 21st century, and plenty of once-successful news outlets have closed. But there is no question about the central role traditional news outlets continue to play even amid massive economic and technological shifts. In his book *Losing the News*, the Pulitzer Prize–winning journalist Alex Jones (2009) points to an "iron core" of serious news that is at the center of a functioning democracy and argues that most of it—an estimated 85–95 percent—is produced by traditional newspapers. While it may seem like plenty of news is available via television and the web, the information provided by these news sources often originates from a newspaper and is merely being passed along by these other content providers. A Pew Research study (2010) that examined 53 news outlets in the city of Baltimore found that most of what the public learns is still overwhelmingly driven by traditional media, especially newspapers. Eight out of every 10 stories analyzed were simply repurposed or repackaged information, but of those stories that did contain original reporting, almost all—95 percent—originated from traditional media. More than half of the original reporting came from print publications, mostly *The Baltimore Sun*, the city's primary metropolitan daily newspaper. This state of affairs, in which the work of newspapers and other outlets dedicated to investigative journalism is appropriated and regurgitated to fill cable news programming and website space, remains a major, if underappreciated, reality of today's news media environment.

On many cable news channels and websites, viewers are also more likely to be subjected to opinion and commentary rather than original reporting, and studies indicate that there is a good chance that consumers of content from these sources are being misled. According to an analysis by the fact-checking website Politifact (Sharockman 2015), on Fox and Fox News, 60 percent of claims examined were found to be "mostly false," "false," or "pants on fire." MSNBC and NBC fared slightly better, at 44 percent. CNN performed the best with only 21 percent of claims rated as false. Another study by the Union of Concerned Scientists (2014) examined cable news coverage of climate science. Fox News was the worst offender. Out of 50 segments on climate science in 2013, only 28 percent were deemed accurate while 72 percent included misleading portrayals of the state of climate science. CNN fared better with an accuracy rate of 70 percent, and MSNBC did best at 92 percent accurate. While there are some occasional bright spots on cable news, journalists and scholars have long lamented the decline of serious reporting on cable television. Many have noted a trend away from a "journalism of verification" in favor of a "journalism of assertion." Journalism of verification requires a careful assessment of the facts, which must be subjected to a thorough vetting process. Journalism of assertion, on the other hand, simply allows sources and pundits to make claims that go unchecked, regardless of their veracity (Kovach and Rosenstiel 2014).

Television news outlets generally invest fewer resources in their reporting as compared to newspaper outlets. Television media are less tolerant of losses because local and cable stations are generally parts of much larger corporations that are more concerned about the bottom line than fulfilling a public function or responsibility. In this view, all media content is simply a way to attract eyeballs that can be sold to advertisers and cable companies. Local broadcast television outlets make money by selling ads and from retransmission fees paid by cable providers, and cable television outlets are funded by a roughly even mix of advertising and subscription revenue (i.e., the money paid by cable providers to be able to offer a given channel such as CNN). Ultimately, this formula has paid off. In 2016, an election year marked by extensive coverage of Donald Trump's often sensational and controversial rallies and statements, prime-time average viewership for Fox, CNN, and MSNBC was up 55 percent to nearly 5 million viewers over the previous year. Total revenue was projected to increase by 19 percent to a total of nearly $5 billion. The three networks did increase their overall newsroom spending by 9 percent for a total of $2.1 billion in spending (Pew Research Center 2017a), but even that level of spending leaves room for large profits. In October 2016, CNN's gross profits were predicted to approach $1 billion for the year, while Fox accrued more than $1.67 billion (Farhi 2016).

Local television viewership has declined over recent years but has seen modest changes compared to newspapers and has remained profitable, in part because the public airwaves over which they broadcast their programming are licensed to them free of charge by the Federal Communications Commission (FCC). Over-the-air advertising revenue exceeded $20 billion in 2016. Political advertising helped make 2016 particularly good for the largest local television station companies, such as Tribune, Sinclair, and Tegna. The seven major local TV companies reported a total of $843 million in political advertising revenue (Pew Research Center 2017b).

Newspapers are not immune from profit motives and revenue maximization, and historically, they have often enjoyed large profit margins as compared to other industries. However, changes in technology and economics have made it increasingly difficult for newspapers to make a profit. Print newspaper advertising revenue peaked in 2000 at $67 billion (adjusted for inflation) and fell to $16.4 billion by 2014. Adding in digital ad revenue brings the 2014 total to $19.9 billion (Perry 2015; Thompson 2016), which remains the lowest level seen since 1950.

These declines parallel the ongoing decreases in circulation. In 2016, U.S. newspapers saw a 10 percent decrease in weekday print circulation and a 1 percent decrease in weekday digital circulation. Total weekend circulation fell to 35 million, down from a peak of around 63 million in the 1980s and the lowest level seen since 1945 (Pew Research Center 2017c). Despite these declines, circulation revenue is actually up a bit (to $10.9 billion in 2016), due in part to a "subscription-first" model being pursued by some newspaper outlets that have put their focus on growing their subscriber base rather than trying to hang on to disappearing ad dollars. But these modest gains in circulation don't come close to covering the declines in advertising revenue over the past three decades.

Most newspapers are facing cuts as they explore new business models. But at the same time, newspapers remain the main producers of original reporting. For example, *The New York Times* employs somewhere around 1,000 journalists. For comparison, CBS News—one of the strongest news brands in broadcast television—has around 150 (Anderson, Downie, and Schudson 2016). *The New York Times* has weathered the digital storm better than most. Despite cutting hundreds of jobs, the *Times* had the largest combined print and digital circulation of any daily newspaper in the United States in 2016. It has 200 million online users around the world, employs journalists in 150 countries, finances reporting bureaus around the world, and publishes around 200 pieces of journalism per day. In 2015, the *Times* made almost $500 million in digital-only revenue, and its direct-from-consumer revenue now exceeds advertising revenue (*New York Times* 2017). Other large daily newspapers have also seen significant growth, such as *The Wall Street Journal*, which saw a 23 percent increase in digital subscriptions in 2016, and *The Chicago Tribune*, which saw a 76 percent rise (Barthel 2017).

In the new media ecosystem, the real gains have gone to the new digital giants. While revenue is declining for the traditional news organizations that produce most original reporting, business is booming at Facebook and Google. These two giants absorb around two-thirds of all digital ad revenue in the United States, and they continue to grow. Total Internet advertising revenue grew 22 percent in 2016, up $12.9 billion, but almost all of that growth—99 percent—went to Facebook and Google, according to an industry research report (Baysinger 2017). Total digital advertising revenue reached $72 billion in 2016, and 65 percent of that, or $47 billion, appears on mobile devices. Of all digital ad revenue, 73 percent goes to the top 10 ad-selling companies.

While some assume the Internet offers a level playing field, to the contrary, it is a highly concentrated business environment. The problem for journalism is that companies like Google and Facebook are only profitable in large part because they repackage and repurpose content that has been produced and paid for by other entities, whether that entity is *The New York Times* or a local newspaper. Google and Facebook profit by selling advertising against content that cost them nothing to produce. Critics assert that this business model enables them to make lots of money but leaves original news producers scrambling to figure out how to remain financially viable.

FURTHER READING

Alterman, Eric. 2008. "Out of Print." *The New Yorker*, March 24. https://www.newyorker.com/magazine/2008/03/31/out-of-print.

Anderson, C. W., Leonard Downie, and Michael Schudson. 2016. *The News Media: What Everyone Needs to Know*. New York: Oxford University Press.

Barthel, Michael. 2017. "Despite Subscription Surges for Largest U.S. Newspapers, Circulation and Revenue Fall for Industry Overall." *Pew Research Center* (blog). June 1. http://www.pewresearch.org/fact-tank/2017/06/01/circulation-and-revenue-fall-for-newspaper-industry/.

Baysinger, Tim. 2017. "Digital Ad Spend Jumps 22 Percent to $72.5 Billion in 2016: Report." Reuters, April 26. https://www.reuters.com/article/us-digital-advertising/digital-ad-spend-jumps-22-percent-to-72-5-billion-in-2016-report-idUSKBN17S2V3.

Farhi, Paul. 2016. "One Billion Dollars Profit? Yes, the Campaign Has Been a Gusher for CNN." *The Washington Post*, October 27, sec. Style. https://www.washingtonpost.com/lifestyle/style/one-billion-dollars-profit-yes-the-campaign-has-been-a-gusher-for-cnn/2016/10/27/1fc879e6-9c6f-11e6-9980-50913d68eacb_story.html?utm_term=.b64cff9be345.

Jones, Alex S. 2009. *Losing the News: The Future of the News That Feeds Democracy*. Institutions of American Democracy. Oxford; New York: Oxford University Press.

Kovach, Bill, and Tom Rosenstiel. 2014. *The Elements of Journalism: What Newspeople Should Know and the Public Should Expect*. Revised and updated 3rd ed. New York: Three Rivers Press.

The New York Times. 2017. "Journalism That Stands Apart." January 17, sec. Insider. http://www.nytimes.com/projects/2020-report/.

Perry, Mark J. 2015. "Creative Destruction: Newspaper Ad Revenue Continued Its Precipitous Free Fall in 2014, and It's Likely to Continue." AEI, April 30. https://www.aei.org/publication/creative-destruction-newspaper-ad-revenue-continued-its-precipitous-free-fall-in-2014-and-its-likely-to-continue/.

Pew Research Center. 2010. "How News Happens." http://www.journalism.org/2010/01/11/how-news-happens/.

Pew Research Center. 2017a. "Cable News Fact Sheet." http://www.journalism.org/fact-sheet/cable-news/.

Pew Research Center. 2017b. "Local TV News Fact Sheet." http://www
.journalism.org/fact-sheet/local-tv-news/.

Pew Research Center. 2017c. "Newspapers Fact Sheet." http://www.jour
nalism.org/fact-sheet/newspapers/.

Sharockman, Aaron. 2015. "MSNBC, Fox, CNN Move the Needle on
Our Truth-O-Meter Scorecards | PunditFact." January 27. http://www
.politifact.com/punditfact/article/2015/jan/27/msnbc-fox-cnn-move-
needle-our-truth-o-meter-scorec/.

Thompson, Derek. 2016. "The Print Apocalypse of American
Newspapers—The Atlantic." November 3. https://www.theatlantic
.com/business/archive/2016/11/the-print-apocalypse-and-how-to-
survive-it/506429/.

Union of Concerned Scientists. 2014. "Science or Spin? Assessing the
Accuracy of Cable News Coverage of Climate Science (2014)." April.
https://www.ucsusa.org/global-warming/solutions/fight-misinformation/
cable-news-coverage-climate-change-science.html.

Q7. DO PUBLIC RELATIONS PROFESSIONALS INFLUENCE JOURNALISTS?

Answer: Yes. While good journalists always strive for independence, many of their news stories—estimates say at least half—originate from public relations professionals. As the journalism profession has declined in size in the online era, the field of public relations or PR has exploded, making the ratio of PR practitioners to journalists as high as 5–1. The relationship between the two professions can be both cooperative and adversarial: PR people help journalists learn about important events and issues, and they help provide quick access to information. On the other hand, the influence of PR can mean less access to high-ranking sources, tightly controlled messaging, and a diminished opportunity to hear the voices of those who cannot afford expensive PR services. Recent trends toward sponsored content online represent ways of spreading PR messages in the guise of news and circumventing journalists altogether.

The Facts: PR is the process of influencing public perceptions, often through news media. It is a broad field encompassing a range of disci-plines, which can include marketers, event planners, public information officers, lobbyists, corporate communication specialists, and many oth-ers. According to the Public Relations Society of America, "Public rela-tions is a strategic communication process that builds mutually beneficial relationships between organizations and their publics" (Public Relations

Society of America n.d.). There are many ways of doing PR, but most PR professionals spend at least some of their time interacting with journalists in order to generate favorable news coverage of an organization, individual, event, or issue. Press releases and conferences are still the industry standards for getting information out to the news media, although the digital realm offers many new opportunities and platforms, including Twitter, Facebook, and search engine optimization strategies. Regardless of method, when working with news media, the goal of PR is to generate "free media."

Of course, PR is not "free" to produce; an organization must pay for PR services or hire its own in-house PR staff. It is "free" because a successful PR message makes its way to the news media without an exchange of money. Free media coverage (also called "earned media") is often preferred and more effective because it appears to be coming from a neutral arbiter rather than obviously originating from a paid sponsor as with a television commercial. News coverage gives legitimacy and authenticity to a client's PR message. Thus, the best PR campaigns are likely to be ones that the public never knows about. The process of influencing the news is meant to take place behind the scenes, invisible to the end consumer of the message.

In a real-world example, a new microbrewery in Idaho once hired a PR firm to generate publicity by creating an outdoor billboard on its building. The brewery was located at a freeway entrance traveled by more than 37,000 cars per day, so the firm created a billboard that mimicked the yellow and green colors of nearby traffic signs with text that read "Craft Beer, Right Here." On the surface, this seems like any ordinary ad. But when the state transportation department ordered the removal of the sign, that's when the PR began. As the PR firm later explained on its blog, "the brewery received notice that the billboard was in violation of state regulations, which was exactly what we wanted. We immediately issued a news release and spread the story via social media. From there it took on a life of its own, begetting publicity, engagement, social sharing and more. In the media, the story ran on all local newscasts and the front page of the leading paper. It also appeared across the country on TV stations and in newspapers, business trades, and industry rags" (Oliver Russell n.d.).

In the context of news media, PR differs from advertising primarily because it surreptitiously generates free media coverage for an organization or event, whereas advertising relies on "paid media" and is generally much easier to spot. PR is also more likely to focus on an overall brand, industry, or issue, while advertising is often more narrowly focused on specific products or services. For example, a PR campaign by the National

Rifle Association or the Brady Campaign to Prevent Gun Violence might try to influence news coverage of gun control legislation; PR by the Warner Music Group would work to generate favorable coverage of their musical artists; PR by a local developer might aim to show journalists the economic benefits of building a new downtown sports stadium; and PR from a university athletic department might encourage journalists to downplay a scandal involving sexual assault by coaches or players.

In many ways, PR professionals are valuable resources for journalists. PR practitioners keep journalists aware of important events and issues, they generate all kinds of ready-to-use information, and they are almost always available when journalists need answers to their questions. Whether they work as political reporters or music writers, many journalists see developing relationships and open lines of communication with PR representatives as crucial to their work.

On the other hand, there are several common complaints about PR. One is that its practitioners stand between journalists and the sources they really need to talk to. Rather than being able to ask a tough question of the town mayor or member of Congress, a journalist might be limited to the "spin" of a public information officer. Another concern is that powerful interests unduly control the news agenda with their public relations strategies. And when journalists rely too heavily on PR, the public can suffer. Marginalized voices often go unheard when they cannot afford expensive PR campaigns, giving the tilted impression that society is composed primarily of wealthy elites and their interests (Shoemaker and Reese 2014).

The ratio of PR practitioners to journalists was roughly even in 1980. But as the number of working reporters has plummeted, the number of PR specialists has risen dramatically. Today the ratio is somewhere between one journalist to every four or five PR professionals (McChesney and Nichols 2010), and many of those PR professionals are former journalists. This can mean cozy relationships between those who have moved to PR and their former journalism colleagues. Also, former journalists often make the best PR people because they are highly knowledgeable about the newsmaking process, and they know how to influence it. Finally, many former journalists have turned to PR as a way to earn better pay with better working conditions, such as more regular hours and a more sustainable pace.

Ultimately, this means the number of independent reporters striving to reach the closest possible version of the truth has been slashed at the same time that the number of self-interested influencers with a one-sided message has exploded. This can create significant challenges in a self-governing democratic society in which the public needs reliable, accurate, and comprehensive information to make good public policy decisions. At the end of the day, it is the job of journalists to apply their well-honed editorial judgment and decide if a PR message is worthy of coverage just as they would with any other topic of potential public concern or importance. But the reality is that journalists often are severely limited in what they can accomplish in a day, especially in today's economic climate, where they are often required to turn out multiple stories per day.

An easy solution for journalists under pressure to complete reports is to turn to an eager PR professional who can quickly supply basic facts, quotes, anecdotes, and photos. A diligent journalist will then take the time to consult other sources, check the facts, seek other points of view, and gather relevant context, which can lead to a fair and responsible story from which the public can benefit. In a less ideal scenario, a journalist writes a story from the PR materials and calls it a day. The story is not necessarily wrong in this case, but it is probably incomplete. In a worst-case scenario, a journalist could take a press release from a PR professional, slap on his or her own byline, and call it done. Not only is this dishonest and unethical but it is also a total abdication of the journalistic mission. It's one thing to pass along press materials promoting a county fair or artist profile. This should be avoided when possible, but it's a much more serious offense to pass off as news the political spin or advocacy of a one-sided publicity effort.

Determining the exact amount of influence PR has on journalism is difficult. Many factors affect the news product, so it is hard to know exactly how powerful PR can be among the other factors. Scholars have found, however, that journalists and PR professionals alike feel that PR has a strong influence on news. One study found that even journalists say an average of 44 percent of news content is influenced by PR (Sallot and Johnson 2006). PR campaigns work to manage news messages and create events, sometimes called "pseudo-events," for the express purpose of generating news coverage. Many scholars tend to assume that PR, like advertising, has a significant effect if for no other reason than the tremendous resources that go into it (Shoemaker and Reese 2014; Shoemaker and Vos 2009).

PR is also practiced by the American military and has a long history, dating to at least World War I. During the Vietnam War, the press had relative freedom to cover the conflict. But after images of death and destruction began to appear on American televisions and journalists posted reports and accounts that challenged the official U.S. position that the war was going well, military image handlers devised plans to limit journalists' access (Iyengar 2015). When American forces invaded Grenada in 1983, several days passed before journalists were allowed on the island and they were limited to receiving briefings from military officials. The 1991 Gulf War introduced the use of "press pools" and "embedded" reporters, which would be taken individually or in groups to predetermined sites rather than being allowed to report freely. The trend toward limited access only increased with the invasions of Afghanistan and Iraq in the early 2000s. Partly as a result, some journalists have turned to leaked information to cover aspects of military conflict, as with the Abu Ghraib prison photos that documented torture and abuse by U.S. forces. Journalists almost always avoid disclosure of information that would interfere with military strategy or put U.S. troops in danger, and many are actually quite supportive of military messaging. While there are reasonable limits to be placed on reporting of military action, when it comes to foreign conflict, Americans need access to reliable information about the actions of their government.

PR dates back to the 1800s when "publicity" agents used a variety of underhanded tactics, such as fake stories and staged events, to generate interest for clients. By the 20th century, early PR professionals realized their work could be better received if they were honest and direct. A growing understanding of human psychology led to new ways to influence perceptions, particularly through selective framing of information and appeals to emotion. Since then, a variety of tools and tactics have emerged that help the practice of PR reach further than ever, consistently making it one of the top 10 growing professions in the United States. Social media messaging, digital marketing, sponsored content, native advertising, and a variety of other practices have helped PR expand across the media environment whether the public notices or not. Ultimately, it remains the job of journalists to use their critical news judgment skills and processes of verification to evaluate PR messages and determine whether and to what extent they can be used to serve the public.

FURTHER READING

Iyengar, Shanto. 2015. *Media Politics: A Citizen's Guide.* 3rd ed. New York: W. W. Norton & Company.

McChesney, Robert, and John Nichols. 2010. *The Death and Life of American Journalism: The Media Revolution That Will Begin the World Again.* 1st Nation Books. Philadelphia, PA: Nation Books.

Oliver Russell. n.d. "Woodland Empire." *Work* (blog). Accessed April 25, 2018. http://www.oliverrussell.com/work/woodland-empire.

Open Secrets. n.d. "Lobbying Database." Influence and Lobbying. Accessed April 25, 2018. https://www.opensecrets.org/lobby/.

Public Relations Society of America. n.d. "All about PR." Accessed April 25, 2018. https://www.prsa.org/all-about-pr/.

Sallot, Lynne, and Elizabeth Johnson. 2006. "Investigating Relationships between Journalists and Public Relations Practitioners: Working Together to Set, Frame and Build the Public Agenda, 1991–2004." *Public Relations Review* 32 (2): 151–59. https://doi.org/10.1016/j.pubrev.2006.02.008.

Shoemaker, Pamela J., and Stephen D. Reese. 2014. *Mediating the Message in the 21st Century: A Media Sociology Perspective.* 3rd ed. New York: Routledge/Taylor & Francis Group.

Shoemaker, Pamela J., and Tim P. Vos. 2009. *Gatekeeping Theory.* New York: Routledge.

2

❖❖❖

News Media Law and Economics

News media content can be fully understood only within the context of the legal and economic system where it is produced. While journalists and their organizations have a great deal of control over their news products, they are subject to a range of outside influences in the form of laws, policies, regulations, corporate ownership, and commercial pressures. The legal and economic framework for news media can range from the protections of the First Amendment to licensing by the Federal Communications Commission (FCC) to government subsidies for public media to the financial demands of shareholders. These often-hidden influences can tell us a great deal about the structure of the news media system and its potential effects on news content, which ultimately helps shape our views of the world around us. Comparing the legal and economic structures of U.S. news media with those of other developed nations helps reveal both the promise and the pitfalls of the American system.

Q8. DOES THE FIRST AMENDMENT GIVE JOURNALISTS ANY SPECIAL LEGAL RIGHTS?

Answer: The First Amendment is a part of the U.S. Constitution, and it protects five individual freedoms: religion, speech, press, assembly, and petition. While the First Amendment says Congress shall make "no law" restricting these freedoms, there are some limits, such as making a false statement of fact that produces harm. In particular, many laws and policies influence news content and regulate the structure of news media systems. The First Amendment protections for the press are generally interpreted by courts alongside the freedom of speech, with no special protections generally provided to *journalists* not enjoyed by all persons. However, other federal and state laws provide those working as journalists with some special rights and privileges.

The Facts: The First Amendment is the starting point for understanding the relationship between government and the press, but it does not end there. The amendment's language, which states that "Congress shall make no law . . . abridging the freedom of speech, or of the press," sounds clear enough. Indeed, courts have a long history of protecting the rights of the press and ensuring a free exchange of ideas among journalists and citizens alike. But despite the apparent absolutism of the First Amendment (i.e., "no law"), many laws and policies restrict what journalists can do and say, especially defamation laws and privacy torts. This is because the judicial system aims to balance competing interests in society. Freedom of speech and the press are undeniably important to democracy, but courts have balanced these important goals with other interests such as the right to privacy and the right to a fair trial. Other laws and policies that create the structure of the media system also influence press freedom, such as the licensing of broadcasters by the FCC or limits on contributions to political campaigns.

Overall, the press in the United States ranks among the most free in the world, according to watchdog organizations such as Freedom House and Reporters without Borders. If there are threats to a free press in the United States, they often come from political and economic factors such as the concentration of ownership in news media, which often limits the diversity of content that appears in the news. It's important to recognize that the First Amendment only protects the rights of journalists (and citizens) from infringement by government, not by private corporations or other entities.

The First Amendment was signed into law in 1791 as part of the first 10 amendments to the Constitution known as the Bill of Rights. In addition to protecting press and speech rights, it established religious freedom, as well as the rights to peaceably assemble and to petition the government. However, just a few years later, in 1798, Congress passed the Alien and Sedition Acts, which included the criminalization of "false, scandalous, and malicious writings against the government." Many at the time criticized the punishment of "seditious libel" as a violation of the First Amendment, but others who had supported the First Amendment had no problem with the new act. This shows that even those who crafted and approved the First Amendment were not entirely in agreement on its meaning and intent. This leaves it to the courts to interpret and apply constitutional law. This often means a review of federal and state laws as well as administrative rulemaking by the FCC and other regulatory agencies.

The prohibition of "prior restraint," perhaps the most important principle regarding government and the press, was established by the Supreme Court in 1931. In the case *Near v. Minnesota* (283 U.S. 697), a small local paper in Minnesota devoted to exposing scandal and intrigue was censored by a state "gag law" on the grounds that the paper's work constituted a "public nuisance." In a 5–4 ruling, the Supreme Court ruled that such censorship, otherwise known as prior restraint, would be unconstitutional. Although the Court left leeway for censorship in the interest of national security, the precedent set by the Court means that governments generally cannot stop the press from publishing. The idea here is that no law has potentially been broken until after publication occurs.

A later case expanded this principle, making it harder to use national security as grounds for prior restraint. In 1971, in *The New York Times Co. v. United States* (403 U.S. 713), also known as the "Pentagon Papers case," the Nixon administration attempted to stop publication of classified documents related to the Vietnam War. In a 6–3 ruling, the Court held that the freedom of the press to print the documents was more important than the government's interest in keeping them secret. The Court found that the Nixon administration failed to show that publication would cause a "grave and irreparable" danger and thus could not legally halt publication. Today, due to organizations such as WikiLeaks and Anonymous, it has become more commonplace to publish secret government information on the Internet. However, the general prohibition of censorship by government remains a bedrock of press freedom in the United States.

While government censorship is generally forbidden, other laws apply to the published works of journalists. These are often thought of as exceptions to free speech and press rights, which are designed to balance free expression with other societal interests. The most significant exception for journalists is defamation, or a false statement of fact that produces harm. When spoken, defamation is referred to as slander, and when published via writing or broadcast, it is called libel. Libel cases are commonly brought against journalists and their organizations, but they are hard to win in the United States. For private individuals, plaintiffs must show that a journalist published false information that resulted in some kind of damage or injury and that the journalist was negligent in attempting to ascertain the truth. For a public figure such as a movie star or government official, the standard is even harder to meet. In addition to meeting the requirements for private individuals, public figures must show that a journalist acted with "actual malice," which means the journalist knew the information was false and published it anyway or acted with "reckless disregard for the truth."

The actual malice standard was developed by the Supreme Court in the 1964 case *New York Times v. Sullivan* (376 U.S. 254). In this case, a city commissioner from Alabama sued *The New York Times* for libel because of a published advertisement criticizing law enforcement tactics in the South. While the ad contained errors of fact, the Court held that the First Amendment protected the news organization against charges of libel brought by a public figure. The hard-to-meet standard for public figures gives journalists greater leeway to publish erroneous material as long as they are not acting with malice. This makes it difficult for public figures to win libel suits because it is hard to prove that a journalist knew something was false or acted recklessly. In a unanimous decision, the Supreme Court said that "debate on public issues should be uninhibited, robust, and wide-open" and thus required public officials prove actual malice to sue for defamation to provide that required "breathing room" for such debate.

Libel laws in the United States require that the plaintiff (the one alleging he or she was defamed) carry the burden of proving that the defendant (the one who the plaintiff alleges did the defaming) published a false statement of fact that produced harm and should therefore pay damages. The fact that the burden is on the plaintiff is a significant advantage for those engaging in political speech or journalism, and it differs from laws in some other countries. Additionally, if the defendant can prove the statement is true, that is an absolute defense against a libel claim. That said, some plaintiffs will threaten a lawsuit purely to silence opposition. These lawsuits, known as SLAPPs (short for Strategic Lawsuits against Public Participation), can present problems for press freedom, especially for small news organizations who feel they might not be able to afford to defend themselves legally. More than 30 states and several federal appeals courts recognize anti-SLAPP statutes or regulations, which generally allow the person being sued to ask the court to dismiss the case because it involves speech of public concern, requiring plaintiffs to prove early on that they have a probability of winning the case.

In addition to libel, journalism is limited by privacy law, most notably what are referred to as the four privacy torts. These laws are structured in such a way that someone who alleges he or she was the subject of a violation can sue those who violated his or her privacy for monetary damages. These include appropriation, which is using another person's name or likeness for commercial gain without permission; intrusion, which is intruding on another's privacy, such as by using technology to peer into a private space; disclosure of private facts, which is publicizing personal, private, embarrassing information about someone; and false light, which is intentionally publishing false and highly offensive information about someone. Some states don't recognize false light because of its similarities to libel. In addition, there are several defenses to these privacy torts that particularly protect journalists. For example, publishing a person's name or likeness for news purposes is generally not regarded as "appropriation," and disclosing embarrassing private facts is generally acceptable when those facts are newsworthy and of legitimate public concern.

That said, journalists do not have a blank check to violate privacy. For example, the First Amendment doesn't allow journalists special rights to enter private spaces. In one case, *Life* magazine journalists doing a story on an individual who claimed to heal people with unusual remedies entered that individual's home, posing as patients and using hidden cameras to take photos and record conversations. The Ninth Circuit U.S. Court of Appeals rejected claims that the First Amendment provided protections for such conduct: "The First Amendment has never been construed to accord newsmen immunity from torts or crimes committed during the course of newsgathering. The First Amendment is not a license to trespass, to steal, or to intrude by electronic means into the precincts of another's home or office. It does not become such a license simply because the person subjected to the intrusion is reasonably suspected of committing a crime" (*Dietemann v. Time*, 449 F.2d 245 (1971)).

Indeed, the Supreme Court has largely interpreted the First Amendment as providing little protection for press rights beyond the free speech rights guaranteed to individuals more generally. One of the landmark cases that limited freedom of the press was *Branzburg v. Hayes* (408 U.S. 665 (1972)). In this case, journalists argued that the First Amendment protected them from having to testify in front of grand juries and reveal information from and about confidential sources, including their identities. The Court ruled that requiring reporters to reveal such information does not violate the First Amendment. In coming to that conclusion, the Court outlined a variety of ways that the press is not exempt from laws applying to the public generally. Though the Court said that there may be some First Amendment protection for newsgathering (without which "freedom of the press could be eviscerated"), the First Amendment "does not guarantee the press a constitutional right of special access to information not available to the public generally." Though the Court ruled against the journalists, one of the majority votes in the 5–4 decision was that of Justice Lewis F. Powell, who wrote a concurring opinion that noted the "limited nature" of the decision. Powell emphasized that a journalist's ability to claim a privilege should be evaluated on a case-by-case basis and allowed if the information requested isn't relevant to a case or serves no legitimate law enforcement purpose. Powell's narrowly worded concurrence, together with a dissenting opinion from Justice Potter Stewart, effectively limited the impact of *Branzburg*. Many lower courts have interpreted these opinions to suggest that there is a limited journalists' privilege. Journalists could claim a privilege unless (1) they have information relevant to a specific violation of law, (2) the information they have isn't obtainable through other sources, and (3) there was a compelling and overriding interest in the information.

Though some courts have interpreted a limited privilege under *Branzburg*, many states have developed shield laws through legislation or case law that protect journalists from being held in contempt of court for refusing to reveal confidential information or the identities of confidential sources. At the time of the *Branzburg* decision, 17 states had such laws or rules; by 2018, 48 states, Guam, and the District of Columbia had such laws in force, either through statute or case law. However, they vary widely in their application and who can use them. For instance, some states' laws say only those who are employed and receive income from a traditional media outlet like a newspaper or TV station are covered, thereby excluding citizen journalists, student journalists, and others who might produce journalism for nontraditional news operations. Additionally, the laws vary in what they protect; for example, some protect journalists from revealing the source of confidential information but don't protect them from having to reveal the confidential information itself. Further, these protections work in state and local courts only, not federal courts. There is no federal shield law, and attempts to pass one have failed in part because of the difficulty in defining who is a journalist and thus qualified to claim protection.

A few years after *Branzburg*, the Supreme Court reinforced the principle that journalists enjoy the same rights and responsibilities as the general public. In *Zurcher v. Stanford Daily* (436 U.S. 547 (1978)), the Court ruled that journalists are subject to search warrants of newsrooms. However, in 1980, Congress responded to *Zurcher* by passing the Privacy Protection Act, which limited the ability for law enforcement to search or seize journalists' work product or documentary materials through a search warrant. Instead, the law requires that officials use a subpoena, which can be legally challenged before any information is collected.

Finally, journalists also receive some special rights under freedom of information and open records laws. Such laws require that most government documents be available to the public unless they fall under certain legally protected categories. Though anyone may use open records laws to request information, some states' laws, as well as the federal Freedom of Information Act, specify that searching and copying fees should be waived for journalists.

Though there are some special protections and privileges available to journalists, they are limited. Courts have been hesitant to interpret the First Amendment as providing much more protection for journalists than it does for the general public, legislatures have been reluctant to grant new rights, and the press as an institution has been subject to heavy criticism from both main political parties (although the complaints leveled by Republicans and Democrats are dramatically different). Doing so is also challenging at a time when the definition of journalist is in flux, as the granting of any special right must include a clear definition of who would enjoy that right.

FURTHER READING

Freedom House. 2017. "Freedom of the Press." Accessed April 24, 2018. https://freedomhouse.org/report/freedom-press/freedom-press-2017.

Peters, Jonathan. 2016. "Shield Laws and Journalist's Privilege: The Basics Every Reporter Should Know." *Columbia Journalism Review*, August 22. https://www.cjr.org/united_states_project/journalists_privilege_ shield_law_primer.php.

Reporters Committee for Freedom of the Press. n.d. Accessed April 24, 2018. https://www.rcfp.org/.

Reporters without Borders. n.d. Accessed April 24, 2018. https://rsf. org/en.

Trager, Robert, Susan Dente Ross, and Amy Reynolds. 2017. *The Law of Journalism and Mass Communication.* Thousand Oaks, CA: CQ Press.

Q9. DOES THE FEDERAL GOVERNMENT REGULATE NEWS MEDIA?

Answer: Yes, but not much. Communication law and policy, which includes media regulations, come from acts of Congress and from the Federal Communications Commission (FCC), an independent agency of the federal government and the chief regulatory body for communications and media in the United States. Because of the protections afforded by the First Amendment, Congress and the FCC are severely limited in their ability to exert direct control over news media content. Instead, laws and policies tend to focus on media structure and ownership issues, but acts of Congress and FCC rulemaking (or lack thereof) can have a significant impact on the content produced by the news media system. Today, many consider the FCC a classic case of "regulatory capture," where the agency is controlled by the very industries it is supposed to regulate, resulting in policies favorable to those in power.

The Facts: In the early days of radio, around the start of the 20th century, amateurs and inventors tinkered with the original "wireless" technology. The ability to send signals over the airwaves became important to ships at sea to communicate with each other and with stations onshore. However, an absence of regulations meant that the airwaves could become cluttered with competing signals from the variety of emerging broadcasters, which included the U.S. Navy and private companies. A lack of policies regarding the consistent use of radio equipment limited the potential use of wireless for emergency communication. The scope of the problem crystallized with the sinking of the *Titanic* in 1912; the ship's distress signal went unheard by nearby ships that had turned off their radios for the night, and rescue efforts were hampered by competing signals from amateur operators (Douglas 1987; Rosen 1980). The growing cacophony of the airwaves had already prompted Congress to begin working on a plan for broadcast regulation, but the *Titanic* disaster left no uncertainty about the need for some kind of regulatory framework.

The result was the Radio Act of 1912, which adopted international standards requiring ships at sea to continuously monitor emergency frequencies, something most European nations had done as early as 1903. Furthermore, to combat the problem of signal interference, the act also required for the first time that all broadcasters be licensed by the federal government, and it empowered the Department of Commerce to do the licensing, although no guidelines for granting licenses were given. As World War I drew closer, the navy gained dominance over the airwaves, which led many officials to advocate for a full government monopoly over broadcasting in the hands of the navy. Others argued that the Post Office Department was best equipped to administer the airwaves as a public service (Rosen 1980). Amateur operators thought of radio as the "people's medium" and wanted to preserve their access to the airwaves (Douglas 1987). Others with a stake in radio included department stores, newspapers, universities, and churches, all of which competed for limited spectrum as radio began to boom in the 1920s.

Meanwhile, a commercial broadcasting industry began to emerge, consisting of the major radio equipment manufacturers: RCA, GE, AT&T, and Westinghouse (Barnouw 1966; Rosen 1980). Even they had become frustrated by the lack of a clear regulatory framework. Herbert Hoover, who then served as secretary of the Department of Commerce, famously noted, "I think this is probably the only industry of the United States that is unanimously in favor of having itself regulated." The end result was the Radio Act of 1927, which created the Federal Radio Commission (FRC) and empowered it to grant licenses to operate based on the "public interest, convenience and necessity." Notably, there was to be no pure government monopoly over radio nor was there any attempt to sell licenses to the highest bidder. Rather, a system was conceived that would grant free licenses to the established commercial broadcasters—those with the best technology, the clearest signals, and the most "neutral" programming—and wipe virtually all others off the airwaves (McChesney 1993; Rosen 1980). It was hardly a democratic solution to the problem of how to allocate access to the naturally occurring airwaves, which are said to belong to the public.

With the subsequent Communication Act of 1934, which remains the framework for communication policy in the United States today, the new FCC replaced the FRC and was tasked with the regulation of all interstate and foreign wired and wireless communication. Despite ongoing debate about the need for noncommercial and educational access to the airwaves, the established licensing system and the commercial broadcasting industry it supported remained in place (McChesney 1993; Stole 2006). This is how the American media system as we know it today was born, constructed by human actors making deliberate public policy decisions about who gets to speak and who does not. They did not place restrictions on content per se, but by creating the structure of the system through laws and policies, the result certainly was to privilege some speakers and their content over others.

This outcome can be attributed largely to the growth of market society in early-20th-century America (Marchand 1998). As American culture became synonymous with corporate power, the "public interest" was increasingly viewed as the ability to participate in consumer society, and the regulatory framework for broadcasting was designed to facilitate exactly that. As sociologist Paul Starr noted, "Commercial radio did not merely become entrenched as an interest group; it became embedded in culture and consciousness, and it gathered legitimacy until it seemed impossible that it could be any other way" (Starr 2004, 363). While it may seem that the supposedly laissez-faire, or "hands off," approach to the licensing of broadcasters was the best way to guarantee the First Amendment's protection of speech and the press, the effect was to concentrate a large amount of influence in the hands of a powerful few (Streeter 1996). This trend has played out in much of American media (and American life in general), where a lack of regulatory intervention actually encourages and facilitates this concentration of power, which generally leads to the marginalization of minority voices and dissenting viewpoints (Bagdikian 2004; McChesney 1993).

In the early days of the FCC, the agency took seriously its mission of regulating in the public interest as radio (and later television) came to dominate American life and as critics became increasingly vocal about problems of commercialization (Pickard 2015). The FCC's 1941 *Report on Chain Broadcasting* required the breakup of the National Broadcasting Corporation (NBC) due to its domination of radio broadcasting; NBC Blue was sold and eventually became the American Broadcasting Corporation (ABC). In the 1940s, the FCC also issued a series of rules limiting ownership of multiple stations and networks. The Department of Justice also played a role in using antitrust law to limit concentrations of ownership, as with the forced divestiture of RCA by GE in 1930 or the 1945 ruling against restrictions on news distribution by the Associated Press.

In 1941, the FCC's Mayflower Doctrine required radio stations to refrain from editorializing and remain neutral in news and politics. Its repeal paved the way for the Fairness Doctrine, a 1949 rule that required broadcasters to meet their public interest obligations by providing adequate coverage of public affairs and to fairly represent opposing views. The Fairness Doctrine is one of the few policies to ever place direct restrictions on news content, but it received lax enforcement (Rowan 1984). The constitutionality of the Fairness Doctrine was challenged in 1969 but was upheld by the Supreme Court due to the special obligations of broadcasters as stewards of the public airwaves. (In another case, the Supreme Court ruled that the same logic could not be applied to newspapers. Because of the theoretically unlimited nature of print publications, newspapers generally have faced no government restrictions except for the occasional antitrust violation.) Also, in the 1940s, the FCC published a report titled *Public Service Responsibility of Broadcast Licensees*. Known as the FCC Blue Book, the report spelled out specific public service requirements for licensees, but fierce opposition from commercial broadcasters led to its defeat and demise (Pickard 2015).

The explosion of television into American homes through the 1950s led to a surge in new programming, but this "golden age of television" came to be dominated by commercially successful entertainment rather than aiming for the cultural and educational aspirations as many had hoped (Baughman 2007). This led then FCC chairman Newton Minnow to announce to the National Association of Broadcasters in 1961 that commercial television programming constituted a "vast wasteland" and to call for greater programming in the public interest. Despite the tough talk, broadcast licensees were rarely challenged and licenses almost always were renewed.

In 1967, Congress passed the Public Broadcasting Act, which created the Corporation for Public Broadcasting in an effort to support the creation of noncommercial and educational programming on television and radio. The result was the creation of the Public Broadcasting Service, or PBS, known for producing children's shows such as *Sesame Street* and *Mister Rogers' Neighborhood*, and National Public Radio, or NPR. Although PBS and NPR remain well-known American institutions, they reach relatively small niche audiences, and public funding for them is paltry compared to the public media systems of other developed nations (Benson and Powers 2011). Most of the funding for American public media comes from donations and grants.

Beginning in the late 1970s, widespread deregulation across American industries led communication policy makers to take an even stronger market-oriented view than had historically dominated communication law and policy. Then FCC chairman Mark Fowler famously noted that a television is merely a "toaster with pictures," or just another consumer product deserving of no special treatment or restrictions on content or ownership despite the long-held public interest obligations of broadcasters. During this period, the duration of a broadcast license was extended, ownership restrictions were eased, programming guidelines and advertising limitations were dropped, and, in 1987, the Fairness Doctrine was eliminated. Many saw these deregulatory moves as necessary due to the emergence of cable and satellite technology; others saw them as further capitulation to corporate power.

The deregulatory trend culminated in the sweeping Telecommunications Act of 1996, which amended the 1934 act and "rewrote the basic law that governs communications policy from top to bottom" (Aufderheide 1999, 9). Propelled by massive changes in ideology and technology, the new approach to communications policy intended to remove regulatory hurdles from the market's ability to grow in the new, converged media environment. The result was increased consolidation in media industries and what many consider to be steadily declining quality in media products and services (Bagdikian 2004; McChesney 1999). Most recently and notably, the FCC has gone back and forth on a policy of "net neutrality," or the idea that all Internet traffic should be treated equally in order to protect freedom of speech and preserve the open Internet. In 2015, the FCC under President Barack Obama passed net neutrality rules that classified the Internet as a "common carrier," which must treat all content equally as opposed to an "information service," which can give selective preference to some types of content over others. In 2017, the FCC under President Donald Trump repealed that rule, arguing that it would impede economic growth, innovation, and competition. The deregulatory trend continued as the FCC voted in November 2017 to eliminate a 42-year-old ban on cross-ownership of a newspaper and TV station in a major market and to allow media companies to own multiple TV stations in a single market. The likely effect will be further consolidation of media ownership and less competition as fewer companies come to own more local outlets.

As this history shows, American media regulation consists of a somewhat contradictory mix of strong speech protections combined with a supposedly laissez-faire approach that actually ends up giving preference to some speakers over others. The big question is, should the government use the force of law to help promote diversity of speech and limit the concentrations of power that dominate media industries? Many believe the government should do more to improve the quality and diversity of media content due to the failure of the marketplace to do so; others hold that the "hands off" approach is the best way to ensure political and economic freedom and growth. Either way, law and policy will always create the structure of the media system, which has an undeniable effect on the content produced.

FURTHER READING

Aufderheide, Patricia. 1999. *Communications Policy and the Public Interest: The Telecommunications Act of 1996*. The Guilford Communication Series. New York: Guilford Press.

Bagdikian, Ben H. 2004. *The New Media Monopoly*. Boston: Beacon Press.

Barnouw, Erik. 1966. *A Tower in Babel: A History of Broadcasting in the United States to 1933*. Vol. 1. New York: Oxford University Press.

Baughman, James L. 2007. *Same Time, Same Station: Creating American Television, 1948–1961*. Baltimore: Johns Hopkins University Press.

Benson, Rodney, and Matthew Powers. 2011. "Public Media and Political Independence: Lessons for the Future of Journalism from around the World." Free Press. http://rodneybenson.org/wp-content/uploads/Benson-Powers-2011-public-media-and-political-independence-1.pdf

Douglas, Susan J. 1987. *Inventing American Broadcasting, 1899–1922.* Baltimore: Johns Hopkins University Press.

Marchand, Roland. 1998. *Creating the Corporate Soul: The Rise of Public Relations and Corporate Imagery in American Big Business.* A Director's Circle Book. Berkeley: University of California Press.

McChesney, Robert. 1993. *Telecommunications, Mass Media, and Democracy: The Battle for the Control of U.S. Broadcasting, 1928–1935.* New York: Oxford University Press.

McChesney, Robert. 1999. *Rich Media, Poor Democracy: Communication Politics in Dubious Times.* The History of Communication. Urbana: University of Illinois Press.

Pickard, Victor W. 2015. *America's Battle for Media Democracy: The Triumph of Corporate Libertarianism and the Future of Media Reform.* Communication, Society and Politics. New York: Cambridge University Press.

Rosen, Philip T. 1980. *The Modern Stentors: Radio Broadcasters and the Federal Government, 1920–1934.* Contributions in Economics and Economic History. Westport, CT: Greenwood Press.

Rowan, Ford. 1984. *Broadcast Fairness: Doctrine, Practice, Prospects: A Reappraisal of the Fairness Doctrine and Equal Time Rule.* Longman Series in Public Communication. New York: Longman.

Starr, Paul. 2004. *The Creation of the Media: Political Origins of Modern Communications.* New York: Basic Books.

Stole, Inger L. 2006. *Advertising on Trial: Consumer Activism and Corporate Public Relations in the 1930s.* History of Communication. Urbana: University of Illinois Press.

Streeter, Thomas. 1996. *Selling the Air: A Critique of the Policy of Commercial Broadcasting in the United States.* Chicago, IL: University of Chicago Press.

Q10. IS AMERICA'S NEWS MEDIA LANDSCAPE DOMINATED BY JUST A FEW CORPORATIONS?

Answer: Yes. Diversity of ownership of the news media landscape has always been limited, but it has become even more drastically reduced since the 1980s. A small handful of large corporations have come to dominate the newspaper, magazine, radio, television, and now digital industries. This matters because ownership, in the pursuit of profits, can influence the kinds of content produced and the diversity of voices that are represented. New voices have emerged online, but while the web theoretically allows anyone to contribute, most page views go to the same small handful of corporate-owned Web sites, and—crucially—most revenue flows to only a few Internet giants—namely, Facebook and Google.

The Facts: Historically, the creation of media products in the United States has been the purview of the few, not the many. Before electronic media, newspapers could be printed and distributed only by those with access to a printing press (Smith 1990). The telegraph arrived in the mid-1800s and was quickly dominated by the monopoly power of Western Union (John 2010). Radio broadcasting was subsumed in its infancy by the primary manufacturers of radio equipment—namely, RCA, AT&T, GE, and Westinghouse (Rosen 1980). Television was dominated by the established radio broadcasters (Baughman 2007). Just as cable and satellite technology began to introduce competition to the television broadcasting industry, the arrival of deregulation in the 1980s and 1990s made it easier than ever for large corporations to consolidate their holdings and reduce competition. Companies that once focused entirely on media products became small parts of much larger corporations, as with the 1986 reacquisition of National Broadcasting Corporation (NBC) by General Electric, which was by then in the business of making home appliances and jet engines, and providing financial services. (In 2003, NBC merged with Universal Studios' parent company to become NBC Universal, which was acquired in 2011 by Comcast, which became the sole owner in 2013.) As for newspapers, the 20th century began with local ownership and diverse competition; more than 500 U.S. cities had two or more competing daily newspapers. As group ownership increased and circulation began to decline, metropolitan areas saw less competition and less local control. Today, 85 percent of newspapers are under group ownership, and only 10 U.S. cities have two or more competing papers (Dirks, Van Essen, Murray & April 2017).

Today, with hundreds of channels on television, endless streaming video, and a billion Web sites on the Internet, it might seem like diversity of ownership and control has exploded. Surely, with all that media, there is something for everyone, including a sufficient supply of quality news content. In reality, the trend toward consolidation and commercialism has only accelerated, and the effect is significant. As larger companies take ownership of more news media outlets, quality journalism suffers (Bagdikian 2004; Croteau and Hoynes 2006; McChesney 2013). This is because real news reporting is expensive to produce and is not especially popular when compared to entertainment and sports programming. Today, the major owners of media producers include large corporations such as Comcast, the Walt Disney Company, Time Warner, 21st Century

Fox, and National Amusements. All of these companies generate annual revenues in the tens of billions of dollars, and the production of news is a tiny part of their operations. In the online environment, most page views and revenues go to a small handful of web operators, especially Google, Facebook, Amazon, and Microsoft, and web access is controlled by a small number of Internet service providers, particularly Comcast, Charter, AT&T, and Verizon (McChesney 2013). None of the major web companies produce any amount of journalism; rather, they merely aggregate and distribute—and profit from—the work of others.

Local newspapers and television outlets have followed similar trends. Local television continues to reach more adults than any other platform but is dominated by a handful of major companies including Sinclair, Nexstar, Gray, Tegna, and Tribune. These companies controlled 179 stations in 2004 and 443 stations in 2016. Sinclair, in particular, has been criticized for forcing local stations to air conservative content (Kroll 2017) and was fined $13 million by the Federal Communications Commission (FCC) in 2017 for failing to disclose the airing of sponsored or paid content (Battaglio 2017). While local television news can be a good source of impartial information, most news broadcasts contain very little serious news but rather are dominated by commercials, soft features, weather, and sports. While broadcast audiences have declined, revenues have increased, with many of these owners reporting 30–40 percent profit margins. Many of these companies also own local newspapers, though they have begun to spin off their broadcast divisions into other companies in order to protect these more profitable enterprises (Williams 2016). Newspapers still provide much of the serious journalism in the United States, but they have been hardest hit by technological and economic transformations. Even major metropolitan newspapers that have managed to survive the reading public's dramatic shift to free digital content have been forced to cull their news staffs and shut down unprofitable departments and news bureaus. "For more than two centuries, newspapers have been the indispensable source of public information and a check on the abuses of government and other powerful interests," wrote Richard Perez-Pena in *The New York Times*. "But no one yet has unlocked the puzzle of supporting a large newsroom purely on digital revenue, a fact that may presage an era of news organizations that are smaller, weaker and less able to fulfill their traditional function as the nation's watchdog" (Perez-Pena 2009).

If concentrated ownership in the hands of a few large corporations resulted in loads of quality journalism, it wouldn't really matter who was in control. If citizens were getting the information they needed, would it matter where it came from? However, research studies indicate that in news media institutions, concentrated ownership means lower quality news and less of it (Baker 2002, 2007; Croteau and Hoynes 2006; Iyengar 2015). Less diversity of ownership means less competition, which often means less incentive to cover local news; to produce serious fact-based reporting; to include a multitude of voices and opinions; or to provide substantive, issue-oriented reporting, as opposed to sensationalized crime and scandal news (sometimes called "infotainment"). When news media is primarily thought of as a business, the impulse to provide a valuable public service can be easily sidelined.

Critics assert that under these current arrangements, media operations are decided by a small handful of powerful industry actors making top-down decisions about who gets to speak and what one gets to say. Many free market proponents argue that this is the best approach for maximizing freedom and innovation because the success of any media producer depends on attracting consumers—generally by giving people what they want. This is theoretically true but in reality is subject to a few problems. First, people do not necessarily know what they want, which is why companies, including news media owners, often spend large amounts of money marketing their products. Second, when it comes to news media and journalism, what people want (e.g., sports and entertainment news) might be very different from the information they need to participate in democratic society as well-informed, self-governing citizens. While freedom of choice includes the option of remaining uninformed, the bedrock of democracy is an informed citizenry capable of making good judgments about the organization of society. A basic problem of democracy is that the vote of a poorly informed citizen counts just as much as that of a well-informed citizen. A third problem with concentrated ownership is that it gives a tremendous amount of power to a small handful of actors to dictate the national conversation. Critics contend that when this power rests in the hands of a few corporate owners, the messages they produce and issues they emphasize will be generally supportive of their interests. A fourth problem is that concentrated ownership means high barriers to entry into the marketplace. If the media landscape is dominated by a few players, it becomes nearly impossible for newcomers to generate the resources needed to compete at the same level.

It is for these reasons that many democratic nations have chosen to make strong commitments to public, nonprofit, and noncommercial news media, which can operate independent of political and economic pressures (other than requirements to produce certain levels of public affairs content). This is thought to be one way to produce the best information for democratic self-governance, and research supports the importance of these efforts. Studies regularly show that consumers of nonprofit and noncommercial news media tend to be better informed than those who consume commercial news, especially on television (Curran et al. 2009; Hallin and Mancini 2004). The U.S. news media, which is almost entirely commercial and for-profit, stands alone among developed nations, which generally have hybrid systems with robust public service broadcasting and other publicly funded news options.

Despite these problems, a market-oriented approach to providing news and information can have some benefits. To help identify these benefits, scholars Croteau and Hoynes (2006) differentiate between a "market model" and a "public sphere model" for media businesses. In the ideal market model, media businesses sell products to the public, and the laws of supply and demand mean that consumers get what they want. Competitive markets promote efficiency and innovation because businesses are always working to produce new and better products at lower costs as long as they are not burdened by cumbersome regulations. Supply and demand dictate that markets will respond to consumer preferences, and the flexibility of the marketplace makes it easy for businesses to quickly adapt to changing desires.

These principles make sense in the context of competitive markets producing diverse products, but as noted earlier, media markets often lack much competition due to concentration of ownership. Furthermore, markets can be undemocratic, meaning they do not represent the whole of society, and markets can be amoral, meaning that producers don't necessarily care if products are beneficial or harmful as long as they generate revenue. In this sense, markets don't always meet social or democratic needs. David Croteau and William Hoynes point out that the media business is different from other industries for a few reasons. One, media is the only industry specifically cited in the Constitution ("the press" in the First Amendment) as deserving of special protection. Two, media products are often sold on a "dual product" model, where the media product appears to be "free," but the real product is the consumer's attention, which is being sold to advertisers. Scholars call this the "audience commodity," noting that consuming advertising is the "work" audiences must often perform to receive media content. Finally, most people agree that news media outlets play some kind of role in the success of democratic society and thus have some duty to do more than simply generate profit. "Market failure" is the term used to describe a situation when markets are not capable of providing a product or service in a sufficient quality or quantity to meet the needs of society.

This brings us to the public sphere media model, which builds on the work of scholar Jürgen Habermas (1989), who is well known for his description of the need for vibrant social spaces for critical discourse and debate; he charted the decline of the public sphere with the arrival of consumer capitalism and the growing power of public opinion and mass media, especially in the 20th century. The public sphere model for media includes public resources serving citizens rather than private companies selling products to consumers. Media outlets promote education and citizenship over profit generation. Media content is diverse and substantive rather than merely striving to provide whatever is popular, and success is measured by service to the public interest rather than profits for owners and shareholders. Thus, many believe that institutions of journalism and news media, if they are to perform a vital public service and help create an informed citizenry, are best viewed under this public sphere model.

Since the Cold War era of the 1950s and 1960s, many people have tended not to criticize free market capitalism because of a perception that it is what makes democracy possible. Any critique of capitalism and the free market could be viewed as an attack on democracy and a free society. The silence on this issue gave way to more vocal critics after the Cold War ended, and scholars, citizens, and activists began to publicly question the merits and logic of markets particularly as applied to media content. This trend has led to a modern reform movement, calling for an increase in media democracy. This includes reforming the corporate media model, strengthening public service broadcasting, providing subsidies for quality journalism, increasing the prevalence of citizen journalism, and using media to promote democratic ideals, including the values of diversity and pluralism.

FURTHER READING

Bagdikian, Ben H. 2004. *The New Media Monopoly*. Boston: Beacon Press.

Baker, C. Edwin. 2002. *Media, Markets, and Democracy*. Cambridge, UK: Cambridge University Press.

Baker, C. Edwin. 2007. *Media Concentration and Democracy: Why Ownership Matters*. Communication, Society, and Politics. Cambridge, UK; New York: Cambridge University Press.

Battaglio, Stephen. 2017. "Sinclair Broadcast Group Is Fined $13 Million by FCC for Failing to Identify Sponsored Programming." *Los Angeles Times*, December 21. http://www.latimes.com/business/hollywood/la-fi-ct-sinclair-fcc-fine-20171221-story.html.

Baughman, James L. 2007. *Same Time, Same Station: Creating American Television, 1948–1961*. Baltimore: Johns Hopkins University Press.

Croteau, David, and William Hoynes. 2006. *The Business of Media: Corporate Media and the Public Interest*. 2nd ed. Thousand Oaks, CA: Pine Forge Press.

Curran, James, Shanto Iyengar, Anker Brink Lund, and Inka Salovaara-Moring. 2009. "Media System, Public Knowledge and Democracy: A Comparative Study." *European Journal of Communication* 24 (1): 5–26. https://doi.org/10.1177/0267323108098943.

Dirks, Van Essen, Murray & April. 2017. "History of Ownership Consolidation." March 31. http://dirksvanessen.com/articles/view/223/history-of-ownership-consolidation-/.

Habermas, Jürgen. 1989. *The Structural Transformation of the Public Sphere: An Inquiry into a Category of Bourgeois Society*. Studies in Contemporary German Social Thought. Cambridge, MA: MIT Press.

Hallin, Daniel C., and Paolo Mancini. 2004. *Comparing Media Systems: Three Models of Media and Politics*. Communication, Society, and Politics. Cambridge, UK: Cambridge University Press.

Iyengar, Shanto. 2015. *Media Politics: A Citizen's Guide*. 3rd ed. New York: W. W. Norton & Company.

John, Richard R. 2010. *Network Nation: Inventing American Telecommunications*. Cambridge, MA: Belknap Press of Harvard University Press.

Kroll, Andy. 2017. "Ready for Trump TV? Inside Sinclair Broadcasting's Plot to Take Over Your Local News." *Mother Jones*. https://www.motherjones.com/politics/2017/10/ready-for-trump-tv-inside-sinclair-broadcastings-plot-to-take-over-your-local-news-1/.

McChesney, Robert Waterman. 2013. *Digital Disconnect: How Capitalism Is Turning the Internet against Democracy*. New York: The New Press.

Perez-Pena, Richard. 2009. "As Cities Go from Two Papers to One, Talk of Zero." *The New York Times*, March 11. https://www.nytimes.com/2009/03/12/business/media/12papers.html.

Rosen, Philip T. 1980. *The Modern Stentors: Radio Broadcasters and the Federal Government, 1920–1934*. Contributions in Economics and Economic History. Westport, CT: Greenwood Press.

Smith, Jeffery Alan. 1990. *Printers and Press Freedom: The Ideology of Early American Journalism*. New York: Oxford University Press.

Williams, Alex T. 2016. "Newspaper Companies Lag behind Their Broadcast Siblings after Spinoffs." http://www.pewresearch.org/fact-tank/2016/08/09/newspaper-companies-lag-behind-their-broadcast-siblings-after-spinoffs/.

Q11. DO NEWSGATHERING ORGANIZATIONS ONLY PUBLISH CONTENT THAT WILL MAKE THEM MONEY?

Answer: Yes and no. Many factors influence what content is published, including commercial pressures, though their influence is often indirect. Many journalism organizations—and especially the journalists who work there—try to operate around public service missions. But most news organizations in the United States are commercial businesses, so they are subject to the commercial pressures that affect any business. Additionally, most media organizations have traditionally relied on a dual-product model, in which they sell content to consumers while also selling the consumers' attention to advertisers. With numerous channels competing for audiences' money and attention, the popularity of content—which translates to a bigger audience and more revenue—becomes a driving force in the decisions of what content to publish. Though journalists and content producers have traditionally been somewhat shielded from this structural bias toward commercial interests, that firewall between the content and business operations of a media organization has eroded in the 21st century. Additionally, digital tools have allowed individual content producers and journalists to see in real time what content is being read or viewed, which at least implicitly pushes journalists to increase those numbers.

The Facts: The motivations to publish any media content are multifaceted and complex. The process often involves many people, and the forces that drive decisions are often indirect. Gatekeeping (Shoemaker and Vos 2009) and hierarchy of influences (Shoemaker and Reese 2014) theories explain how media content decisions are made through several hierarchical levels: individuals, their routines, the organizations they work for, the social institutions and other organizations they work alongside, and the broader society and culture they work within. These levels interact with one another, exerting influence on lower levels. For example, individuals make decisions based in part on their personal backgrounds and life experiences (e.g., going to an elite and expensive college but having little debt because of high socioeconomic status), but those life experiences exist within a broader social and cultural context (e.g., a capitalist economy that emphasizes wealth). As such, broader structural characteristics within a media system can influence organizations, processes, and people to influence content.

The U.S. economy is based primarily on free-market principles, and decisions over the course of the past 100 years or so, as mass media developed, have established most media as for-profit, commercial enterprises. That means that media organizations are expected to bring in revenue and hopefully turn a profit to operate. The philosophy behind this structure is that market forces put the audiences in charge, and the content that audiences want will be produced because media businesses will work to respond to those market desires and innovate out of necessity to create the supply that the audience demands. However, commercial media is structured to respond to other factors beyond audience desires. In the United States, many see journalism as a vital institution of democracy. It is the so-called fourth estate, charged with speaking truth to power and giving voice to the voiceless. Market forces may not encourage, and may in fact discourage, such democratic goals. Though other media systems and structures exist that have less market impact because they are often publicly funded and somewhat free from market forces (Croteau and Hoynes 2006), most media organizations in the United States are commercial enterprises that rely on audience consumption behavior to make content decisions.

To fully understand the market-based decisions of media companies, it's important to understand just what a media company is selling. At first glance, it may seem like the content is the product. But the content is just one of the products. Scholars David Croteau and William Hoynes argue that media businesses operate in a "dual product market," selling media content to consumers and then selling consumers to advertisers. Of course, though some media organizations still operate with some money directly from consumers in the form of cable subscriptions or book purchases, for example, many news media organizations have traditionally operated primarily with advertising revenue. That's especially true with Internet and broadcast media, which are main sources of news for many Americans. If the audience is the product, then the consumer of that product is the advertiser. This is one of the central critiques according to this dual-product market media model—that media organizations might be more responsive to advertiser desires than audience wants or needs. They might focus, for example, on getting more attention for products at the expense of important social stories that might distract from attention paid to the advertiser.

Advertising has been a major source of revenue for news media. In the mid-20th century, for example, advertising accounted for nearly two-thirds of newspapers' revenues. With such heavy reliance on ads, journalists and newsroom leaders tried to limit the influence of advertiser interest. For many years, it worked reasonably well. There were few mass media options for advertisers to market their products to consumers—primarily newspapers, local television stations, local radio stations, and magazines. And those consumers were in the habit of reading and consuming those media. That meant that news businesses in particular could sometimes pursue public service goals despite a potential negative impact on a relationship with an advertiser. In some organizations, especially larger ones, the decisions of the news reporting side of an organization were somewhat insulated from business concerns. Robert McCormick, the longtime *Chicago Tribune* publisher, went so far as to require journalists and those involved on the business side of the paper to take separate elevators, restricting the business elevators from stopping on the newsroom floors of the building. But as cable TV in the 1970s and 1980s and online media in the 1990s and 2000s developed, the number of sources for information—and thus competitors for the advertisers' business—grew exponentially. Though many journalists believe a firewall between business and news/editorial operations should exist, some suggest such a structure is unrealistic, an "anachronistic relic of a time when the news industry's survival wasn't threatened" (Coddington 2015, 68). With the ability to very narrowly target consumers with new social media and digital marketing tools developed in the late 2000s and 2010s, advertisers have many more—and some would argue, more effective—options to put their products in front of consumers. As print media advertising decreases and TV advertising stays flat or grows slowly, digital advertising—especially mobile advertising—is becoming more dominant. Though the majority of advertising dollars still go to nondigital sources, that's rapidly changing. According to eMarketer estimates, digital advertising made up about 44 percent of all advertising revenue in 2017, up from 37 percent in 2016. Mobile advertising accounts for nearly two-thirds of that figure. Additionally, nearly 52 percent of all digital display advertising revenue goes to just Facebook and Google, which some refer to as the "digital duopoly" of the digital advertising world.

Because of increased competition, especially in the digital realm, news organizations have tried new advertising strategies, which, some argue, weaken the barrier between the news and business sides of a media company. For example, many newsrooms have experimented with so-called native advertising, which is a sponsored message that tends to adopt the same look, feel, and tone of the actual news content produced on a site or app. The Interactive Advertising Bureau (2013) defined native advertising as "paid ads that are so cohesive with the page content, assimilated into the design, and consistent with the platform behavior that the viewer simply feels that they belong." Although as many as three-quarters of online publishers in the United States offer some form of "native" advertising

(Gilley 2013), the practice remains the topic of some controversy in journalism circles. Some critics say that the lines between journalism and advertising are blurred when publishers run native ads, especially as several studies have shown that audiences often do not notice paid advertising labels even when they are present. When people do recognize native advertising for what it is, however, that also can have negative repercussions for publishers. One study found that when audiences noticed native advertising, attitudes about the publisher and perceptions of its credibility declined, especially among digital-only publishers (Amazeen and Muddiman 2018). Newsroom leaders might perceive this to be a risk to credibility that they cannot afford in a political and social climate that seems hostile to journalism.

In addition to the pressures from within news organizations and between news organizations and other institutions with which they interact, subtle structural bias present in the routines of individual journalists influences the content that is published. One scholar provided a lengthy list of such biases:

- Commercial bias: Most news organizations are moneymaking businesses and need to create content that is attractive to their customers, which are both audiences and advertisers.
- Temporal bias: New information is preferred over old information.
- Visual bias: Stories that include visually compelling videos or photographs may be more likely to attract audiences.
- Bad news bias: Good news is perceived as boring, and bad news is perceived as having a more pressing impact on audiences.
- Narrative bias: News is presented as stories that follow familiar narrative structures, so news that includes narrative elements like a beginning, middle, and end and characters like clear antagonists, protagonists, and so forth may be more likely to be chosen.
- Status quo bias: A belief in the underlying social system and its norms, especially as it relates to larger political and economic social structures.
- Fairness bias: A practice stemming from the desire to be fair that pushes journalists to always get opposing sides of stories, even if perspectives are not equal, creating potential false equivalences.
- Expediency bias: Journalists are busy and deadline driven, and reporting resources are often scarce, so the most expedient path to publishing a story may be taken, such as using the first expert source a journalist can get on the phone for a story, even if that person might not be the best choice.

- Glory bias: Journalists, especially TV journalists, want to maintain cultural capital and be seen as knowledgeable insiders, so they tend to put themselves into stories more than necessary.
- Class bias: Journalists, for the most part, do not reflect the demographics of the communities they cover. They are more likely to be white, male, middle-aged, more educated, and more highly paid and are more likely to consider themselves politically independent compared to the general U.S. population (Cline 2009).

While the commercial bias is just one of many listed, it is embedded in several other biases. For instance, visuals help attract and keep audiences' attention, so stories with compelling videos or photographs might be chosen because more attention equals more potential advertising revenue. Additionally, staffing realities in newsrooms caused by economic pressures to maintain profits despite decreased advertising revenue can increase the influence of the expediency bias. For instance, as profit-driven media owners cut newsroom staffs, fewer journalists are left doing the same or even more work, so more expedient paths to accomplishing tasks and publishing material may be taken.

Though most journalists say that they perceive a significant amount of professional autonomy in selecting what to cover, some feel pressure from owners and from advertisers to toe a more business-friendly line. The extent of this influence often depends on factors like the size of the media operation or the platform. One study found that advertising managers at small newspapers and those owned by chains were more likely to approve of scenarios that blurred the lines between the advertising and editorial sides of the paper (An and Bergen 2007). Another study found that among various organizational influences on content decisions, owners and top-level executives had the biggest influence, followed by staff-size pressures (Colistra 2018). Though some journalists do perceive pressure from owners and advertisers, most business influence is indirect. "Commercial imperatives" from decreased staffing and newsroom resources have increasingly played a role in journalists' work. One 2013 survey of U.S. journalists found that about half said they felt they were expected to do more work with fewer resources (Willnat, Weaver, and Wilhoit 2017).

Additionally, journalists are increasingly pressured to pay attention to and make decisions based on the popularity of their work. Many newsrooms are now equipped with large television screens displaying the most popular or trending stories in a newsroom. These displays often show minute details, such as the audience size for each piece of content, how much of a video was watched, or how much of an article was read. Scholars look at audience metrics as a particularly powerful form of audience feedback. Of course, journalists have varying views on the use of analytics, with some journalists flatly rejecting their use for fear of threats to independence. But one study found that journalists with organizational policies that push the use of analytics are more likely to say they intend to and ultimately use audience analytics in making decisions in their work, including what stories to cover and how to cover those stories (Tandoc and Ferrucci 2017). Indeed, many news organizations have started not only displaying analytics around the newsroom but also sending personalized reports to journalists with their own numbers. A report from the Tow Center noted that organizational culture is a major driver for how metrics are used and the influence they have on content decisions (Petre 2015). For example, metrics can drive internal competition among journalists in a news organization rather than toward competing media businesses. But they can also be used to simply provide additional data to support decisions already made through more traditional journalistic processes. There is still much research to be conducted on the role of analytics in shaping newsgathering decisions.

Journalists and newsgathering organizations have traditionally taken pride in the independence from market influences on their work, establishing proverbial firewalls between the economic pressures of running a business and decisions about what news to cover. Though those separations exist, commercial bias is embedded in various levels of influence, even if indirectly. However, as newsgathering organizations face increased competition for advertising dollars, some may face hard decisions on how such separations can exist in the future. Additionally, journalists may face increasing pressure to produce content that meets organizational audience and financial goals.

FURTHER READING

Amazeen, Michelle A., and Ashley R. Muddiman. 2018. "Saving Media or Trading on Trust?" *Digital Journalism* 6 (2): 176–195. https://doi:10 .1080/21670811.2017.1293488.

An, Soontae, and Lori Bergen. 2007. "Advertiser Pressure on Daily Newspapers: A Survey of Advertising Sales Executives." *Journal of Advertising* 36 (2): 111–121.

Cline, Andrew. 2009. "Bias." In *21st Century Communication: A Reference Handbook*, edited by William F. Eadie, 479–486. Thousand Oaks, CA: Sage.

Coddington, Mark. 2015. "The Wall Becomes a Curtain: Revisiting Journalism's News-Business Boundary." In *Boundaries of Journalism: Professionalism, Practices and Participation*, edited by M. Carlson and S. C. Lewis, 67–82. New York: Routledge.

Colistra, Rita. 2018. "Power Pressures and Pocketbook Concerns: Perceptions of Organization Influences on News Content in the Television Industry." *International Journal of Communication* 12 (18): 1790–1810. http://ijoc.org/index.php/ijoc/article/view/8121/2331.

Croteau, David, and William Hoynes. 2006. *The Business of Media: Corporate Media and the Public Interest*. 2nd ed. Thousand Oaks, CA: Pine Forge Press.

Gilley, Stephanie. 2013. "Blurred Lines: Advertising or Content?—An FTC Workshop on Native Advertising." Federal Trade Commission, December 4. http://www.ftc.gov/news-events/events-calendar/2013/12/blurred-lines-advertising-or-content-ftc-workshop-native.

Interactive Advertising Bureau. 2013. "The Native Advertising Playbook." December 4. https://www.iab.com/wp-content/uploads/2015/06/IAB-Native-Advertising-Playbook2.pdf.

Petre, Caitlin. 2015. *The Traffic Factories: Metrics at Chartbeat, Gawker Media, and the News York Times*. New York: Tow Center for Digital Journalism. https://towcenter.org/research/traffic-factories/.

Shoemaker, Pamela J., and Stephen D. Reese. 2014. *Mediating the Message in the 21st Century*. New York: Routledge.

Shoemaker, Pamela J., and Timothy Vos. 2009. *Gatekeeping Theory*. New York: Routledge.

Tandoc, Edson C., and Patrick R. Ferrucci. 2017. "Giving In or Giving Up: What Makes Journalists Use Audience Feedback in Their News Work?" *Computers in Human Behavior* 68 (March): 149–156. https://doi: 10.1016/j.chb.2016.11.027.

Willnat, Lars, David H. Weaver, and G. Cleveland Wilhoit. 2017. *The American Journalist in the Digital Age: A Half-Century Perspective*. New York: Peter Lang Publishing.

Q12. IS THE AMERICAN NEWS MEDIA SYSTEM THE SAME AS THAT OF THE REST OF THE DEVELOPED WORLD?

Answer: Yes and no. The United States enjoys one of the freest press systems in the world, but among developed nations, the United States is uniquely reliant on a highly conglomerated commercial media system to meet the information needs of the public. Other developed nations generally offer a more robust mix of commercial and noncommercial outlets, typically including a well-funded public media system that operates independent of government and politics.

The Facts: Media systems around the world vary a great deal. At one end of the spectrum, some countries—such as North Korea and Iran—have little to no press freedom. The only news media that exist in these nations are owned and controlled by the government, and the only messages citizens hear from these entities are ones that support the interests of the state. Dissenting views are nonexistent, and anyone who challenges the official message is imprisoned or worse. Countries at the other end of the spectrum—notably Denmark and Finland—have robust hybrid media systems, including a diverse mix of public and private ownership; large subsidies for noncommercial media; and laws and policies that help provide access to information, reduce concentrations of ownership, and restrict hate speech. Citizens have access to a rich diversity of information from a variety of points of view. Still other countries—such as Brazil and India—fall somewhere in between. They might have laws protecting speech and press rights in theory, but the reality faced by journalists might involve undue amounts of political pressure, government censorship, violence and intimidation, and highly concentrated ownership. Citizens in these countries have access to a limited diversity of information that might include different viewpoints on certain issues and topics but not on others.

So where does the United States fall? According to independent, nongovernmental watchdog groups such as Freedom House and Reporters Without Borders, while the United States has generally ranked among the "most free" nations, it is quite far from the top of the list, and its ranking has been on the decline over the past decade. According to Freedom House's 2017 Press Freedom rankings, the United States is tied for 33rd place out of 199, behind countries such as Iceland, Costa Rica, and Estonia (Freedom House 2017). Reporters Without Borders places the United States at number 43 out of 180, behind the Czech Republic, Ghana, and South Africa, among others (Reporters Without Borders 2017). Other countries that top the United States for press freedom include Austria, New Zealand, Australia, Germany, Spain, Chile, France, and the United Kingdom. The very top of these lists almost always features the Scandinavian countries—namely, Norway, Sweden, Denmark—as well as Finland and the Netherlands.

Why does the United States appear where it does? The United States provides very strong legal protections for the press by virtue of the First

Amendment, and courts routinely uphold the rights of the press. However, the lack of a federal "shield law" means journalists can be forced to reveal sources and secrets, and federal authorities have regularly cracked down on leaks and whistle-blowers who attempt to provide information to journalists. The Obama administration was heavily criticized by free press advocates in this regard. The Obama administration did expand the federal Freedom of Information Act, which guarantees public access to government documents, but also reduced transparency and set a record high number of request denials. The trend has continued under the Trump administration. As of March 2018, requests were denied or censored in 78 percent of 823,222 cases, a new record for the past decade (Bridis 2015, 2018).

Economically, compared to many nations, the U.S. media system—despite overwhelmingly private ownership—offers access to a range of information sources, including some publicly funded noncommercial media, most notably PBS (television's Public Broadcasting Service) and NPR (National Public Radio). The economics of the news industry remain in flux as newspapers continue to struggle for viability, and concentration of ownership remains a concern. The United States fails to receive top marks because of its comparatively low level of funding for public media and its relative lack of regulations ensuring access to information and diversity of ownership.

The United States' ranking takes its biggest hit in terms of political interference. While censorship is rare, American news media outlets are increasingly and aggressively partisan, especially on cable television and online. Most newspapers and over-the-air broadcasters continue to strive for impartial coverage, but journalists routinely face harassment and intimidation in the highly charged political landscape. This trend intensified dramatically during the 2016 presidential campaign and Donald Trump's subsequent presidency. President Trump routinely taunted and harassed news media outlets and journalists during the 2016 campaign and the first two years of his time in the Oval Office, calling them an "enemy of the people," characterizing their work as "fake news," and threatening to revoke the press credentials of any journalist who failed to cover him in a positive light. As Trump himself proclaimed, "I have a running war with the media. They are among the most dishonest human beings on earth" (Davis and Rosenberg 2017). Critics suggest that Trump aims to undermine trust in news media and its traditionally independent watchdog role. On the other hand, he often praises Fox News, which almost always covers him and his administration with a high degree of favorability. Other developed nations with high marks for press freedom do not face such a climate of incivility toward news media or journalists.

Overall, while the United States is far from perfect, it's important to note that only 13 percent of the world's population enjoys a free press (Freedom House 2017). Most citizens of the world live in countries with moderate to severe restrictions on access to diverse information. And press freedom worldwide has been on the decline in the 21st century due to threats to journalists and crackdowns on independent media, both in democratic nations and in regions facing growing authoritarianism. Press freedom in general began to increase in the late 1980s as the Cold War came to an end and authoritarian governments began to fall, so a reversal of this trend is seen as alarming to proponents of press freedom. Obviously, press freedom is important for journalists to do their work, but restrictions on press freedom often serve as early warning signs of future crackdowns on other kinds of freedom. Scholars emphasize that historically, authoritarian regimes target news media in the early stages of a broader campaign to destabilize and undermine other institutions such as court systems and elections that, when healthy, act as checks on totalitarian impulses.

More narrowly, the media systems of nations in the developed world offer different approaches to press freedom, but these generally include less private ownership and more regulation when compared to the United States (Iyengar 2015). For example, a political candidate in the United States has to raise enormous amounts of money to buy access to the airwaves; in most European democracies, free access is guaranteed for candidates and parties alike. The U.S. approach theoretically means anyone can gain access, but the financial reality means campaigning is mainly the province of the wealthy. The typical European approach ensures that citizens have a chance to hear from a variety of voices regardless of the amount of money they have or can raise. This is illustrative of the general difference in approaches to liberty between the United States and Europe. The U.S. approach is generally "negative," meaning an absence of government involvement is seen as the best way to ensure freedom. The European approach is more "positive," meaning the government is expected to play a more active role in leveling the playing field and ensuring equality of opportunity.

In any democracy, important roles of news media include contributing to informed citizenship and serving as a watchdog over the powerful on behalf of citizens. Market forces have an effect on journalists' ability to perform this role. In the United States, where news media organizations are almost entirely privately owned, the drive to be profitable means more entertainment content and less news—and even the news content must be entertaining. In Europe, most countries have mixed systems with substantial public subsidies for broadcasters, which limit the influence of market forces and increase the amount of news content that supports informed citizenship. In most of the European Union, public television channels rank at the top of audience share; European audiences for public television range from a low of 23 percent in Spain to a high of 67 percent in Denmark (Iyengar 2015).

While the public media systems of Europe were formed relatively early in the 20th century, the United States did not establish its own public media outlets until Congress passed the Public Broadcasting Act of 1967, which created Public Broadcasting Service (PBS). However, significant funding was never allotted, and today, most funding comes from private grants and donations rather than from public revenue. Overall, PBS reaches only about 2 percent of the American television audience, much lower than its European counterparts (Iyengar 2015). Nonetheless, the audience for PBS programming has grown recently, with the *PBS News-Hour* attracting around 1 million viewers in 2016. A majority of Americans report having a high degree of trust in PBS and consider it a good use of public revenue. The Corporation for Public Broadcasting (CPB) oversees federal funding for public media and distributes 70 percent of its funds to nearly 1,500 locally owned public radio and television stations. In 2017, CPB received $445 million in federal appropriations, or around $1.35 per American (Corporation for Public Broadcasting 2017). Compare that to the per capita spending on public media in other developed nations, which ranges from $30 per person in Canada and $34 in Australia to $90 in the United Kingdom and $133 in Norway (Benson and Powers 2011). Some of these subsidies go to commercial news outlets, which are then required to meet requirements for quality and quantity of public affairs programming. Many of these public broadcasting channels attract one-third or more of the national television audience.

There is no one way to create a media system, and every developed nation has a different approach. But scholars have shown that mixed or hybrid systems with robust commitments to public media routinely produce the best outcomes in terms of quality of information and benefit to citizens (Curran et al. 2009; Hallin and Mancini 2004; Iyengar 2015). Furthermore, historians have shown a significant precedent for public subsidies for journalism in the United States. In the early days of the republic, postal subsidies and government printing contracts amounted to today's equivalent of billions of dollars in public spending on news and information production and distribution (McChesney and Nichols

2010). Finally, comparing media systems helps show that the current American system is neither natural nor inevitable but rather is the result of policies and practices established over time by human actors with their own priorities and presumptions. History shows how media systems, rather than being predetermined by culture or technologies, are shaped by political struggles (McChesney 1993; Starr 2004). As always, the public should ask who benefits from the current arrangement and whether public resources are being properly allocated to provide sufficient public benefit. As scholars Rodney Benson and Matthew Powers (2011, 3) noted, "In fact, government has always and will always influence how our media system functions, from the early newspaper postal subsidies to handing out broadcast licenses and subsidizing broadband deployment. The question is not if government should be involved, but how, and that is a question that demands an in-depth conversation, not a shouting match."

FURTHER READING

Benson, Rodney, and Matthew Powers. 2011. "Public Media and Political Independence: Lessons for the Future of Journalism from around the World." Free Press. http://rodneybenson.org/wp-content/uploads/Benson-Powers-2011-public-media-and-political-independence-1.pdf

Bridis, Ted. 2015. "Obama Administration Sets New Record for Withholding FOIA Requests." *PBS NewsHour*, March 18. https://www.pbs.org/newshour/nation/obama-administration-sets-new-record-withholding-foia-requests.

Bridis, Ted. 2018. "US Sets New Record for Censoring, Withholding Gov't Files." AP News, March 12. https://apnews.com/714791d91d7944e49a284a51fab65b85.

Corporation for Public Broadcasting. 2014. "About CPB." September 22. https://www.cpb.org/aboutcpb.

Curran, James, Shanto Iyengar, Anker Brink Lund, and Inka Salovaara-Moring. 2009. "Media System, Public Knowledge and Democracy: A Comparative Study." *European Journal of Communication* 24 (1): 5–26. https://doi.org/10.1177/0267323108098943.

Davis, Julie Hirschfeld, and Matthew Rosenberg. 2017. "With False Claims, Trump Attacks Media on Turnout and Intelligence Rift." *The New York Times*, January 21, sec. Politics. https://www.nytimes.com/2017/01/21/us/politics/trump-white-house-briefing-inauguration-crowd-size.html.

Freedom House. 2017. "Freedom of the Press 2017." April 18. https://freedomhouse.org/report/freedom-press/freedom-press-2017.

Hallin, Daniel C., and Paolo Mancini. 2004. *Comparing Media Systems: Three Models of Media and Politics*. Communication, Society, and Politics. Cambridge, UK: Cambridge University Press.

Iyengar, Shanto. 2015. *Media Politics: A Citizen's Guide*. 3rd ed. New York: W. W. Norton & Company.

McChesney, Robert. 1993. *Telecommunications, Mass Media, and Democracy: The Battle for the Control of U.S. Broadcasting, 1928–1935*. New York: Oxford University Press.

McChesney, Robert, and John Nichols. 2010. *The Death and Life of American Journalism: The Media Revolution That Will Begin the World Again*. 1st Nation Books. Philadelphia, PA: Nation Books.

Reporters without Borders. 2017. "2017 World Press Freedom Index." Accessed February 15, 2018. https://rsf.org/en/ranking.

Starr, Paul. 2004. *The Creation of the Media: Political Origins of Modern Communications*. New York: Basic Books.

3

❖❖❖

News Audiences

Audiences play an important role in shaping news content, both directly and indirectly. Audience interest and behavior can influence the stories that journalists cover, especially as journalists use increasingly sophisticated tools to measure responses to specific stories. While the highest ideals of journalism are to provide citizens with the information they need to make informed decisions as self-governing members of a democracy, journalists also want to entertain readers and to provide them with information about the stories and people they want to hear about, so journalists are sometimes said to be seeking a balance between giving readers what they want and what they need. Meanwhile, social media and participatory media, in general, have enabled audiences to participate more in the creation and dissemination of news and information. Another important trend in today's information-rich media environment is the escalating fragmentation of news audiences, as readers and viewers increasingly seek out news sources that conform to their existing worldviews.

Q13. DO MOST AMERICANS GET THEIR NEWS ONLINE TODAY?

Answer: No. Television, including cable, local, and network television news programs, was still the most popular way for Americans to get their news in 2016, with online sources coming second, ahead of radio and print media. However, half of Americans ages 18–29 get their news online, so these consumption patterns may shift to favor online news in the coming years. The vast majority of Americans say they consume news in some form, although there are differences when it comes to age and preferred medium. Generally, older Americans consume the most news.

The Facts: Nearly 90 percent of Americans used the Internet in the late 2000s. The growth of the Internet and the wide adoption of smart-phones mean that the majority of people in the United States have almost constant access to information. Smartphones, which approximately two-thirds of Americans now own, are a portal to various kinds of infor-mation, connecting people with personal social networks, professional and business content, entertainment, and news of public interest in the same device. Users learn about political news and family events through the same handheld technology, and sometimes the same application or social media site. Even the public interest news they receive may be per-sonalized due to cultivation of a news feed by users and algorithms that select information based on a user's history and apparent preferences.

What people consider news may be shifting, but the notion of news is still largely shaped by modern journalism and the 20th-century develop-ment of the journalistic profession. As Barbie Zelizer (2005, 66) noted, "The term *news*—originally derived from the word *new* during the late 16th century—tends to signal a commercial aura that surrounds the ongoing provision of information about current events." This definition of news was shaped in part by the practices and principles of journalists, whose ethics codes were built around a commitment to serve the public interest and provide a truthful account of the day's events in a meaning-ful context. Bill Kovach and Tom Rosenstiel studied journalists' views of their role through a series of surveys and forums and summarized their findings as follows: "The primary purpose of journalism is to provide citi-zens with the information they need to be free and self-governing" (2001, 17). The understanding of news as information that has some significance or importance in people's lives and has happened recently and in the proximity of the audience shapes the common understanding of what we call news today.

News, as generally conceived, continues to be important to a majority of Americans. According to the Pew Research Center, more than 70 per-cent of adults in the United States reported in 2016 that they follow "national and local news somewhat or very closely" (Mitchell et al. 2016), and 65 percent said they follow international news. However, beyond sharing a broad interest in the news, there are differences in how much news people consume and the medium they use to get the news. There has also been an increased fracturing of the news audience with the growth of cable news networks; the proliferation of online news sites, blogs, and even YouTube channels producing news; and the trend toward consuming news from postings on Facebook and other social media—all of which have varying degrees of professionalism and ethical standards.

When it comes to regular news consumption habits, television is still the most popular medium, but the Internet is now second, ahead of radio and print. Of the respondents in a 2018 Pew survey, 50 percent said they often get news from television, compared with 38 percent who say they often get news online (Matsa 2018). Twenty-five percent said they often get news from the radio, and 20 percent identified print newspapers as their primary source of news. Social media is a popular way to get news, particularly for younger people, and the Pew data indicate that age is a strong factor determining people's preferred medium for getting news.

Generally, older Americans favor television and print newspapers, and those numbers decline in younger age groups, while the reverse is true for online news. Just 5 percent of those in the 18- to 29-year-old demographic said they often get news from a print newspaper, while almost half of those over the age of 65 said they often read a print paper (Mitchell et al. 2016). There were similar disparities in the ages of those who watch television news. Significant majorities of Americans ages 50–64 (72 percent) and over 65 (85 percent) said they often get news on TV, but only 27 percent of those ages 18–29 said they do. Younger Americans were much more likely to get news online, with 50 percent of 18- to 29-year-olds and 49 percent of 30- to 49-year-olds saying they often get news from the Internet. Diddi and LaRose (2006) found that people's news consumption habits are set by the time they turn 30, which may explain why newspapers are most popular in the oldest demographics, gradually decreasing in each younger group.

The shift to digital news has been developing over the past couple decades with the growth of the Internet. Many news organizations have moved their content online and expanded online content offerings beyond what was available through print. Other news organizations have grown out of the Internet, and the proliferation of easy-to-use blogging sites has made the online publication of information accessible to a great many more people—and enabled the survival of more niche sites that serve smaller audiences.

Social media have further extended the power to create and share content to everyone with Internet access and the ability to set up an account. The increased number of voices means that Americans can seek the exact content they want. Enthusiasts celebrate the idea that we are all journalists now, excited by the dismantling of gatekeeping institutions and the democratization of information. Critics worry that the public service provided by journalists is being threatened, that citizen journalists and social media cannot replace it, and that consumers of news are increasingly limiting themselves to news sources that confirm their pre-existing political beliefs and ideologies. The traditional news media is at risk, as the business model that supported those organizations for so long has become unsustainable.

At the same time, widespread concerns have been expressed that the proliferation of nonprofessional information sources without ethics codes or editorial oversight will lead to a public that is so misinformed or so differently informed that citizens cannot discuss a shared set of facts. Although professional news organizations may also produce content targeted at a particular political audience, social media may exacerbate political divisions by allowing users to connect with like-minded individuals and curate their news feeds to include only those sources they would like to see. Most social media sites also employ algorithms to filter content to show users information that may conform to their preferences and previous behaviors (Pariser 2011). Users are therefore unlikely to encounter information that contradicts their previously held beliefs.

Although there are differences in regular news habits, most Americans have used the Internet to get news, and a majority get news through social media, even if they indicate that these are not the sources they turn to most often. In 2016, 81 percent of adults in the United States said they get news online, according to Pew. Many of those news consumers were using the Internet to access traditional news media, such as newspapers and television news networks that offer their content online, but by 2017, 67 percent of U.S. adults reported that they get news through social media at least occasionally (Shearer and Gottfried 2017). Facebook is by far the most popular site to get news, with 45 percent of Americans saying they got news from the site. The next-most popular social media site for getting news was YouTube, which only 18 percent of Americans said they used for news, followed by Twitter, Instagram, and Snapchat (Shearer and Gottfried 2017). While Facebook has more users overall, a much higher percentage of Twitter's users turn to that site for news, indicating that there is some difference in how users perceive and use the site. So, although 74 percent of Twitter users say they use the site for news, that represents just 11 percent of Americans who get news on Twitter.

While many Americans use social media to get news, respondents to the Pew survey indicated that they don't trust news they get from social media very much. Only 4 percent of Internet users said they trust the news they get on social media "a lot," and 30 percent said they trust the news they get on social media "some" (Mitchell et al. 2016). Confidence in local and national news organizations, in contrast, is relatively high: 22 percent of American adults said they trust information they get from local news organizations a lot, and 60 percent said they trust it some. National news organizations were just slightly less trusted: 18 percent said they trust information from them a lot, and 59 percent said they trust it some. Similarly, a study by the NORC research center at the University of Chicago found that "90 percent of Americans who use [newspapers], in print or digital form, said they 'can completely or mostly trust' newspapers as a source" (Bradburn et al. 2016).

Social media provides some benefits to news consumers, as social media sites and apps make it easy to access news content while interacting with content from friends and social connections, bringing the news to where the users are already spending time and attention. One 2017 media study found that "the ideal-typical mode in which young users consume news on social media can be characterized with the notion of 'incidental news'. Most young users get the news on their mobile devices as part of being on platforms like Facebook or Twitter. They encounter the news, rather than looking for it" (Boczkowski, Mitchelstein, and Matassi 2017, 1785). Other research suggests that while people may be following the news generally on social media sites, they may not be reading full stories. Gabielkov et al. (2016) found that 59 percent of links shared on Twitter, for example, were shared but not clicked, so the users passed them on without reading the article they're linking to.

FURTHER READING

Boczkowski, Pablo, Eugenia Mitchelstein, and Mora Matassi. 2017. "Incidental News: How Young People Consume News on Social Media." Proceedings of the 50th Hawaii International Conference on System Sciences. http://scholarspace.manoa.hawaii.edu/bitstream/10125/41371/1/paper0222.pdf.

Bradburn, Norman, Jennifer Benz, Brian Kirchoff, Emily Alvarez, David Sterrett, and Trevor Tompson. 2016. "How Americans Navigate the Modern Information Environment." NORC, University of Chicago.

Diddi, Arvind, and Robert LaRose. 2006. "Getting Hooked on News: Uses and Gratifications and the Formation of News Habits among College Students in an Internet Environment." *Journal of Broadcasting & Electronic Media* 50 (2): 193–210.

Gabielkov, Maksym, Arthi Ramachandran, Augustin Chaintreau, and Arnaud Legout. 2016. "Social Clicks: What and Who Gets Read on Twitter?" ACM SIGMETRICS/IFIP Performance, Antibes, Juan-les-Pins, France.

Kovach, Bill, and Tom Rosenstiel. 2001. *Elements of Journalism: What Newspeople Should Know and the Public Should Expect.* New York: Three Rivers Press.

Matsa, Katerina E. 2018. "Fewer Americans Rely on TV News; What Type They Watch Varies by Who They Are." Pew Research Center. http://www.pewresearch.org/fact-tank/2018/01/05/fewer-americans-rely-on-tv-news-what-type-they-watch-varies-by-who-they-are/.

Mitchell, Amy, Jeffrey Gottfried, Michael Barthel, and Elisa Shearer. 2016. "The Modern News Consumer: News Attitudes and Practices in the Digital Era." Pew Research Center. http://www.journalism.org/2016/07/07/the-modern-news-consumer/.

Mitchell, Amy, Jeffrey Gottfried, Jocelyn Kiley, and Katerina E. Matsa. 2014. "Political Polarization and Media Habits." Pew Research Center. http://www.journalism.org/2014/10/21/political-polarization-media-habits/.

Pariser, Eli. 2011. *The Filter Bubble: What the Internet Is Hiding from You.* New York: Penguin Press.

Shearer, Elisa, and Jeffrey Gottfried. 2017. "News Use across Social Media Platforms 2017." Pew Research Center. http://www.journalism.org/2017/09/07/news-use-across-social-media-platforms-2017/.

Zelizer, Barbie. 2005. "Definitions of Journalism." In *The Press*, edited by Geneva Overholser and Kathleen H. Jamieson, 66–80. New York: Oxford University Press.

Q14. DO LIBERALS AND CONSERVATIVES CONSUME DIFFERENT MEDIA?

Answer: Yes, political ideology is a strong factor determining the audience of different news media, with liberals and conservatives expressing markedly different levels of trust in specific media outlets and the news media in general. This divide has grown with the increase in online news consumption and cable news shows catering to partisan audiences. Social media and algorithms in search engines and news aggregators may serve to further isolate divergent audiences from each other. However, some scholars suggest there is still significant overlap around centrist media sources. In addition, research indicates that liberals tend to consume diverse media, even while conservatives coalesce around a single primary news source—Fox News.

The Facts: Not all Americans strongly identify with a political party, but a survey by the Pew Research Center (2017) found that about 51 percent of Americans identified as being on the left side of the political spectrum, 8 percent were "bystanders" in the middle, and 42 percent were on the right side. On either end of the spectrum were core partisans: 16 percent of Americans whose views are solidly liberal and 13 percent who were identified as solidly conservative. These views translate more or less to party affiliation, with 20 percent identifying as strong Democrats, 11 percent moderate Democrats, 18 percent leaning Democrat, 10 percent not leaning to either party, 15 percent strong Republicans, 9 percent moderate Republicans, and 16 percent leaning Republican. The extreme partisans in these groups have more in common, in terms of media habits, with other extreme partisans than they do with moderates, but they tend to get their news from entirely different sources. As the Media Insight Project (2017) concluded, "The bigger differences come between people who identify with one of the two major political parties and those who consider themselves independents or nonpartisans."

Differences in news habits of audiences were markedly different and correlated with ideology. Almost half of those who had "consistently conservative" views cited Fox News as their primary source for news about government and politics. Consistent liberals, on the other hand, named an array of news sources, including CNN (15 percent), NPR (13 percent), MSNBC (12 percent), and *The New York Times* (10 percent) (Mitchell et al. 2014). These primary sources, particularly Fox News as the main source for conservatives, may contribute to political polarization, as cable news networks have become increasingly polarized over the past two decades. A Pew Research Center (2009) study found that the Fox News audience was 14 points more Republican than the general public and 3 points less Democratic, while the CNN audience was 15 points more Democratic and 7 points less Republican than the general public.

This trend has been growing in part because some news media outlets, eager to attract and retain audiences with strong political beliefs, have adopted more partisan views over time. This state of affairs has resulted in a movement of some news media toward both ends of the political spectrum. A study by Gregory Martin and Ali Yurukoglu (2017) found that the partisan slant of cable news channels (CNN, MSNBC, and Fox News) increased over the period from 2000 to 2012 and attributed a general increase in political polarization in the U.S. population over the same period to the influence of those channels. They identify the 1990s as the period during which Fox News coverage began moving to the right and 2006 as the year that MSNBC began adopting a more liberal slant. They specifically noted that the Fox News effect on elections grew over the period from 2000 to 2008 due to increasing viewership of the network and an increasingly conservative slant. Martin and Yurukoglu (2017) found that in 2008, Fox News was to the right of the median Republican voter and MSNBC was to the left of the median Democratic voter. Notably, they attribute the cable news-driven increasing polarization to consumers' taste for like-minded news.

Besides consuming different media, liberals and conservatives demonstrate different levels of trust of the media and general opinions about the news media. Overall, trust in the media has been measured as low as 32 percent, according to Gallup polls (Swift 2016), with as few as 14 percent of Republican respondents expressing trust of news media. The Pew Research Center (2017) found similar results: "Views of the impact of the national news media for the most part break down along partisan lines, with Democratic-leaning groups expressing more positive opinions than GOP groups." That study further noted that the most partisan respondents had the most extreme views: consistent liberals were the only ideological group in which a majority (57 percent) said that "the news media has a positive effect on the way things are going in the country," while 95 percent of consistent conservatives said news media has a negative effect (Pew Research Center 2017).

While trust of the news media in general may be low, trust of specific news organizations is high, as partisan viewers have favorable views of their preferred news sources. When asked about specific sources, consistent conservatives expressed more distrust than trust of 24 of 36 news sources measured in the survey (Mitchell et al. 2014), while consistent liberals expressed more trust than distrust of 28 of the 36 sources. At the same time, however, 88 percent of consistent conservatives said they trust Fox News, while consistent liberals named NPR, PBS, and the BBC as the news sources they trust most. Trust also differs based on medium. A study from the NORC research group at the University of Chicago found that people who read newspapers show a high level of confidence in them: "90 percent of Americans who use them, in print or digital form, said they 'can completely or mostly trust' newspapers as a source" (Bradburn et al. 2016). These opinions contribute to what is perceived as the polarization of American news audiences: viewers get news from different sources, and trust their source, while distrusting other sources. However, politically moderate Americans were more diverse in their media consumption. Americans also show loyalty in their news consumption habits but differ in expressing that loyalty. In 2016, half of Americans said they feel loyal to their news sources, while half did not feel loyal to the sources they get news from (Mitchell et al. 2016). However, their habits indicate that they go back to the same sources again and again: in that same study, 76 percent of Americans said they turned to the same news sources repeatedly.

These differences in news sources, as well as the tendency to seek like-minded information, are replicated or even amplified on social media, where conservatives and liberals have displayed an increasing inclination to only pay heed to news organizations, social critics, scholars, celebrities, and other influencers and opinion leaders who hold the same political beliefs and world outlooks as themselves. Eli Pariser (2011) argued that these "filter bubbles"—wherein social media and Internet users reside in information bubbles that support their existing views—exacerbate these political divisions and divergent news consumption habits. Filter bubbles are created by algorithms on social media sites and search engines that select content for users based on their previous behaviors and demonstrated preferences. Analogous to movie recommending systems that suggest movies to users based on previous viewing and the preferences of other users who have demonstrated shared preferences, these algorithms function to show people information that agrees with or confirms their preexisting views. However, others have suggested that some sites, such as online newspapers, cause people to encounter views quite different from their own.

People who identify as conservatives and liberals both report behaviors on social media sites that may increase the likelihood they will encounter like-minded information, leading to further polarization in terms of information exposure. Pew found that consistent liberals who said they "pay attention to politics on Facebook" are also more likely than others to "like" or follow issue-based groups, with 60 percent doing so, while 46 percent of consistent conservatives did, and only 33 percent of undecideds did (Mitchell et al. 2014). Consistent conservatives and consistent liberals also reported following political parties or elected officials at higher rates, with 49 percent of consistent conservatives and 42 percent of consistent liberals reporting doing so, compared to 29 percent of overall Facebook users.

The Pew survey found that consistent conservatives on Facebook "were more likely than respondents in other ideological groups to hear political opinions that are in line with their own views" (Mitchell et al. 2014) and more likely to have friends with the same political views, with 66 percent reporting that most of their close friends have the same views on government and politics. Consistent liberals, meanwhile, were more likely than those in other ideological groups to block or break off friendships, both online and offline, because of political differences. Both groups were more likely than others to be exposed to views similar to their own: 47 percent of consistent conservatives and 32 percent of consistent liberals who said they pay attention to politics said the opinions they see are "mostly or always in line with their own views" (Mitchell et al. 2014). Respondents on the far partisan extremes were also more likely to say that most of their close friends share the same political views, as compared to those with self-described moderate views. These issues were not as common for moderates, which indicates that there is still a centrist majority that is not suffering from the same divisive tendencies (Prior 2013).

The tendency to seek out, favor, recall, and give credence to information that confirms one's existing beliefs is known as confirmation bias and has been observed in many settings and in individuals expressing views across the political spectrum. Confirmation bias may be a strong factor guiding audiences' perceptions and consumption of news media, especially partisan audiences. Another factor may be hostile media bias, the phenomenon in which partisans of opposite views both perceive the same news story to be biased against their side. Hostile media bias has been found to be strongest when people's feelings of partisanship are stimulated prior to reading an article and is mitigated most when readers are prompted to see themselves as part of the same group and as unified (Reid 2012). However, news programming and social media content that appeals to partisan viewers remains very commercially successful, generating high numbers of page views and high levels of viewership for cable news programming.

FURTHER READING

Bialik, Carl. 2016. "People Who Oppose Gay Marriage Are Less Likely to Value Expert Opinion." FiveThirtyEight. https://fivethirtyeight .com/features/people-who-oppose-gay-marriage-are-less-likely-to-value-expert-opinion/.

Bradburn, Norman, Jennifer Benz, Brian Kirchoff, Emily Alvarez, David Sterrett, and Trevor Tompson. 2016. "How Americans Navigate the Modern Information Environment." NORC, University of Chicago.

Martin, Gregory J., and Ali Yurukoglu. 2017. "Bias in Cable News: Persuasion and Polarization." *American Economic Review* 107 (9): 2565–2599.

Media Insight Project. 2017. "Partisanship and the Media: How Personal Politics Affect Where People Go, What They Trust, and Whether They

Pay." Associated Press and NORC. https://www.americanpressinstitute
.org/publications/reports/survey-research/partisanship-news-behavior/.

Mitchell, Amy, Jeffrey Gottfried, Michael Barthel, and Elisa Shearer.
2016. "The Modern News Consumer: News Attitudes and Practices
in the Digital Era." Pew Research Center. http://www.journalism.org/
2016/07/07/the-modern-news-consumer/.

Mitchell, Amy, Jeffrey Gottfried, Jocelyn Kiley, and Katerina E. Matsa.
2014. "Political Polarization and Media Habits." Pew Research Center.
http://www.journalism.org/2014/10/21/political-polarization-media-
habits/.

Pariser, Eli. 2011. *The Filter Bubble: What the Internet Is Hiding from You.*
New York: Penguin Press.

Pew Research Center. 2009. "Partisanship and Cable News Audiences." Pew
Research Center. http://www.pewresearch.org/2009/10/30/partisanship-
and-cable-news-audiences/.

Pew Research Center. 2017. "Political Typology Reveals Deep Fissures
on the Right and Left." Pew Research Center. http://www.people-press
.org/2017/10/24/political-typology-reveals-deep-fissures-on-the-right-
and-left/.

Prior, Markus. 2013. "Media and Political Polarization." *Annual Review
of Political Science* 16 (1): 101–127. https://doi.org/10.1146/annurev-
polisci-100711-135242.

Reid, Scott A. 2012. "A Self-Categorization Explanation for the Hostile
Media Effect." *Journal of Communication* 62 (3): 381–399.

Swift, Art. 2016. "Americans' Trust in Mass Media Sinks to New Low."
Gallup News. http://news.gallup.com/poll/195542/americans-trust-
mass-media-sinks-new-low.aspx.

Q15. DO AMERICANS TRUST THE NEWS MEDIA?

Answer: It depends. While many widely publicized polls show low and
even decreasing levels of trust in news media compared to just a couple of decades ago, public opinion varies widely when accounting for
demographics. In addition, most polls lump all media together, but audiences often differentiate among media organizations in the level of trust
assigned. Importantly, trust in news media has fallen to historically low
levels at the same time that trust in other political and social institutions
like government, organized religion, and educational institutions has
also declined. Finally, trust is a vague concept, sometimes conflated with

related terms like "reliability," "truthfulness," "lack of bias," and "accuracy," making trust hard to assess.

The Facts: According to many recent polls, journalists are not faring well. A 2017 poll from Gallup showed that just 41 percent of Americans have a fair amount or a great deal of "trust and confidence" in the media to report the news "fully, accurately, and fairly." Gallup first started asking this question in 1972 and has done so every year since 1997. Trust in the media was at its highest—72 percent—in 1976, after significant in-depth war reporting on the Vietnam War and the investigative journalism surrounding Watergate. Other polls show similar results. The public relations firm Edelman, for example, publishes an annual Trust Barometer that looks at a variety of social institutions. Edelman's 2018 report found that just 42 percent of Americans trust media "to do what is right." That figure marked a five-point decrease since 2017 among the general U.S. population. The Trust Barometer also reported a 22-point decrease in media trust among what Edelman called "informed publics"—college-educated high-earners who are aged 25–64 and report significant business news consumption and engagement.

However, trust and other opinions about the news media often vary widely depending on demographic characteristics, especially political affiliations and preferences. For example, a 2017 Gallup/Knight Foundation survey combined four questions about the media (overall satisfaction, level of perceived bias, perceived ability for media to separate fact from opinion, and perceived ability for media to provide objective news reports) to create a trust score, ranging from 0 (least trust) to 100 (most trust). The average score for respondents overall was 37. Democrats' average score was 54 compared to Republicans' 21. In another 2017 Gallup poll, while 41 percent of Americans overall trusted and had confidence in news media, only 14 percent of Republicans did. That compares to 72 percent of Democrats and 37 percent of Independents expressing the same level of confidence and trust. In fact, the 2017 overall figure showing 41 percent is an increase from 32 percent in 2016, which Gallup attributes to Democrats' overall strong opinion of news media. There has been a split between Republicans and Democrats in this poll since Gallup starting asking annually in 1997, but the difference between the two in 2017—58 points—was the largest in the poll's history. The Pew Research Center has found similar partisan divides among opinions of the news media and its role in society. Pew has been asking since 1985 whether Americans "think that criticism from news organizations keeps political leaders from doing things that shouldn't be done." In 2017, 89 percent of Democrats agreed with this statement compared to 42 percent of

Republicans. However, in 2016, slightly more Republicans (77 percent) than Democrats (74 percent) supported this statement. In fact, Republican support for the watchdog role of the press had been consistently higher since 2011, when Democrat Barack Obama was in his third year in the White House. Republicans and Democrats' belief in the watchdog role tends to flip depending on which party is in power, but the gap has never been wider than 2017's 47 points. Until then, the largest gap was 28 points, in the middle of the George W. Bush administration.

Other attitudes about media similarly diverge along party lines. More Republicans (87 percent) than Democrats (53 percent) in Pew's 2017 survey thought that "news organizations tend to favor one side." Gallup in 2017 found that 62 percent of Americans said that the media "favors one political party over the other." Of that 62 percent who said the media favors one party, 64 percent said it favors Democrats, and 22 percent said it favors Republicans. Between 1995 and 2003, Americans were almost evenly split on whether they thought media favored one party over the other, but since 2003 the percentage who thinks the media plays favorites—as well as those who think the favorites are the Democrats—has increased steadily each year. Support for national news organizations, in particular, is split along party lines. For instance, the 2017 Pew survey showed that more Democrats (34 percent) than Republicans (11 percent) thought "information from national news organizations is very trustworthy." In addition, Pew found that more Democrats (33 percent) than Republicans (18 percent) thought "national news media do very well in keeping them informed." A 2018 Gallup/Knight Foundation survey found that about 75 percent of Democrats but only about 30 percent of Republicans were confident that news from national newspapers and national TV newscasts was "mostly accurate and politically balanced." This suggests that Republicans, especially, see the news media as biased, favoring Democrats, and that perception may be fueled especially by how they evaluate the work of national news outlets.

Many of the polling and research organizations mentioned here have referenced the 2016 presidential election and the ongoing criticism of the press from the Trump administration as contributing to public opinion about the news media. A 2017 national survey from the Poynter Institute for Media Studies dug a little deeper into these issues, in part looking to see whether support for Trump (and not necessarily party affiliation) relates to opinions of the press. President Trump has made several comments referring to news media as the "enemy of the people" and arguing that news media keeps political leaders from doing their jobs. Indeed, while 31 percent of Americans overall agree with these statements, they differ substantially depending on whether they support Trump (about 65 percent of supporters agreed with Trump's criticisms) or not (about 15 percent). Poynter found that about 25 percent of Americans (including 42 percent of Trump supporters) believe that the government should be able to prevent news stories that are "biased or inaccurate" from running, a finding especially troubling for free press advocates. Currently, such prior restraint is unconstitutional according to a number of Supreme Court cases. General trust also diverges among supporters of different political candidates. For example, the 2018 Edelman Trust Barometer showed that 61 percent of Americans who voted for Hillary Clinton in the 2016 presidential election said they trust "media," compared to just 27 percent of those who voted for Donald Trump.

While political ideology, party affiliation, and candidate support are strong predictors of trust and other opinions of media, other demographic factors play a role as well. According to the 2017 Gallup/Knight Foundation survey, media trust scores differ among race, with whites having a lower score (32) than blacks (52), Hispanics (43), or Asians (44). Age was a factor as well, with 18- to 29-year-olds posting an average score of 33 compared to an average score of 41 for those 65 or older. Respondents differed also by income level, with those making more money showing lower average media trust scores (ranging from 32 for those with households making $100,000 or more to 42 for those with household income below $50,000). Rural residents also averaged lower media trust scores (32) compared to those respondents from big cities (43), with a steady increase in trust as community types got bigger.

Though the use of social media sometimes obscures the source of information, Americans seem to differentiate their opinions on media and journalism, in part based on the organization or institution providing information. Many polls ask for opinions about "media" in general or "news media," sometimes providing examples like newspapers, television, and so on. But according to the 2018 Edelman Trust Barometer, people view both platforms and content publishers as "media." The research asked people what they "assume was meant by the phrase 'media in general.'" Though the survey uses a global sample, it's illustrative of just how broad a term "media" is. For instance, while 89 percent of respondents said that media includes journalists, about half (48 percent) said it includes social media platforms, and one-quarter (25 percent) said it includes search platforms. These results indicate that media is seen as a multifaceted concept and that levels of trust differ markedly among the individual elements. For instance, Edelman found that in the United States, 53 percent of respondents said they trust "journalism" compared to 42 percent who trust platforms. In fact, in the United States, trust in platforms—such as social media feeds, search tools, and news applications—decreased by 11 points between 2017 and 2018, the steepest decline among all countries surveyed that year. Other organizations found similar opinions about trust in news organizations versus trust in social media. According to Pew, about 20 and 25 percent of Americans said they trust "a lot" of information that comes from national and local news organizations, respectively. A much higher percentage trust "some" information from national (52 percent) and local (60 percent) news organizations. Only 5 percent said they trust "a lot" of information from social media, with 33 percent saying they trust "some" information from social media. The Reuters Institute for the Study of Journalism found in its "Digital News Report 2018" that while only 34 percent of Americans said they trusted news overall, 50 percent said they trusted the news they use. Twenty-six percent said they trust news found through search engines, and 13 percent said they trust news found via social media. Among different news brands, local TV news, national network news, and national newspapers ranked highest, with cable and online sources ranked lower.

While several measures show low trust in news media, it's important to note that trust and confidence in public institutions overall are low. Gallup has perhaps the most comprehensive set of public trust and confidence measures to assess public confidence in 14 institutions, including public schools, banks, organized labor, the Supreme Court, the criminal justice system, Congress, big and small businesses, the military, the health care system, and the presidency. An average across all institutions showed that 35 percent of individuals in 2017 said they had "a great deal" or "quite a lot" of confidence in them. That was up a couple points from some historic lows in the late 2000s and throughout the 2010s but still indicated significant public distrust and skepticism of foundational American institutions.

Other research has found similar declines in trust. The 2018 Edelman Trust Barometer, for example, showed a deep decline in trust in several institutions in the United States between 2017 and 2018. Those who trusted nongovernment organizations (e.g., nonprofits) decreased from 58 percent to 49 percent, those who trusted business dropped from 58 percent to 48 percent, and those who trusted government declined from 47 percent to 33 percent. Trust and confidence in public institutions have been much lower in recent years than decades past. For instance, Gallup data show that confidence in public schools has decreased to 36 percent in 2017 from the high point in the mid-1970s of about 60 percent. Confidence in religion has decreased to 41 percent in 2017 from about

65 percent in the mid-1970s. While confidence in institutions ebbs and flows, sometimes tied to news coverage such as that of low confidence in banks during the Great Recession in the late 2000s, many institutions have seen declining trends in confidence over the past few decades.

Lastly, trust in media—and really trust in general—is a complex concept that often suffers from lack of consistency in how it is measured. Much of the research in media "trust" uses that term and media "credibility" almost interchangeably, and it can be divided into three main areas: message credibility (trust in the information), source credibility (trust in the source of the information, such as a particular media organization), and media credibility (trust in the medium through which information is relayed, such as TV or newspapers). However, the terms "trust" and "credibility" may be interpreted differently, and few surveys provide definitions to respondents (Fisher 2016). Scholars reviewing the research on trust and credibility have found many other terms used in its place, such as believability, accuracy, fairness, bias, ease of use, completeness, and reliability. One group of scholars (Metzger et al. 2003, 309) even argued that the "intense focus on measurement has perhaps come at the cost of developing clear conceptual definitions of media credibility that could be used to form consistent operationalizations of the concept." Additionally, some scholars (e.g., Fisher 2016; Sundar 2008) suggest that assessing credibility among the three traditional areas of media, source, and message is difficult for most average media consumers because of the increasingly complex, interconnected ways we use digital media.

FURTHER READING

Barthel, Michael, and Amy Mitchell. 2017. "Americans' Attitudes about the News Media Deeply Divided along Partisan Lines." Washington, DC: Pew Research Center. http://assets.pewresearch.org/wp-content/uploads/sites/13/2017/05/09144304/PJ_2017.05.10_Media-Attitudes_FINAL.pdf.

Edelman. 2018. "Edelman Trust Barometer: Global Report." http://cms.edelman.com/sites/default/files/2018-02/2018_Edelman_Trust_Barometer_Global_Report_FEB.pdf.

Fisher, Caroline. 2016. "The Trouble with 'Trust' in News Media." *Communication Research and Practice* 2 (4): 451–465. doi:10.1080/22041451.2016.1261251.

Gallup Inc. n.d. "Confidence in Institutions." Accessed June 21, 2018. https://news.gallup.com/poll/1597/confidence-institutions.aspx.

Gallup/Knight Foundation. 2017. "American Views: Trust, Media and Democracy." Washington, DC: Gallup Inc. https://knightfoundation .org/reports/american-views-trust-media-and-democracy.

Guess, Andrew, Brendan Nyhan, and Jason Reifler. 2017. "'You're Fake News!' The 2017 Poynter Media Trust Survey." St. Petersburg, FL: Poynter Institute for Media Studies. https://poyntercdn.blob.core.windows .net/files/PoynterMediaTrustSurvey2017.pdf.

Metzger, Miriam J., Andrew J. Flanagin, Keren Eyal, Daisy R. Lemus, and Robert M. Mccann. 2003. "Credibility for the 21st Century: Integrating Perspectives on Source, Message, and Media Credibility in the Contemporary Media Environment." *Annals of the International Communication Association* 27 (1): 293–335. doi:10.1080/23808985.2003. 11679029.

Newman, Nic, Richard Fletcher, Antonis Kalogeropoulos, David A.L. Levy, and Rasmus K. Nielsen. 2018. "Digital News Report 2018." Oxford, UK: Reuters Institute for the Study of Journalism. http://www .digitalnewsreport.org/survey/2018/overview-key-findings-2018/.

Newport, Frank. 2017. "Americans' Confidence in Institutions Edges Up." *Gallup Inc.* (blog). June 26. https://news.gallup.com/poll/212840/ americans-confidence-institutions-edges.aspx.

Sundar, S. Shyam. 2008. "The MAIN Model: A Heuristic Approach to Understanding Technology Effects on Credibility." In *Digital Media, Youth, and Credibility*, edited by Miriam J. Metzger and Andrew J. Flanagin, 73–100. Cambridge, MA: The MIT Press. doi:10.1162/dmal .9780262562324.073.

Swift, Art. 2017a. "Democrats' Confidence in Mass Media Rises Sharply from 2016." *Gallup Inc.* (blog). September 21. https://news.gallup.com/ poll/219824/democrats-confidence-mass-media-rises-sharply-2016 .aspx.

Swift, Art. 2017b. "Six in 10 in U.S. See Partisan Bias in News Media." *Gallup Inc.* (blog). April 5. https://news.gallup.com/poll/207794/six-partisan-bias-news-media.aspx.

Q16. DO NEWS MEDIA ORGANIZATIONS SHAPE THEIR COVERAGE TO ATTRACT VIEWERS WITH CERTAIN POLITICAL BELIEFS?

Answer: Yes, but it's nothing new, nor is it the norm. Segments of the American press have always aimed to reach partisan audiences, but most of the news consumed by most people today still comes from traditional, nonpartisan mainstream sources, which continue to target wide mass audiences. Some partisan outlets have succeeded by focusing on niche, fragmented audiences, as with Fox News and MSNBC. It's difficult to say which came first: the partisan outlet or the partisan audience, but it's likely some of both. A potentially bigger problem today is that the proliferation of media choice means many people tune out news altogether.

The Facts: In the early 1800s, before advertising and the commercialization of news, virtually all American newspapers were partisan outlets closely aligned with political parties aiming to target potential voters. A side benefit of this state of affairs was that it created a fertile environment for robust and substantive political debate about the issues of the day (generally limited to literate males, a small subset of the citizenry), but the primary goal was to win elections. Papers were started by political parties to get their candidates into office, and editors did not have to be encouraged to toe the party line; they were typically fervent advocates to begin with. Barriers to entry into the marketplace were low, making it relatively easy to launch a new paper (although many of them failed due to fierce competition). Competition among newspapers was already in place through the political parties, and government patronage—in the form of printing contracts and subsidies—guaranteed competition and diversity of ownership. Government could offer its patronage to all newspapers that competed for its funding (Baldasty 1992).

At the start of the 19th century, American newspapers were narrowly defined, each serving as an apparatus for a particular political party with content limited to partisan advocacy. By the end of the century, newspapers looked much like what readers have come to expect today. As scholar Gerald Baldasty put it, "In the early nineteenth century, editors defined news as a political instrument intended to promote party interests. By century's end, editors defined news within a business context to ensure or increase revenues. News had become commercialized" (Baldasty 1992, 4). By the 1900s, as publishers sought to broaden their audiences, newspapers included a range of information on a variety of topics from business and stocks to sports, arts, literature, and crime. Close political affiliation was no longer a distinguishing factor. Just as papers supported and were supported by political parties in the early century, they supported and were supported by advertisers by the century's end. "These two constituencies, first political parties and later advertisers, were instrumental in defining news," explained Baldasty. "Both helped shape news to reflect their own needs and interests" (Baldasty 1992, 5).

So what changed? American life in general underwent significant changes with the arrival of the Industrial Revolution and the rise of a market economy. Rapid urbanization, greater leisure time, and increased literacy all brought about drastic shifts in American society. Each of these factors and more contributed to the evolution of American newspapers. Suspicion and dislike of politics increased, and a broader readership—beyond educated males involved in politics—meant an increased desire for a greater diversity of content and news of the wider world. Journalism was increasingly seen as a profession rather than something that could be done by anyone with a notebook and a pen. New technology improved methods of production and distribution, and new economic models lowered the cost of papers and made them available to a much larger segment of the population. As a result of this complex array of factors, politics were sidelined and neutrality became central as a way to appeal to a broader set of readers and to help journalists be seen as professionals rather than political mouthpieces and sensation-seeking hacks. The successful penny papers avoided all political affiliation. *The New York Sun*, for example, included no editorials. Ultimately, the measures of success became large audiences and revenues, not the ability to artfully argue and persuade (Baldasty 1992; McChesney and Nichols 2010; Schudson 1978).

This history is significant because it illustrates the socially constructed nature of news; that is, there is no one way to do news, and the definition at any point in time is highly subjective and influenced by the social, political, and economic contexts that shape the news media. It also illustrates what a truly partisan press looked like. Much of today's news media might seem to harken back to the era of the partisan press, but today's partisan news media, such as the cable outlets Fox News and MSNBC, are still driven by commercial impulses. It just so happens that partisanship sells.

The silver lining is that partisanship can have benefits if done well; some observers advocate for more partisanship as a way to increase transparency and generate more issue-oriented coverage, rather than fleeting coverage of disconnected episodes or a single-minded focus on the "horse-race" qualities of elections. Some observers believe that the nonpartisan model is not necessarily the best for helping citizens understand issues and make decisions. As Shanto Iyengar (2015, 339) has noted, as paid professionals, journalists "are more interested in getting the story right (avoiding any semblance of partisan bias) and less interested in helping voters identify the candidate who has the better ideas, programs, or track record. It is this arm's-length treatment of candidates and parties that is partly responsible for the low level of coverage accorded to issues."

However, cable news outlets such as Fox News and MSNBC are hardly the partisan ideal, according to many critics. They complain that American cable news outlets produce little in the way of original reporting, and that their viewers are not as well informed as those who consume print and public noncommercial media. One study from Fairleigh Dickinson University showed that on international issues, Fox News and MSNBC viewers are less well informed than individuals who consume no news at all (PublicMind 2012). The best-informed individuals in this survey consumed NPR, Sunday morning political shows, and *The Daily Show* on Comedy Central. (The survey did not ask about newspapers.) It's worth noting, however, that Americans overall are not particularly well informed; on average, respondents to the Fairleigh Dickinson survey were able to answer correctly 1.8 of 4 questions about international news—and only 1.6 of 5 questions about domestic affairs.

The fragmentation of the once mass audience has certainly changed the media landscape. Plenty of popular mainstream partisan sources exist, ranging from *Weekly Standard* and *National Review* on the right to *Talking Points Memo*, the Intercept, and Vox on the left (and various media organizations that more brazenly distort the news of the day for nakedly partisan purposes are also thriving in the current polarized environment). No doubt these outlets are produced by partisan individuals, much like the partisan press of the 1800s. However, they still have had to position themselves in terms of a market and have relied on a commercial business model that caters to niche partisan audiences. As media scholar Justin Buchler (2017) has noted, "Just as market incentives supported the development of a neutral press, market incentives, combined with technology, have allowed institutions like Fox News and MSNBC to provide news coverage from decidedly conservative and liberal perspectives, with internet sources further fragmenting the media environment into narrow ideological niches."

Despite this proliferation of partisan outlets, evidence suggests that most news outlets still aim to produce nonpartisan content, which is consumed by large mass audiences. Studies indicate that although some polarization has occurred among media outlets and American citizens alike, most Americans remain fairly moderate in their views, and most news has remained mostly centrist (Prior 2013). Highly partisan news may be the primary choice of highly partisan individuals, who may have an outsized influence on America's political discourse. But even these individuals still expose themselves to a range of content beyond a partisan echo chamber. For example, one 2012 study found high overlap across news outlets and challenged the idea that fragmented audiences are associated with social polarization (Webster and Ksiazek 2012). In the end, some believe popularity will hold audiences together. Consumers will continue to have significant overlap and points of intersection. These findings may seem counterintuitive to observers of today's media landscape, and future research may well find that shifts are occurring as audience fragmentation increases and news outlets seek to define themselves as the preferred source for niche groups of partisan consumers.

Signs of this shift may already exist. As Pew Research has found, there does seem to be a preference for partisan sources among conservatives, while liberals are more likely to prefer traditionally mainstream sources (Mitchell et al. 2014). Conservatives are tightly clustered around Fox News and a few other conservative sources; liberals are more likely to prefer a greater range of news outlets.

If there is an increasing preference for partisan sources among conservatives, it began in 1987 with the repeal of the Fairness Doctrine, a rule created by the Federal Communications Commission (FCC) in 1949 in an attempt to bring balance to the airwaves, which were thought of as a limited public resource deserving of special protections. Because broadcasters received free licenses to use the airwaves, they were obligated to "devote reasonable attention to the coverage of controversial issues of public importance" and had to provide "reasonable although not necessarily equal" opportunities for opposing sides to express competing views. Competition from cable and satellite as well as sweeping deregulation by the Reagan administration provided the impetus for scrapping the rule (Rowan 1984). The effect was to turn the airwaves into a private marketplace where maximizing profits became paramount and public service took a back seat. Not coincidentally, *The Rush Limbaugh Show* was nationally syndicated in 1988, a year after the Fairness Doctrine's demise.

Limbaugh is one of the best-known conservative commentators and radio personalities in the United States. Still on air today, his is the top-rated talk radio show and enjoys an audience of 14 million. Limbaugh is not alone, as the top 10 talk radio shows are dominated by conservatives and are heard by tens of millions of listeners (Talkers 2018). This consistent conservative commentary on the airwaves would not have passed FCC muster under the Fairness Doctrine (Wallace 2005). Furthermore, a central theme offered by Limbaugh and others is the prevalence of liberal bias in the mainstream media, even as conservatives came to dominate talk radio and went on to gather large audiences on cable television and some newspapers. In any case, much of talk radio uses a market approach to gathering large audiences by presenting a strong conservative voice rather than striving for neutrality. Of course, talk radio is entertainment and commentary, not news. No journalism is produced; instead, the content centers on punditry and opinion, often delivered with high levels of emotion and anger.

Ultimately, the rise of conservative talk radio showed the potential profitability of this format and set the stage for the rise of Fox News in the 1990s. As a cable outlet, Fox News would not have been subject to the Fairness Doctrine, which only applied to over-the-air broadcasters, but the success of conservative talk radio established a business model that would prove enduring. In general, as media formats have proliferated and audiences have fragmented, many successful producers and distributors have found ways to reach homogenized niche audiences rather than heterogeneous mass audiences. That's why cable gave rise to whole channels devoted to such narrow interests as golf, comedy, and music videos. This leads to the larger problem of today's news media environment: the ease with which large numbers of citizens can tune out news altogether.

In a high-choice media environment, the effect of having so many choices may be that a majority of Americans, rather than tuning in to partisan media outlets and getting lost in homogenous echo chambers, are actually taking the opportunity to tune out the news altogether. As political science scholar Matt Levendusky has noted:

> While the political can tune into Fox and MSNBC, those who dislike politics also have more options than ever for avoiding it. In lieu of the nightly news—or a televised presidential address—they can watch *Sports Center*, *Entertainment Tonight*, or a rerun of *The Big Bang Theory*. When confronted with a political option, they simply change the channel to something else that they find more agreeable. Even the most popular cable news programs get 2 to 3 million viewers on a typical evening in a country of 300 million Americans. In earlier decades, some of these individuals would have been incidentally exposed to political news and information (by, say, watching the television news at 6 o'clock, when there were no other options). Now that they can avoid news altogether, they know less about politics and are less likely to participate. So the growth of media choice strengthens the extremes while hollowing out the center, making the electorate more divided. (2014 n.p.)

This is not entirely new. Recall that the commercialization of news in the 19th century led to less news and engagement partly because citizens had more choice regarding content options. Based on this history, it makes sense that today's extremely high level of choice would have a similar and much more drastic effect. As media scholar Marcus Prior wrote, "Content preference indeed becomes a better predictor of political knowledge and turnout as media choice increases. Cable TV and the Internet increase gaps in knowledge and turnout between people who prefer news and people who prefer entertainment" (Prior 2005, 577). It remains to be seen how this mix of trends will play out. The best hope for American democracy is that all citizens (not just the politically interested) continue to find their way to common sources of information—even if they disagree with some of what they find.

FURTHER READING

Baldasty, Gerald J. 1992. *The Commercialization of News in the Nineteenth Century*. Madison: University of Wisconsin Press.

Buchler, Justin. 2017. "Does Nonpartisan Journalism Have a Future?" *The Conversation*. January 5. http://theconversation.com/does-nonpartisan-journalism-have-a-future-70384.

Iyengar, Shanto. 2015. *Media Politics: A Citizen's Guide*. 3rd ed. New York: W. W. Norton & Company.

Levendusky, Matt. 2014. "Are Fox and MSNBC Polarizing America?—The Washington Post." *The Washington Post*, February 3. https://www.washingtonpost.com/news/monkey-cage/wp/2014/02/03/are-fox-and-msnbc-polarizing-america/?utm_term=.a1dd09956ec4.

McChesney, Robert, and John Nichols. 2010. *The Death and Life of American Journalism: The Media Revolution That Will Begin the World Again*. 1st Nation Books. Philadelphia, PA: Nation Books.

Mitchell, Amy, Jeffrey Gottfried, Jocelyn Kiley, and Katerina E. Matsa. 2014. "Political Polarization & Media Habits | Pew Research Center." Pew Research Center. October 21. http://www.journalism.org/2014/10/21/political-polarization-media-habits/#.

Prior, Markus. 2005. "News vs. Entertainment: How Increasing Media Choice Widens Gaps in Political Knowledge and Turnout." *American Journal of Political Science* 49 (3): 577–592. https://doi.org/10.1111/j.1540-5907.2005.00143.x.

Prior, Markus. 2013. "Media and Political Polarization." *Annual Review of Political Science* 16 (1): 101–127. https://doi.org/10.1146/annurev-polisci-100711-135242.

PublicMind. 2012. "What You Know Depends on What You Watch: Current Events Knowledge across Popular News Sources." Fairleigh Dickinson University. http://publicmind.fdu.edu/2012/confirmed/final.pdf.

Rowan, Ford. 1984. *Broadcast Fairness: Doctrine, Practice, Prospects: A Reappraisal of the Fairness Doctrine and Equal Time Rule.* Longman Series in Public Communication. New York: Longman.

Schudson, Michael. 1978. *Discovering the News: A Social History of American Newspapers.* New York: Basic Books.

Talkers. 2017. "Top Talk Audiences." *TALKERS Magazine—"The Bible of Talk Media"* (blog). May 3. http://www.talkers.com/top-talk-audiences/.

Wallace, David Foster. 2005. "Host." *The Atlantic*, April. https://www.theatlantic.com/magazine/archive/2005/04/host/303812/.

Webster, James G., and Thomas B. Ksiazek. 2012. "The Dynamics of Audience Fragmentation: Public Attention in an Age of Digital Media." *Journal of Communication* 62 (1): 39–56. https://doi.org/10.1111/j.1460-2466.2011.01616.x.

Q17. DO AUDIENCES INFLUENCE NEWS CONTENT?

Answer: Yes, audiences can have a great deal of influence on news content, both directly and indirectly. Many journalists working in media aim to serve the public, and that means not only giving their audience as they understand it the information it needs but also responding to audience demands for what it wants, which may not be as beneficial for the health and vitality of America's cultural and political institutions. More directly, citizens can contribute to news content by creating and sharing original work; sending information directly to journalists in the form of photos, videos, reports, or commentary on their work; participating in crowdsourcing projects; and interacting with news content through online news sites and social media sites.

The Facts: The role of the audiences in the creation, analysis, and spread of news content has increased dramatically with the widespread adoption of new media tools for recording, creating, and posting content online. This shift has led to debate about the merits of increased participation and the democratization of the media and the downsides to less gatekeeping, increased audience influence on journalists, and the unpaid labor of social media users playing a bigger role in the chain of media distribution, among other things. The enthusiasm about citizen journalism in the early part of the 21st century has been subsumed by the growth of social media, which emphasized the social sharing aspect of users' involvement in media over the citizen or journalism aspect, despite the fact that social media became a primary way to share and discuss news.

The downsides of anonymity, fake accounts, bots, and algorithms that reward popularity and virality above all have become more salient in the past few years.

Consumers of news may have some indirect influence on its content simply by being part of the audience that journalists are trying to serve. Journalists may consider their audience, as far as they understand it, in selecting stories or guiding coverage of those stories. Reporters working for print publications and on local radio and broadcast television networks may think about the geographic community they serve, while there is some evidence that cable news channels have tried to appeal to partisan demographics. Many observers, including media scholars, political scientists, and journalists, have suggested that Fox News and MSNBC have deliberately slanted their coverage and programming to appeal to more partisan viewers. Public radio and television services have a wider audience and a mission to serve the public, so they may consider their audience to be the local community, broadly considered, although the audience is often skewed to be more white, affluent, and educated than the general population.

The increasing use of website analytics means that journalists who publish online have even greater knowledge about their audiences and also about the response of their audience to particular content. Web analytics are "instant, specific, time-related and provide behavioral information, all at once" (Hanusch 2017, 1571). Responses through social media also provide feedback to journalists about how audiences perceive and use their work. Folker Hanusch (2017) has found that journalists are becoming more open to taking audience feedback into account, and that audience feedback is causing journalists to become more consumer oriented, leading to changes in practices, values, and norms. Hanusch has argued that the adoption of web analytics, while giving journalists a better understanding of how their audiences interact with news content, also leads to an increasing dependence on the economic field. Critics suggest that a consumer orientation may lead to journalists giving audiences "what they want," while a citizen orientation should encourage journalists to give audiences the kind of information they need to be self-governing citizens in a democracy. There is some evidence that what audiences want may be negative news. One 2015 study, for example, found that news consumers preferred bad news, perceiving it to have more value and provide a greater advantage for them, even if it also made them more depressed (McCluskey, Swinnen, and Vandemoortele 2015). Increasing knowledge about the audience's reaction to content may have the effect of driving journalists to cover more news that is popular or provokes strong reactions and may lead to narrower coverage, as journalists may have less incentive to pursue original or unusual stories with unproven audience reaction.

Audiences exert a more direct influence on news content through playing a role in gathering, publishing, analyzing, and disseminating information. Although attention to audience contributions to news has grown with the Internet, and especially Web 2.0 and social media, nonprofessionals have long contributed to news content in every medium, through such activities as writing letters to the editor, calling in to radio shows, doing "man-on-the-street" interviews, and providing tips or feedback to journalists. Developments in recording technology (cameras and video recorders) and in Internet technology brought content creation to a larger portion of the public and began to expand the ability of nonprofessionals to contribute to news content in a variety of ways and to create their own news content. Barriers to posting original content were lowered by the introduction of more simple interfaces, such as blogging sites and WYSIWYG ("what you see is what you get") editors. Knowledge of programming languages and purchase of a web domain were no longer necessary to share original content in a variety of formats. Photo-sharing sites, such as Flickr, and video-sharing sites, such as YouTube, allowed users to easily post content without creating their own sites, further simplifying the process. Twitter did the same for sharing brief thoughts, news, and commentary. Social networking sites, such as Facebook, allowed users to share stories and add commentary within their social circles. Additionally, as many news organizations moved online, they introduced comment fields that allowed reader comments to appear with each new story.

Citizen journalism is a label that has been used for the contributions of nonprofessionals to the news, although there is some debate about the use of the word "citizen," given the particular legal status it implies (see Costanza-Chock 2008). Media scholar Jay Rosen (2008) famously put it as follows: "When the people formerly known as the audience employ the press tools they have in their possession to inform one another, that's citizen journalism." Citizen journalism was part of a broader period of the growth of "mass self-communication" (Castells 2007) and user-generated content. This growth led to the enthusiastic declarations of such scholars as Scott Gant (2007), in *We're All Journalists Now*, and Clay Shirky (2008), in *Here Comes Everybody*.

Discussion about citizen journalism primarily has been centered around bloggers and random acts of journalism, or "accidental journalism," when citizens happen to be present for newsworthy events and use the tools in their possession to capture the event and share with others. In some cases these contributions have simply added more eyewitness views to newsworthy events that would already have been covered, such as the bombing of the London Tube in 2005. In other cases, citizen journalism has brought attention to events that may have been ignored by the mainstream media and not gained public attention, such as in the case of many shootings of unarmed citizens by police in the United States.

One of the first prominent examples of citizen journalism often cited is the video recording made by George Holliday of the beating of Rodney King by Los Angeles Police Department officers in 1991. Holliday sent the recording (made on a VHS recorder) to the local television news channel, KTLA, and its airing revealed to the public the brutality of the officers' behavior, a reality that undoubtedly played a role in protests that happened after the officers were acquitted. Recordings of police using excessive force or in other ways misusing the power they have been granted by the government have become a common use of citizen journalism, one that prompted the creation of organizations like Witness.org, which encourages the use of video technology to promote human rights, and continues today in many officer-involved shootings. This role of citizen journalists in monitoring the police and other authorities has given more power to citizens to hold officials accountable, a shift conceptualized by the term "sousveillance," a counter to surveillance that means watching from below. Capturing and sharing videos that show police abusing their power is one way citizens have been able to influence journalists to cover stories and larger narratives that might otherwise have been ignored.

Creating original content in the form of videos, pictures, blog posts, and commentary is not the only way audiences can contribute to news content. Crowdsourcing projects by news organizations have produced meaningful contributions to investigative journalism, for example. Crowdsourcing is a distributed problem-solving model in which small parts of a task are assigned or offered to a large group of participants online. *The Guardian* in the United Kingdom famously used crowdsourcing in 2009 to examine hundreds of thousands of pages of expense reports from members of parliament to identify wasteful or corrupt spending. A particularly infamous example in this regard was the case of Sir Peter Viggers, who had expensed to the government 30,000 British pounds in gardening expenses, including 1,700 British pounds (more than $2,000), for the construction of a floating duck island feature on his estate. The newspaper posted the documents it had received from the government online with an easy-to-use interface and asked readers to examine documents and identify those that were worth further scrutiny or reporting. Reporters were then able to take a closer look at a smaller subset of documents. Thousands of readers helped sort through the documents in the first few days the site was up.

The political blog *Talking Points Memo* pursued a similar strategy with the Department of Justice (DOJ) report on the political firings of attorneys general in 2007, posting documents it had received from the DOJ and asking readers to help go through the documents.

Crowdsourcing differs from the sort of opportunistic or "accidental" journalism that characterizes many cases of well-known citizen journalism in that it is led by professional journalists. Journalists leading a crowdsourcing effort select the issues, the targets of the project, and the questions being asked, and may provide materials or documents for contributors to work with. This keeps the journalists in the role of gatekeeper but utilizes the power of the vast number of people online to accomplish tasks that might have been excessively time-consuming for an individual journalist or news organization. The efforts of journalists to find sources through social media can also be seen as a kind of crowdsourcing. Journalists can reach out through social media to ask questions and find people who have knowledge or experience of an issue about which they're reporting. This kind of reporting may bring journalists a different, more diverse set of sources than they might reach simply by reaching out through their own contacts and networks. National Public Radio stations have formalized this through the creation of the Public Insight Network, which allows listeners to share their contact information, background, and other personal details that will allow a journalist to identify potential sources to talk to when reporting stories.

Audiences also contribute to the news process by commenting on and sharing news through social media, acting as part of a chain of dissemination. Sharing can help more viewers see a story and generate conversations in the public, but it is also an important aspect of web analytics used by journalists to gauge the popularity of particular stories, as mentioned earlier. Comments, of course, can add to or counter the perspective initially offered by a story, or can function as press criticism (Craft, Vos, and Wolfgang 2015), holding journalists accountable for the work they produce and creating a public conversation around a news item. Comments may also be ignored by readers, or become contentious and affect the experience of other readers, altering perceptions of media bias, for example (Lee 2012).

Sue Robinson (2011) has advocated rethinking news as a discrete product created by journalists, putting forward the idea of "journalism as process," which considers the production of news as a shared, distributed act done by not only various actors, including journalists, but also members of the audience. This conceptualization of journalism as process would mean thinking about news stories as a starting point for a conversation and shared process of analysis and evaluation by the audience, rather than news stories as a finished product and final word on an event. Journalism as a process can be seen as fitting within the principles of "produsage"—a portmanteau of production and usage—described by Axel Bruns (2008), specifically the principle of "unfinished artefacts, continuing process," which views content as never finished, and part of a continuing process of constant revision.

These changes, however, place a greater burden and responsibility on the audience, giving them power to shape public conversations, with results that are both negative and positive. Empowering more people to share their stories and perspectives can broaden our public understanding of issues and can also have positive effects for participants. On the other hand, this power requires more user education and media literacy. Users who are unprepared to engage with complicated content or encounter hostile users may cause and also suffer negative effects. For example, a great deal of fake news—false information produced with full knowledge of its falsehood and made to look like real news content—was spread by social media users motivated by partisan biases. There are also privacy concerns around the information these sites ask users to reveal before granting them access and the information gathered about users while they are on the sites.

Additionally, there are concerns about the political economy of the user-generated content model, which relies on unpaid labor by users to generate content and interactions that lead to advertising income for corporate-owned sites. Most sites justify their economic exploitation of users' time and effort by noting that they provide the use of the platform for free, but the major social media sites (Facebook, Twitter, Instagram, YouTube) all advertise to users and employ data about user behavior to target advertising. They are operating on the "audience as product" model of older media like television, but they further exploit the audience by collecting and selling data, and they do all of this without investing in content creation themselves.

FURTHER READING

Bruns, Axel. 2008. *Blogs, Wikipedia, Second Life and Beyond: From Produc-tion to Produsage.* New York: Peter Lang.

Castells, Manuel. 2007. "Communication, Power and Counter-Power in the Network Society." *International Journal of Communication* 1 (1): 238–266.

Costanza-Chock, Sasha. 2008. "The Immigrant Rights Movement on the Net: Between 'Web 2.0' and Comunicación Popular." *American Quarterly* 60 (3): 851–864.

Craft, Stephanie, Tim Vos, and David J. Wolfgang. 2015. "Reader Comments as Press Criticism: Implications for the Journalistic Field." *Journalism* 17 (6): 677–693.

Gant, Scott. 2007. *We're All Journalists Now: The Transformation of the Press and Reshaping of the Law in the Internet Age*. New York: Free Press.

Gillmor, Dan. 2004. *We the Media: Grassroots Journalism by the People, for the People*. Sebastopol, CA: O'Reilly Media.

Hanusch, Folker. 2017. "Web Analytics and the Functional Differentiation of Journalism Cultures: Individual, Organizational and Platform-Specific Influences on Newswork." *Information Communication & Society* 20: 1571–1586.

Lee, Eun-Ju. 2012. "That's Not the Way It Is: How User-generated Comments on the News Affect Perceived Media Bias." *Journal of Computer-Mediated Communication* 18 (1): 32–45.

McCluskey, Jill J., Johan Swinnen, and Thijs Vandemoortele. 2015. "You Get What You Want: A Note on the Economics of Bad News." *Information Economics and Policy* 30 (1): 1–5.

Robinson, Sue. 2011. "Journalism as Process: The Organizational Implications of Participatory Online News." *Journalism & Communication Monographs* 13 (3): 137–210.

Rosen, Jay. 2008. "A Most Useful Definition of Citizen Journalism." *PressThink* (blog). July 14. http://archive.pressthink.org/2008/07/14/a_most_useful_d_p.html.

Shirky, Clay. 2008. *Here Comes Everybody: The Power of Organizing without Organizations*. New York: Penguin.

Surowiecki, James. 2004. *The Wisdom of Crowds: Why the Many Are Smarter Than the Few and How Collective Wisdom Shapes Business, Economies, Societies and Nations*. New York: Random House.

4

❖

News and Politics

News and politics are undeniably linked in the American democratic system. Politicians use the media to get information to their constituents, and journalists cover politics to inform citizens. While citizens need journalists to find out what their elected officials are doing, the relationships between journalists and politicians raise important questions and deserve scrutiny as well. Journalists often must balance their public service obligation to act as a "watchdog" with the need to develop relationships with politicians and get information from anonymous sources. The appearance of political bias on the part of journalists, as well as the bias of the reader or viewer of the news, affects how political news may be perceived by the audience. However, constraints and routines that influence how journalists cover politics may play an even stronger role in determining how and to what extent political news is covered.

Q18. ARE ALL NEWS MEDIA BIASED?

Answer: Yes, but not in the ways people typically think. Subjectivity does not arise so much from personal opinion as much as from journalistic norms and routines. It's true that political bias can be found in some news media, but this kind of bias is typically easy to identify, or it exists primarily in the eye of the beholder. Partisan individuals often orient themselves toward the partisan sources they agree with, but research suggests most news products are not highly partisan, instead hewing toward some version of political neutrality. What's harder to see are the more subtle structural biases and frames at work in all news content. Scholars tend to focus on the broader systematic conventions that influence the framing of news content. Just like a photograph that depicts only a selection of reality, news producers must decide what is included and what is left out.

The Facts: Today, a perceived failure to be objective often leads to accusations of political bias. There are a few problems with this. First, there is no absolute center that can be used to evaluate neutrality. Bias is relative. Judging bias in the United States, for example, is different from judging bias in Europe, where the political "center" tends to be more left than America's "center." Second, bias is often in the eye of the beholder. When something we hear doesn't fit with our preconceived notions, we tend to view the report as biased. This basic component of human psychology is a type of cognitive bias. This is evident in the well-documented "hostile media effect," where partisans on competing ends of the political spectrum can view the same news report as biased against their point of view. Third, a narrow focus on political bias assumes that political influence is the only factor that should be considered when evaluating news content. It is also important to be aware of the other types of influence that shape news (Schudson 2012; Shoemaker and Reese 2014).

Bias is not necessarily bad. Sometimes having a bias for certain things leads to what we typically identify as social and cultural progress such as civil and human rights. For instance, few people today would consider an "anti-slavery" bias to be a bad thing or a "pro-human-trafficking" bias to be a good thing. Increasingly, a "pro-earth" bias is becoming the norm in discussions of global warming and its possible solutions. Occasionally, having a bias is just another way of exercising good judgment even if some people have yet to catch on. Some journalists have admitted they failed to adequately challenge the Bush administration's case for the 2003 invasion of Iraq, which was based on flawed evidence (Boyd-Barrett 2004). The few journalists who did exhibit skepticism were met with harsh criticism and even death threats. Were they "biased" against the Bush administration, or were they simply correct? Thousands of American soldiers and Iraqi citizens died in a war based on a false pretext. Perhaps a stronger "bias" for good evidence could have yielded a better outcome.

To further examine the idea of media bias, it's useful to compare the typical conservative and liberal criticisms of biased news (Shoemaker and Reese 2014). The conservative critique tends to center on individual journalists and their organizations. Although half of journalists now identify as political independents, there are more who tend to lean liberal and vote for Democrats than those who lean conservative and vote for Republicans (Willnat and Weaver 2014). Because of their own political biases, the critique goes that their work must inevitably be biased in favor of a liberal perspective. The problem here is that judging news based on the political preferences of individual journalists tells us nothing about the actual content of their work. Instead, it is important to analyze the journalistic content they produce, which can actually veer to the right when liberal journalists overcompensate for their own known biases (or vice versa). Thus, the conservative critique tends to focus heavily on the "agency," or independence, of individual journalists and neglects the influence of journalistic norms and routines as well as the influence of other forces, including markets, audiences, sources, and owners.

Compare this to the typical liberal critique, which tends to focus on these institutional factors while neglecting the agency of individual journalists. According to the liberal critique, because most media outlets are owned by large profit-seeking corporations, journalists and their work will typically reflect the interests of their capitalist bosses and the advertisers that pay their bills. In this sense, it doesn't matter what preferences are held by individual journalists because their work must ultimately serve a larger purpose. Individual agency takes a back seat to organizational goals. This is possible because journalists become acclimated to what is deemed acceptable at their news organization. Through a process of "self-selection," journalists either accept and internalize the expectations for the type of content they will produce or they quit and find somewhere else to work.

So which view is correct? The two critiques play out in different ways depending on the issue at hand. News content related to social issues such as civil rights and welfare can often take a liberal tone as journalists seek to highlight inequality and injustice, both real and perceived. But when it comes to economic and fiscal issues, journalists and their work tend to be more tied to conservative positions related to corporate strategies and growth. However, neither critique tells us much about many of the values that dominate news coverage, such as "ethnocentrism and nationalism," which are most evident in coverage of foreign affairs. The United States is often presented as a global force for good, operating in the best interest of all. This bias is evident anytime the United States is engaged in military conflict and was pervasive in news coverage following the attacks of September 11, 2001, and in the months leading up to the 2003 invasion of Iraq. Other typical news values, as identified by sociologist Herbert Gans (2004), include "altruistic democracy," or the idea that democracy is the best form of government and always operates in the best interest of citizens; "responsible capitalism," or the idea that business and growth are positive forces and government regulation represents a negative interference; "small-town pastoralism," in which news shows a preference for rural communities and "Main Street" values; "individualism," or a preference for the importance of individual liberty over social cohesion; and "moderatism," which counsels against excess or extremism. According to Gans, if there is bias in news content, it is more likely to be oriented around these values than around political ideology.

Other types of bias can also be seen in areas of general consensus about what is acceptable for debate and discussion versus ideas that are taken for granted and rarely challenged in journalism (Shoemaker and Reese 2014). Scholar Daniel Hallin (1986) suggested that the topics for debate exist in the "sphere of legitimate controversy," which includes such topics as health care and immigration policy. Outside of this are ideas that are assumed to be generally settled, such as the ideas that private enterprise and a growing economy are always good or that American-style democracy is the natural and preferred system of government.

While popular discussions of bias tend to center on political questions, news content is just as likely to be influenced by "structural biases," such as a preference for the status quo, a preference for timeliness, and the commercial imperative of most news media outlets. In this sense, the status quo of the American two-party system of government is taken for granted and rarely challenged. A bias toward timeliness dictates that news content is focused on recent developments rather than considering how processes unfold over time. Americans sometimes hear or read about the latest vote on a health care bill, for instance, without much explanation of how it came to be, whose interests it serves, or what impact it would have. Television news is heavily biased toward dramatic visuals, so news that can be easily photographed, such as protests, rallies, military activities, and natural disasters, gets attention, while policy issues go ignored. Another type of bias—a "fairness bias"—can be a good thing, but it can also get reporters into trouble if they fail to examine relevant evidence. For years, for example, news coverage of global warming has taken great pains to represent "both sides" of the debate over the extent and causes of climate change, even though the scientific community reached an overwhelming consensus long ago that climate change is occurring and that it is attributable to human activity (primarily the consumption of fossil fuels that release greenhouse gases). The fairness bias is related to a "narrative bias," which gives preference to good stories that center on conflict and have a strong narrative arc—a beginning, middle, and end. Such stories have clear antagonists and protagonists, and they are driven by drama.

Narratives often become firmly established matters of public opinion regardless of whether they are based in fact, such as the idea of "welfare queens" abusing the social safety net.

Another way to think about bias is in terms of what scholars call "framing." Think of a photographer taking a picture—they have to point the camera somewhere and decide what to include and what to leave out of their photo. When applied to news content, frames are also used to present a story. According to scholar Robert Entman (1993), framing is a mix of "selection" and "salience." Events and actions are selected from a reporter's perceived reality and are then made salient, or prominent, in their report based on their subjective interpretation or evaluation. For example, in a story about a pro-environment protest, a reporter can decide to focus on the message of the demonstrators or the nuisance caused by protesters interfering with traffic. Typical frames center on conflict, winners and losers, and wrongdoing, and certain sources such as government officials, experts, advocates, and industry usually have a major advantage when it comes to setting the terms of a debate. Indeed, a theory known as "indexing" suggests that news reports on politics and policy issues adhere to the parameters of debate set by political elites. In other words, the news is merely an "index" of what government officials say. For example, when few politicians were critical of the 2003 invasion of Iraq, news reports were similarly devoid of dissenting opinions.

Frames can be either episodic or thematic, according to scholar Shanto Iyengar (2015). Episodic frames focus on specific individuals and events, which can lead news consumers to view social problems as personal failings rather than seeing larger social, political, or economic contexts that affect people's lives. For example, when news stories about homelessness or poverty focus on individuals, news consumers are more likely to blame the individuals for their laziness. Similarly, stories of personal success and triumph misleadingly suggest that individuals alone have the power to determine their own fate rather than identifying the social and cultural benefits and privileges that help individuals succeed. On the other hand, thematic frames focus on larger social and national contexts that contribute to social problems. Thematic frames can lead news consumers to see such problems as attributable (at least in part) to wider cultural forces such as high unemployment, widespread poverty, or government policies. News, especially television news, tends to be dominated by episodic frames, which can have the negative effect of simplifying complex issues and depicting reality as a series of unrelated events with no underlying causes and effects. The bias toward personal stories and anecdotes can leave news consumers with a poor understanding of the larger contexts and influences that affect day-to-day life.

So while "political bias" can certainly be found in news media, whether news is biased toward conservative or liberal points of view does not tell the full story about the underlying processes, values, and influences that shape news. Instead of simply asking whether something is biased, news consumers should first ask whether the bias is really their own and then examine the frames, values, and structural factors at play. What perspectives are present in a story? Who is featured, and who is left out? What is the meaning being conveyed?

FURTHER READING

Boyd-Barrett, Oliver. 2004. "Judith Miller, the New York Times, and the Propaganda Model." *Journalism Studies* 5 (4): 435–449.

Entman, Robert M. 1993. "Framing: Toward Clarification of a Fractured Paradigm." *Journal of Communication* 43 (4): 51–58. https://doi .org/10.1111/j.1460-2466.1993.tb01304.x.

Gans, Herbert J. 2004. *Deciding What's News: A Study of CBS Evening News, NBC Nightly News, Newsweek, and Time/Herbert J. Gans*. Visions of the American Press. Evanston, IL: Northwestern University Press.

Hallin, Daniel C. 1986. *The Uncensored War: The Media and Vietnam*. Berkeley: University of California Press.

Iyengar, Shanto. 2015. *Media Politics: A Citizen's Guide*. 3rd ed. New York: W. W. Norton & Company.

Schudson, Michael. 2012. *The Sociology of News*. 2nd ed. Contemporary Societies. New York: W. W. Norton & Company.

Shoemaker, Pamela J., and Stephen D. Reese. 2014. *Mediating the Message in the 21st Century: A Media Sociology Perspective*. 3rd ed. New York: Routledge/Taylor & Francis Group.

Willnat, Lars, and David H. Weaver. 2014. "The American Journalist in the Digital Age." Bloomington: Indiana University School of Journalism. http://archive.news.indiana.edu/releases/iu/2014/05/2013-american-journalist-key-findings.pdf.

Q19. WHEN COVERING ELECTIONS, DO NEWS MEDIA TYPICALLY FOCUS ON THE ISSUES AND POLICIES THAT AFFECT CITIZENS?

Answer: No. When covering election campaigns, many news outlets focus disproportionately on polling and scandals instead of helping the public understand the nuances of candidates' qualifications and their policy positions. The "horse race" approach means constant discussion of who is winning from one day to the next, especially on television. There are legitimate scandals and character flaws and trends in campaign fortunes that deserve reporting, but many media critics (and members of the American public) believe that too often, these elements are covered so exhaustively that virtually no attention is given to issues and policies that actually affect citizens.

The Facts: Covering election campaigns is one of the most important functions of journalism. In a representative democracy like that of the United States, citizens participate in government by selecting elected representatives, participating in ballot initiatives and referendums, and being politically active about selected individuals or issues. Citizens need quality information to make good choices at the polls and in their other political activities, so that's why it's especially important that journalists provide comprehensive and detailed information about what they are likely to get when they cast their ballot. While some news outlets do an outstanding job of producing this kind of journalism, Americans are more likely to consume news from sources that obsess over the daily poll results and political scandals at the expense of substantive reporting.

Americans are fascinated by elections, as evidenced by the uptick in viewership and readership of news media that happens in a typical general election year and the amount of content sharing that has taken place on social media in recent years. In 2016, cable news outlets earned billions in revenue as Americans flocked to their televisions for campaign coverage. According to Pew Research, 74 percent of Americans said they had given a lot or some thought to the candidates in 2015 as presidential primaries began, and 69 percent said they watched at least some of the televised presidential debates, up from 43 percent in 2007 (Pew Research Center 2015).

As for media coverage, Pew Research found that 91 percent of adults learned something from a media source in January 2016 about the U.S. election (Gottfried et al. 2016). And most adults said they consume information from multiple media sources. Almost half of Americans reported learning information from five or more sources, and 35 percent said they learned from at least three or four sources. When the Pew study asked which source was "most helpful," cable television news came in first at 24 percent, followed by social media and local television at 14 percent each, news website or app at 13 percent, radio at 11 percent, and network television nightly news at 10 percent. Only younger audiences aged 18–29 found social media most helpful, at 35 percent.

These relatively high levels of interest and learning contrast with voter turnout, which reached only 55.7 percent of the voting-age population in 2016. American midterm election turnout is even lower, typically around 35–40 percent. In general, American election turnout ranks near the bottom among developed nations (28th out of the 35 member nations of the Organization for Economic Co-operation and Development [OECD]). Compare American turnout to the highest among OECD nations: Belgium at 87.2 percent, Sweden at 82.6 percent, and Denmark at 80.3 percent (DeSilver 2017).

What should we make of this gap between interest and participation in U.S. elections? Many observers point to the role of news media, which can help generate interest and viewership but doesn't necessarily lead to informed participation. There are several possible reasons for this and many ways in which coverage could be improved. First, it's worth noting that the role of news media can vary significantly depending on voter interest, who the candidates are and how they communicate, and what's happening in the nation and world (e.g., wars, economic crises) in any given election year. It's also important to use caution when generalizing about news media broadly. Some news outlets do pay significant attention to policies and issues (mainly large national newspapers), while others are virtually devoid of substantive information. Still, it is possible to point to general patterns of coverage that appear across the media landscape.

Patterns of coverage can be attributed to the pressures journalists face, which center on the need to be commercially successful by gaining large audiences. Thus, the marketplace for news is largely controlled by public desire. As scholar Doris Graber points out:

> It is extremely difficult to mesh the public's preference for simple, dramatic stories with the need to present ample information for issue-based election choices. Information that may be crucial for voting decisions often is too complex and technical to appeal to much of the audience. Hence newspeople feel compelled to write breezy infotainment stories that stress the horse race and skim over policy details. (Graber 2010, 207)

In a market context, it makes sense that a public preference for simplicity would dictate coverage, but it doesn't have to be that way. If the public were provided with a broad array of substantive and even challenging information, it could raise their level of expectations for the press and for themselves. Existing patterns of election coverage include uniformity across news outlets; a focus on candidate qualifications, candidate events, and scandals; and avoidance of the appearance of political bias even while embracing a bias toward the status quo and the immediate.

Regardless of degree of partisan orientation, most presidential election coverage is similar. News outlets within a given media sector (e.g., cable TV, radio, newspaper) devote comparable amounts of time and space to election coverage, and they paint similar portraits of candidates with some variation in tone of evaluation. Journalists follow campaigns in similar ways and tend to focus on the same day-to-day happenings, such as campaign rallies, press conferences, and the release of polling data. This leads to homogeneous coverage, sometimes referred to as "pack journalism" or the "media echo effect" because of the tendency for news outlets to copy each other. Ideally, homogeneous coverage should help produce a shared base of facts that different audiences could agree on. But when presentations of facts become twisted in service to particular political goals and allegiances, partisan audiences can receive quite different interpretations of campaign and candidate activity. Perhaps more important, uniformity of coverage—even when shaped by partisan orientation—means the same substantive issue and policy coverage is omitted across news outlets. Such omissions also apply to third-party candidates, who receive little to no news coverage, reflecting a news bias toward the two-party status quo.

The bias toward immediacy is also pervasive across election coverage. Traditional professional standards for newsworthiness often dictate that a trivial event on the campaign trail or a new revelation about a candidate's personal life is more likely to receive coverage than issues of intrinsic importance. In 1992, a large portion of coverage of Bill Clinton focused on his personal life, including drug use, poor word choice, and sexual escapades. In 2000, coverage of George W. Bush spent days on his drunk-driving charges more than two decades earlier; foreign policy issues as a whole received less coverage over the last few months of the campaign. In the 2008 Democratic primary, Hillary Clinton generated a frenzy of coverage when she teared up at a New Hampshire event; "Can Hillary Cry Her Way Back to the White House?" asked a *New York Times* opinion headline. Also in 2008, coverage of Sarah Palin focused excessively on an out-of-wedlock pregnancy in her family (Graber 2010). In 2016, mainstream reporting of Donald Trump and Hillary Clinton was focused disproportionately on scandal, personality, and horse-race coverage, and it was overwhelmingly negative (Patterson 2016). Notably, the issues on Trump's agenda (e.g., immigration) dictated much of the coverage of both candidates, and polarized media audiences received drastically different portrayals of their preferred candidates. Conservatives paid much of their attention to highly partisan, pro-Trump outlets, while liberals consumed mainstream outlets that observed traditional standards of neutrality and remained highly critical of Clinton (Faris et al. 2017).

The ways news media outlets cover elections are significant because of their ability to generate effects. Scholars point out that news media do not play a major role in Americans' ability to learn facts (Graber 2010; Iyengar 2015). Voters might feel little incentive to learn a great deal of political information because they do not believe government has much influence over their daily life. Voters also take shortcuts to establishing their candidate preferences by copying the preferences of other groups and individuals. Voters can form opinions based on facts they encounter and then discard those facts from memory. However, several theories point to the ability of news media to influence voter preferences and behaviors. "Agenda-setting" theory, which has dominated mass communication research for decades, suggests that wherever the news media directs their attention is where the public will direct its attention (McCombs and Shaw 1972). Only when a topic enters the news agenda does it enter the public agenda. For example, the Ebola virus was not a topic of concern for most Americans until it came to dominate news coverage during a 2014 outbreak. At that point, news media contributed significantly to the public panic that ensued, even though only five Americans were ever infected (Sell et al. 2017). Agenda-setting by news media is particularly likely for national and international issues with which Americans have little to no firsthand experience. In elections, voters are not likely to be concerned about an issue unless it gets significant media attention.

Another theory relevant to understanding election coverage is "framing," or the way news outlets portray an event or issue—by highlighting some aspects and ignoring others—and how it can affect audience perceptions (Iyengar 2015). Psychologists have long known that expressing outcomes in terms of gains or losses can alter preferences. A disease cure that would save 1 in 10 sick people sounds much better than a cure that would allow 9 out of 10 to die. Similarly, news coverage can frame political issues in different ways. Gun control can be an issue of individual liberty or public safety. Public assistance programs can be tied to lazy welfare recipients or the underprivileged poor. Military action can be a patriotic duty or a wasteful intervention. Different frames can affect how voters consider an issue and can influence their evaluation of candidates and their campaigns. Candidates themselves can be framed as relatable men or women "of the people" or as out-of-touch elites.

How can election coverage be improved? Scholars have several ideas for getting news outlets to take their public service responsibilities more seriously (Iyengar 2015). First, the United States has a weak public media sector, particularly as compared to other developed countries. Providing increased funding for public service broadcasting would help generate more news coverage not beholden to market pressures and influences. Regulation of commercial media, especially broadcast outlets holding free licenses to use and profit from the public airwaves, could increase the quantity and quality of public affairs information that Americans are exposed to. Providing candidates with free airtime could level the playing field and make it possible for a greater diversity of voices to reach wide audiences without first raising millions of dollars to buy access. Greater communication between candidates and voters can generate increased interest and participation. The 2016 election was a particularly bad one in terms of news coverage: negative, partisan, and nearly devoid of issue and policy information (Faris et al. 2017; Patterson 2016). Positive change is likely to occur only if the American public demands it.

FURTHER READING

DeSilver, Drew. 2017. "U.S. Trails Most Developed Countries in Voter Turnout." Pew Research Center. http://www.pewresearch.org/fact-tank/2017/05/15/u-s-voter-turnout-trails-most-developed-countries/.

Faris, Rob, Hal Roberts, Bruce Etling, Nikki Bourassa, Ethan Zuckerman, and Yochai Benkler. 2017. "Partisanship, Propaganda, and Disinformation: Online Media and the 2016 U.S. Presidential Election | Berkman Klein Center." Berkman Klein Center for Internet and Society at Harvard University. Accessed March 1, 2018. https://cyber.harvard.edu/publications/2017/08/mediacloud.

Gottfried, Jeffrey, Michael Barthel, Elisa Shearer, and Amy Mitchell. 2016. "The 2016 Presidential Campaign—A News Event That's Hard to Miss." Pew Research Center. http://www.journalism.org/2016/02/04/the-2016-presidential-campaign-a-news-event-thats-hard-to-miss/.

Graber, Doris A. 2010. *Mass Media and American Politics*. 8th ed. Washington, DC: CQ Press.

Iyengar, Shanto. 2015. *Media Politics: A Citizen's Guide*. 3rd ed. New York: W. W. Norton & Company.

McCombs, Maxwell E., and Donald L. Shaw. 1972. "The Agenda-Setting Function of Mass Media." *Public Opinion Quarterly* 36 (2): 176–187.

Patterson, Thomas. 2016. "News Coverage of the 2016 General Election: How the Press Failed the Voters." Shorenstein Center at Harvard University. https://shorensteincenter.org/news-coverage-2016-general-election/.

Pew Research Center. 2015. "Debates Help Fuel Strong Interest in 2016 Campaign." http://www.people-press.org/2015/12/14/debates-help-fuel-strong-interest-in-2016-campaign/.

Sell, Tara Kirk, Crystal Boddie, Emma E. McGinty, Keshia Pollack, Katherine C. Smith, Thomas A. Burke, and Lainie Rutkow. 2017. "Media Messages and Perception of Risk for Ebola Virus Infection, United States." *Emerging Infectious Diseases* 23 (1): 108–111. https://doi.org/10.3201/eid2301.160589.

Q20. DO POLITICIANS SET THE AGENDA FOR JOURNALISTS?

Answer: Politicians have a great deal of influence over what journalists talk about, in part because the policy priorities and decisions of politicians are almost always newsworthy. Politicians also have active press offices that release statements and create events to generate press coverage. This means that they exert a lot of control over what journalists talk about, even if they don't necessarily dictate what journalists say about the issues. However, the way journalists cover issues and which issues they choose to highlight may influence the news agenda and could affect what politicians are compelled to talk about. Some journalists also pursue stories that are not being pushed by politicians, but this kind of reporting often requires more time and resources than simply following the press pool that accompanies politicians.

The Facts: The "agenda" in terms of politicians and journalists is the set of topics or policy issues that are foremost in the minds of the general public. Agenda-setting theory suggests that the media do not tell people what to think, but they influence what people think about. McCombs and Shaw (1972) developed the theory after analyzing coverage of the 1968 presidential election and asserted that journalists "play an important part in shaping political reality" and influence how much importance readers give to certain issues, essentially setting the agenda of the campaign. Agenda-setting has been studied extensively since the original study, but what it demonstrates is that news coverage influences public opinion about the importance of issues. Due to this effect, politicians may be interested in influencing the agenda set by journalists to make sure it reflects their policy priorities and to keep the issues they care about in the news and therefore the minds of the public (and keep other issues out of the public eye).

There are several ways, both overt and subtle, that politicians can influence the reporting of journalists, as well as ways that journalists influence what politicians talk about. Politicians have official mechanisms, such as press officers and public relations teams, to attempt to push their stories and perspectives to journalists. They also have unofficial ways to influence coverage by granting interviews selectively and meeting privately or off-the-record with journalists to share information. Journalists are at least somewhat dependent on politicians to get information about decisions being made in government, so they are subject to these pressures.

Politicians employ communication offices to work on crafting their messages and staging press events. Many politicians have press secretaries who address groups of journalists, providing briefings on the politicians' agendas, as well as answering questions from journalists. This creates an easily identifiable newsworthy event, one which is guaranteed to provide material for a story. Similarly, pseudo-events staged to generate press attention can create the appearance of a newsworthy story that journalists feel they should cover. Politicians can also use social media to try to put issues or ideas in front of the public without going through the press. In addition, politicians can criticize the press, either in statements to other journalists or on social media, putting public pressure on journalists to cover issues differently. However, "Issuing press releases, keeping close relations with journalists, and playing by the media's rules do not in and of themselves guarantee media visibility," because journalists' news values and politicians' ability "ultimately determine whether or not politicians' efforts will bear fruit" (Cohen, Tsfati, and Sheafer 2008, 333).

Part of the power of politicians and press conferences is the pressure they put on journalists to not miss out on a story that may be reported by other outlets. If competitors are attending a press conference, journalists may feel pressured to attend as well. In the case of some high-profile figures, like the president of the United States, journalists have organized press "pools" composed of selected representatives from the various news organizations for each different medium. These representatives share their reporting with all the news organizations that may be interested in reports about a particular event or speech. There is a press pool that travels with the president of the United States on overseas trips and to excursions outside the White House, for example, and sends a pool feed to all organizations involved that they can use and edit for their own publication or broadcast.

For their part, journalists can exert some influence on which issues politicians talk about, through independent reporting, asking questions at press conferences, and selection of stories prioritized on their websites, front pages, newscasts, and social media pages. Bill Kovach and Tom Rosenstiel (2001) suggest that journalists should maintain autonomy from political influence and remember their responsibility to serve the public interest. However, the relationship between politics and journalism is inevitably close, as politicians understand the influence of media in the political process. Others have called this the "mediatization" of politics, which they characterized as an "increasing intrusion of the media in the political process" (Mazzoleni and Schulz 1999, 248), although one study noted that not all politicians respond equally to this process: "Studies reveal large differences in the extent of effort and resources spent in an attempt to receive media coverage on the part of different legislators in the same institution" (Cohen, Tsfati, and Sheafer 2008, 333). The very existence of an independent press may have some influence on the actions of politicians: "Media motivation and effort not only affect politicians' work in their relationships with journalists, but they also relate to their activity in parliament" (Cohen, Tsfati, and Sheafer 2008, 339).

There are pressures that may limit how much journalists can seek out an agenda that is based on news values and what they perceive to be the most important issues or events to their community or audience, rather than simply allowing politicians to set the agenda. Structural biases in the media have a great deal of influence on news content, and perhaps one of the most influential is expediency bias. Expediency bias describes the bias of journalists in favor of information that can be obtained quickly, easily, and inexpensively. This means that they are more likely to call a politician to get a reaction to a story, because they already know that person's name and contact, and there is a press office or press secretary available to respond to their questions and provide them with clear, quotable opinions. This reliance on established sources of information means that they are overrepresented in news coverage compared to the average citizen or even citizen advocacy groups.

Journalists are under a lot of pressure to produce content. They are often competing to come out with stories first, to "break" news before competing reporters. These pressures have increased with the shift to online news, which doesn't have the same publishing deadlines as print newspapers or television news programs and instead demand constant updates. News can break at any time, not just during the evening or morning news programs or in time for the paper going to press. This puts the pressure on journalists to break new stories and generate fresh content all day. They are also under pressure to create new content for online news sites that can get returning viewers throughout the day. Journalists publishing online are also often asked to do more than just write or shoot a story; many are now tasked with creating multimedia versions of stories for the web. In addition, cuts to newsrooms have resulted in fewer journalists working to put out more stories. These pressures on journalists mean they may be more responsive to potential news stories that come to them easily and be less likely to pursue stories that are likely to require extensive independent reporting. If politicians or their press team can put information in front of journalists, giving them an issue or event to write about, and even providing quotations from sources, busy journalists may be susceptible to taking that information and turning it into a news story for their outlet. Jonathan Cohen, Yariv Tsfati, and Tamir Sheafer (2008, 334) noted that "because the great majority of routine news stories involve the intentional promotion of purposive accomplishments by officials, and given that in such routine stories journalists do not often actively seek information that they are not 'fed,' media motivation is necessary for receiving coverage, especially positive coverage."

Some journalists, particularly those empowered by their employers to spend time on stories without a strong time element, still have opportunities to "dig deep" into potential stories. They can report independently and pursue story ideas that come out of their conversations with members of the public about issues that concern them, examinations of public records or other documents, or other indications of lawbreaking or misdeeds that come to their attention. Investigative reporting that reveals illegal activity, misuse of public funds, misconduct by elected officials, and similar stories results from this kind of reporting and is generally off the agenda that politicians are attempting to establish. However, many newsrooms can't afford to have journalists reporting on stories for long periods of time without generating content for print or broadcast, and this problem is exacerbated by the downward trend in advertising revenue for print newspapers, even once they move online.

While cultivating relationships with politicians may lead to access and information, these relationships may make journalists more credulous, impeding their ability to report fairly on the politicians with whom they have close relationships. The need to maintain these relationships also gives politicians some power to influence what journalists say and don't say about them, by offering future access to information or by threatening to cut off ties with particular journalists. In more public settings, politicians may decline to call on specific journalists during press conferences or briefings, if they are concerned that the journalist will ask a difficult question or if they are unhappy with previous reporting by that journalist. For television journalists, politicians can refuse to accept invitations to appear on their shows. For example, President Donald Trump was interviewed 18 times on Fox television networks during the first 10 months of his presidency. During the same period, he appeared on NBC or MSNBC twice, once on CBS News, once on ABC News, and never on CNN (Schwartz 2017). This favoritism, which was uncommon in prior presidencies, may be due to his perception that Fox has been favorable in its coverage, while the other networks have been critical. His choices could affect the content that those news organizations are able to provide to their audiences, their ratings and revenue, and ultimately could influence the coverage of his presidency.

Although politicians have some power to set the agenda, journalists can work to maintain independence and autonomy from political figures, to pursue objective approaches to stories and at least a somewhat adversarial approach to politicians, and to remember their ultimate responsibility to serve the public. This may require seeking to resist the reliance on press releases and press conferences by politicians and to find stories generated by citizen interest groups and others advocating for the public interest. This kind of reporting takes more time and resources and must be supported by the news organizations that employ reporters and ultimately by the audiences that can support those news organizations with their attention and money.

FURTHER READING

Cohen, Jonathan, Yariv Tsfati, and Tamir Sheafer. 2008. "The Influence of Presumed Media Influence in Politics: Do Politicians' Perceptions of Media Power Matter?" *Public Opinion Quarterly* 72 (2): 331–344.

Kovach, Bill, and Tom Rosenstiel. 2001. *Elements of Journalism: What Newspeople Should Know and the Public Should Expect.* New York: Three Rivers Press.

Mazzoleni, Gianpietro, and Winfried Schulz. 1999. "'Mediatization' of Politics: A Challenge for Democracy?" *Political Communication* 16 (3): 247–261.

McCombs, Maxwell E., and Donald L. Shaw. 1972. "The Agenda-Setting Function of Mass Media." *Public Opinion Quarterly* 36 (2): 176–187.

Schwartz, Jason. 2017. "Trump Gives 18th Interview to Fox." *Politico*, October 25. https://www.politico.com/story/2017/10/25/how-many-interviews-has-trump-given-fox-244157.

Q21. IS THE RELATIONSHIP BETWEEN POLITICIANS AND JOURNALISTS ADVERSARIAL OR COOPERATIVE?

Answer: The relationship between politicians and journalists is both adversarial and cooperative, to varying degrees. Journalists need access to politicians in order to find out what policy decisions are being made, and politicians use journalists to get their messages to the public. However, many journalists believe their primary responsibility is to serve the public, not politicians, and to hold those elected officials accountable to their constituents, so they sometimes report stories that politicians would prefer to be kept secret or report them in a way that politicians disagree with. While negative reports are necessary to hold public officials accountable, those reports may cause politicians to refuse future requests for interviews or information, so journalists may weigh the value of a particular report to the public against the cost it may have on future access to politicians.

The Facts: Journalistic ethics promote the idea that journalists' primary obligation is to the public. This point is made in various texts and ethics codes and by journalism scholars and news organizations. Bill Kovach and Tom Rosenstiel (2001, 17), in their authoritative text about journalists, summarized it as follows: "The primary purpose of journalism is to provide citizens with the information they need to be free and self-governing." Others have described this as a "watchdog" role for journalists, positioning them as the "fourth estate," a reference to the three estates in Europe: the clergy, the nobility, and the commoners. These perspectives position journalists as a check on elected officials and other powerful figures and institutions, such as the church, to balance their power with an institution capable of holding them accountable. This idea is reflected in maxims held by some in journalism, such as the idea that newspapers should "comfort the afflicted and afflict the comfortable."

The modern press in the United States began with explicitly partisan newspapers often owned, published, or funded by political parties. These newspapers were not expected to be objective or even to play a role in holding public officials accountable, except perhaps by publishing criticism from competing political parties. The modern understanding of journalism and the role of journalists as having a responsibility to the public, including as a check on elected officials, developed over the course of the 20th century. This view was represented most strongly by the Hutchins Commission on Freedom of the Press (1947), which put forth a social responsibility theory of the press. Several U.S. Supreme Court decisions in the 20th century supported this interpretation of the First Amendment as providing protection for the people and the press to criticize officials and discuss public affairs with impunity.

The watchdog view of journalism suggests that journalists should or would have an adversarial relationship with politicians, one in which they challenge politicians and determine whether politicians are telling the truth to the public, serving the public's best interests, and fulfilling promises they had made to the public, among other things. This view may be interpreted to be at odds with the commitment to objectivity that is also frequently cited as a journalistic value. If journalists claim that objectivity is their guiding principle, they might be unlikely to aggressively pursue leads or question the conduct or statements of public officials. Advocacy journalism is a practice that positions reporters as advocates for a particular cause but still expects them to seek facts and report truthfully.

The public journalism movement in the 1990s specifically sought to position journalists as active participants, enabling the creation and sustained functioning of the public sphere. Its proponents encouraged journalists to see their audiences as citizens rather than consumers, to actively seek input from citizens, and to not just provide a forum for deliberation but to facilitate discussions and seek answers to problems identified by citizens. Compared to mainstream media coverage, "public journalism practices produced more election-related reporting, with mobilizing information and more focus on substantive issues and policy; they de-emphasized polls, campaign strategies, and image-management" (Steiner and Roberts 2011, 194–195). However, this movement did not gain widespread support and ultimately was abandoned even by the editors who had experimented with it. Many journalists were uncomfortable with taking on a proactive role, attacking public journalism as manipulative, propagandistic, or at the very least antithetical to the ideal of objectivity espoused by many journalists. A traditional view of professional journalism in the United States, as it evolved over the 20th century, would not consider advocacy journalism to be the same as what journalists do, but would nonetheless champion the interests of the public.

The view that journalists play a role in holding politicians accountable to the public has become widely accepted. However, in order to report on politicians effectively, journalists also cultivate relationships with them to obtain information about legislation, policy agendas, and other issues. This is called access journalism by some, the kind of journalism that "seeks to provide insider information from powerful institutions and people" (*Columbia Journalism Review* 2014). As the editors of *The Columbia Journalism Review* (2014) noted, "Access journalism is not an inherently bad thing, and is in fact a vital, useful, and inevitable journalistic form," adding, "there will always be a journalism focused on getting close to elites to learn what they are thinking and intending." However, journalists must be careful that the relationships they develop with those sources do not have undue influence on the type of reporting they do about those people. Access journalism can lead to reproducing the discourses being promoted by politicians and other powerful figures and further strengthening the power of a particular group rather than holding those individuals account-able to the public they were elected to serve.

The challenges of holding politicians accountable while relying on them for information and access are further exacerbated by corporate con-solidation of media ownership. As the control of media outlets is concen-trated in fewer companies, the consequences of challenging politicians can become even greater. Pressure from employers to maintain positive relationships with politicians can discourage individual journalists from reporting negative stories, asking tough questions, or investigating certain people or stories. Editors and publishers may be concerned that politicians would punish the whole organization because of critical reporting by one individual—revoking access to press conferences, for example, or refusing to grant interviews.

Some critics have argued that journalists in the United States are sus-ceptible to patriotic fervor and have failed in their watchdog role when it has been most necessary. For example, in the lead-up to the 2003 invasion of Iraq, journalists published many stories based on information provided by Bush administration officials who strongly advocated military interven-tion in Iraq. Journalists were not as skeptical of claims made by the govern-ment to justify starting the war, especially evidence that Saddam Hussein had weapons of mass destruction, and part of their hesitation to rigorously examine those claims had to do with the mood in the country following the terrorist attacks on September 11, 2001. Following that attack, the president's approval rating soared, and the American public displayed a clear inclination to "rally around the flag." Not only were some journalists caught up in the patriotic fervor, but those who were not might also have felt that rigorously questioning the administration's claims about the case for war would have been perceived as antipatriotic. Whether individual trauma or solidarity with the community was the motivation behind the patriotic coverage, Ginosar (2015) has suggested that this kind of patri-otic journalism is common in the coverage of military confrontation and terror attacks and that it deviates from the traditional model of journalism that "endorses neutrality, objectivity, impartiality, and criticism" in favor of more subjective and patriotic coverage. A commitment to act in the public interest could be conflated with a commitment to the national interest, and it can be challenging to separate the two.

Adversarial journalism can have positive effects in a democratic system; it can "excite, involve, and mobilize people in the processes of democ-racy . . . lead to better outcomes, informed by an enhanced understanding of claims and interests" and "foster republican virtues: critical indepen-dence and distrust of authority" (Curran 2005). At its best, adversarial journalism means that the press actively examines claims made by elected officials, investigates business and financial deals to ensure they are made fairly, and generally holds politicians accountable to the public who elected them. However, James Curran (2005) points out that it can also encourage "the circulation of scurrilous information about public figures that has no foundation in truth" and contribute to media partisanship. Journalists should not be so driven to challenge public officials that they seek to attack officials unnecessarily or erode trust in politicians or political institutions.

Agenda-setting theory has suggested that journalists set the public agenda by selecting which stories to cover and how much prominence to give those stories in the overall news coverage (McCombs and Shaw 1972). Politicians, of course, also try to influence that news agenda by inserting their own policies and issues or at least their view of the policies and issues being covered by the news. Critical discourse analysis attempts to explain the relationships between discourse and power and can offer a framework to analyze how politicians and journalists cooperate and compete to set agendas and determine narratives. Not everyone has equal access to the media, and the access that politicians have to communicate with journalists is a further extension of their power. Politicians' ability to control the access that journalists have to state houses, press conferences, and the like gives them even more power over the news agenda.

FURTHER READING

Columbia Journalism Review. 2014. "The Right Debate: Access vs. Accountability Is What Matters" [Editorial]. January/February. https://archives.cjr.org/editorial/the_right_debate.php.

Curran, James. 2005. "What Democracy Requires of the Media." In *The Press*, edited by Geneva Overholser and Kathleen H. Jamieson, 120–140. New York: Oxford University Press.

Ginosar, Avshalom. 2015. "Understanding Patriotic Journalism: Culture, Ideology and Professional Behavior." *Journal of Media Ethics* 30 (4): 289–301.

Haas, Tanni. 2007. *The Pursuit of Public Journalism: Theory, Practice, and Criticism*. New York: Routledge.

Kovach, Bill, and Tom Rosenstiel. 2001. *Elements of Journalism: What Newspeople Should Know and the Public Should Expect*. New York: Three Rivers Press.

McCombs, Maxwell E., and Donald L. Shaw. 1972 "The Agenda-Setting Function of Mass Media." *Public Opinion Quarterly* 36 (2): 176–187.

Steiner, Linda, and Jessica Roberts. 2011. "Philosophical Linkages between Public Journalism and Citizen Journalism." In *Media Perspectives for the 21st Century*, edited by Stylianos Papathanassopoulos, 191–211. New York: Routledge.

van Dijk, Tuen A. 1996. "Discourse, Power and Access." In *Texts and Practices: Readings in Critical Discourse Analysis*, edited by C. R. Caldas-Coulthard and M. Coulthard, 84–104. New York: Routledge.

Q22. DO JOURNALISTS HAVE VALID REASONS TO USE ANONYMOUS OR UNNAMED SOURCES?

Answer: Yes. Journalism can involve reporting on stories that are sensitive or reveal wrongdoing, and the only way to get a source to reveal what they know about these topics is by agreeing not to publish their name in the report. Usually, these sources fear reprisal from employers or others who would prefer to keep damaging information from the public. In these cases, it is assumed that the value of the information to the public is worth the loss of transparency when a journalist is not able to attribute the information to a specific source. Of course, the journalist, and sometimes the editors working above them, knows the identity of the source and tries to identify any potential conflicts or motivation they may have. Many states have "shield laws" meant to protect journalists from having to reveal the identity of an anonymous source in court.

The Facts: Anonymity is a tool journalists can use to offer protection to sources in exchange for sharing what they know. Journalistic ethics emphasizes a responsibility to give citizens the information they need to be self-governing, especially holding public officials accountable to the public. In order to do this effectively, journalists sometimes need to get information from people who do not want to be identified publicly. This means reporting about the activities of elected officials and can include reporting about information that powerful individuals would rather not have made public. As put forth by Bill Kovach and Tom Rosenstiel (2001, 17), "The primary purpose of journalism is to provide citizens with the information they need to be free and self-governing," and their first loyalty is to the public. People working in government or other powerful institutions may have access to information of public interest but fear reprisal from their employers or criticism from family and friends or shy away from the attention they would receive for coming forward to share the information with journalists. Governments need to keep some information secret, but the classified designation is sometimes used to keep embarrassing or politically damaging information from the public. In these cases, people may tell journalists what they know without being identified as the source of that information in any published report.

In other cases, journalists may want to inform citizens about ethical or legal breaches by other powerful figures, including leaders of large corporations or religious institutions. Similar to reporting on government officials, employees or other insiders with knowledge of crimes or abuse may be afraid to report out of fear of reprisal. Journalists may also report on matters that are sensitive or difficult to discuss, such as sex crimes, drug use, or health issues. In order to protect the privacy of a source revealing sensitive personal information, a journalist may grant them anonymity. Reporting on these stories may help the public better understand the issue, and many people who can provide insight into criminal activities may not want to be identified publicly, for their safety or to protect their reputation. In all these cases, anonymity may allow a journalist to gain access to information valuable to the public. The position paper of the Society of Professional Journalists' Ethics Committee (Farrell n.d.) claims, "Anonymous sources are sometimes the only key to unlocking that big story, throwing back the curtain on corruption, fulfilling the journalistic missions of watchdog on the government and informant to the citizens."

Anonymous sources have provided journalists information to report some of the most important news stories in the last century. Daniel Ellsberg shared a study prepared by the U.S. Department of Defense of the country's military involvement in Vietnam with reporters at *The New York Times*, revealing that the U.S. military was misleading the public about the war. *The Washington Post* reporter Bob Woodward learned critical information from an anonymous source within the Federal Bureau of Investigation that helped him and his colleague Carl Bernstein report stories that ultimately led to the resignation of U.S. president Richard Nixon. Reporting in 2013 about the drug-trade links of Doug Ford, a Toronto city councilor and brother of Toronto mayor Rob Ford, relied on anonymous sources.

In other cases, however, anonymous sources have been used badly or falsely cited to insert invented claims or details in stories. *The Washington Post* reporter Janet Cooke invented a story about a child heroin addict in 1981 based on anonymous sources. She was awarded the Pulitzer Prize before it was discovered that the story was fabricated. Cooke returned the prize and lost her job. Jayson Blair, a reporter at *The New York Times*, invented an anonymous law enforcement source in fabricating details in stories about the Washington sniper case in 2002. Blair resigned from the paper. In the run-up to the 2003 U.S. war in Iraq, much of the reporting by *The New York Times* about the case for military action, including the suspected existence of weapons of mass destruction in Iraq, was largely based on unnamed sources in the Bush administration, many of whom were later discredited or discovered to originate from former vice president Dick Cheney.

Most news organizations continue to use anonymous sources in at least some stories. Matt Duffy (2014, 254) noted that the use of anonymous sources became more common following the reporting of the Watergate scandal by *The Washington Post* but that many news organizations "had tightened or clarified their rules surrounding the use of unnamed sources" by the late 2000s, in response to embarrassing episodes such as the Blair case. The use of anonymous sources declined dramatically in the 2000s, following prominent scandals and stricter policies (Duffy 2014). Despite stricter policies, ombudsmen at *The New York Times* and *The Washington Post* have complained about their papers' overuse of anonymous sources. In 2016, *The Washington Post* reneged on an agreement to offer a source anonymity after it was discovered that the woman had invented her story about Roy Moore, candidate for the U.S. Senate in Alabama, in an attempt to discredit the *Post* and its reporting (Boburg, Davis, and Crites 2017). Amid extensive *Post* reporting about allegations against Moore, one woman came forward with a false accusation, presumably to later reveal the accusation was false and undermine the previous reporting. *The Post* determined that her story was false, however, and revealed her identity and her claims to the public.

Most news organizations, and particularly legacy media, such as daily newspapers, have strict rules for when to grant anonymity to a source and how journalists may use information obtained from anonymous sources. For example, the Associated Press (AP) allows reporters to use anonymous sources in the following circumstances: "The material is information and not opinion or speculation, and is vital to the news report. The information is not available except under the conditions of anonymity imposed by the source. The source is reliable, and in a position to have accurate information" (Daniszewski 2017). Generally, journalists are cautious about granting anonymity to sources and aim to do so only when absolutely necessary and after all other options have been exhausted. The Society of Professional Journalists (2014) offers the following guidelines for using anonymous sources in reporting: "Consider sources' motives before promising anonymity. Reserve anonymity for sources who may face danger, retribution or other harm, and have information that cannot be obtained elsewhere. Explain why anonymity was granted."

Anonymity should be agreed upon before interviews between sources and journalists begin, and the conditions of anonymity for a source are often negotiated by a journalist in consultation with their editor or editors. For example, *The New York Times* policy requires "one of three top editors to review and sign off on articles that depend primarily on information from unnamed sources" (Sullivan 2016). Similarly, NPR's (2012) *Ethics Handbook* instructs journalists to "consult with your supervisor and our legal team before you make a promise of confidentiality" and states that individual journalists "do not have the authority to assure any individual that information s/he gives us anonymously will be reported." Sometimes the editor will know the identity of the source, but other times a journalist may keep that information from even the editor. In many organizations, journalists are encouraged to press sources to allow their name to be used in a story and to question why the source wants anonymity in order to identify any personal motivations to reveal damaging information. "Wherever possible, AP journalists are urged to push back against such requests for anonymity, pressing for permission to use the name or bypassing the information if necessary" (Daniszewski 2017).

If a source insists on anonymity, and reporters and editors agree that the source has compelling reasons to request anonymity, journalists will then negotiate how to use the information the source will provide and how to identify the source in a way that allows the reader to understand the context. Some sources will provide information only for background reporting, not to be cited directly in the report but to enable further investigation of the issue. Others will provide information that can be cited directly in a report and attributed to an anonymous source. Most journalists resist directly reporting information from a single anonymous source. When journalists receive information from anonymous sources, they are likely to use that information to do further reporting and to attempt to confirm that information from other sources that are willing to be identified in the story.

Certain kinds of information may not come from anonymous sources. Several organizations have policies against using anonymous sources to report opinions, including the AP and NPR. For example, NPR's (2012) *Ethics Handbook* states, "Unidentified sources should rarely be heard at all and should never be heard attacking or praising others in our reports."

Once a journalist has decided to report material obtained from an anonymous source, the journalist must determine how to describe the source. Journalists aim to help the audience understand who the source was, in terms of their relationship to the information, so that it is clear how the source had access to the information provided and why the source might have been interested in sharing that information to reveal any motivation behind leaks. The NPR (2012) *Ethics Handbook* states, "We describe in as much detail as we can (without revealing so much that we effectively identify that person) how they know this information, their motivations (if any) and any other biographical details that will help a listener or reader evaluate the source's credibility."

Some state supreme courts have recognized the importance of protecting journalists' ability to use anonymous sources and keep those sources confidential. Statutes, known as shield laws, in 40 U.S. states and the District of Columbia protect journalists from having to reveal their sources in court. The U.S. Supreme Court decided in 1972, in *Branzburg v. Hayes*, that requiring journalists to testify in court did not abridge the freedom of speech and of the press protected in the First Amendment. However, Justice Douglas wrote in a dissenting opinion, that the decision would "impede the wide-open and robust dissemination of ideas and counterthought which a free press both fosters and protects and which is essential to the success of intelligent self-government" (*Branzburg v. Hayes* 1972). He argued that "(f)orcing a reporter before a grand jury will have two retarding effects upon the ear and the pen of the press. Fear of exposure will cause dissidents to communicate less openly to trusted reporters. And fear of accountability will cause editors and critics to write with more restrained pens." Despite acknowledging the value of being able to offer anonymity to the fact-finding mission of journalists, the United States has not passed a federal shield law to protect journalists from having to divulge their sources in court.

FURTHER READING

Boburg, Shawn, Aaron C. Davis, and Alice Crites. 2017. "A Woman Approached the Post with Dramatic—and False—Tale about Roy Moore. She Appears to Be Part of Undercover Sting Operation." *The Washington Post*, November 27. https://www.washingtonpost.com/investigations/a-woman-approached-the-post-with-dramatic--and-false--tale-about-roy-moore-sje-appears-to-be-part-of-undercover-sting-operation/2017/11/27/0c2e335a-cfb6-11e7-9d3a-bcbe2af58c3a_story.

Branzburg v. Hayes. 1972. 408 U.S. 665.

Daniszewski, John. 2017. "When Is It OK to Use Anonymous Sources?" AP.org. https://blog.ap.org/behind-the-news/when-is-it-ok-to-use-anonymous-sources.

Duffy, Matt J. 2014. "Anonymous Sources: A Historical Review of the Norms Surrounding Their Use." *American Journalism* 31 (2): 236–261.

Farrell, Michael. n.d. "SPJ Ethics Committee Position Papers: Anonymous Sources." SPJ.org. https://www.spj.org/ethics-papers-anonymity .asp.

Kovach, Bill, and Tom Rosenstiel. 2001. *Elements of Journalism: What Newspeople Should Know and the Public Should Expect.* New York: Three Rivers Press.

NPR. 2012. "Anonymous Sourcing." *Ethics Handbook.* http://ethics.npr .org/tag/anonymity/.

Society of Professional Journalists. 2014. "SPJ Code of Ethics." SPJ.org. https://www.spj.org/ethicscode.asp.

Sullivan, Margaret. 2016. "The Public Editor's Journal: Tightening the Screws on Anonymous Sources." *The New York Times,* March 15. https:// publiceditor.blogs.nytimes.com/2016/03/15/new-york-times-anoymous-sources-policy-public-editor/.

Q23. CAN POLITICIANS CIRCUMVENT JOURNALISTS BY USING SOCIAL MEDIA?

Answer: Yes, social media can provide a way for politicians to communicate messages directly to the public, although those statements may only reach the segment of the public that is following them on social media sites like Twitter or Facebook, and they may lack the authority of news reports that include context and other information to support claims. Sometimes journalists report on statements made by politicians on social media if they are of public interest or generate sufficient conflict. Making statements on social media also allows other politicians, journalists, and the general public to reply or comment publicly back to politicians through those same media, although some data show that people say they trust social media less than they trust professional journalists.

The Facts: Social media has become an increasingly popular way for politicians to communicate messages to the public, and the successful campaign of U.S. presidential candidate Donald Trump brought more attention to how politicians can use social media to speak directly to their political base. Every politician holding a national office in the United States has a social media presence on at least one of the major social media sites and sometimes maintains multiple accounts for official or personal use. Politicians may vary in how much they use social media sites, whether posting their own opinions regularly, or tasking public relations staff with creating social media posts, or some combination of these two, as former secretary of state and 2016 presidential candidate Hillary Clinton did with her Twitter account, signing posts she wrote with her initials. The percentage of Americans who follow politicians on social media has been increasing, as Pew Research showed an increase from 6 percent in 2010 to 16 percent of voters in 2014, with 41 percent of registered voters who follow politicians on social media saying that finding out political news before others was a major reason they did so (Anderson 2015).

Politicians can use social media to respond to news events and media coverage more quickly than through traditional avenues that involved writing press releases and sending them to journalists in hopes the message would appear in news reports or granting interviews to provide sound bites for broadcast. A Pew Research survey on politicians' Facebook pages found that the most ideological members of Congress were more likely to share news stories on Facebook, doing so "more than twice as often as moderate legislators" between January 2015 and July 2017 (Van Kessel, Hughes, and Messing 2018). Social media also allows politicians to publish their own messages, unedited and exactly as they would like them to appear, removing the framing, context, or counter information that a journalist might add to a story. An analysis of the 2012 U.S. presidential election concluded that the Obama campaign "used Facebook as a tool of top-down promotion, focusing on Obama's personality and as a means of strategically guiding followers to act, rather than as a means of bottom-up empowerment or hybridized coproduction" (Gerodimos and Justinussen 2015, 132). Further, the authors found that "followers engaged selectively with campaign messages and often interacted more with policy-oriented posts than with promotional ones" (Gerodimos and Justinussen 2015, 132). The use of social media can contribute to a focus on the individual politician and the politician's personality rather than the political party or policy issues.

One of the advantages of using social media is that it can allow politicians to appear authentic to their followers. Gunn Enli (2017) analyzed and identified several strategies that politicians use to appear authentic on social media: predictability or appearing to "break the rules"; spontaneity; confessions; ordinariness or demonstrating anti-elitism; amateurism, appearing genuine or like an outsider; and imperfection in the form of selected displays of weaknesses, real or staged. Perceived authenticity is a desirable quality in politicians, one that can be difficult to project without appearing too staged or forced. Social media may allow politicians to appear authentic to their constituents or the broader public in a way that they cannot by speaking to journalists, who take their words and put them in context with other information. Donald Trump was evidently successful in using his social media accounts to appeal to a portion of the American public by appearing to flout conventions of political communication, posting tweets that were sometimes offensive, critical, outlandish, or completely unfounded. His use of Twitter contributed to his image among supporters as an anti-elitist outsider, who wasn't afraid to "tell it like it is" or "say what he meant," all of which could be understood as markers of authenticity.

Using social media to promote a message may be less effective than getting a message into the news media. Using social media to connect with constituents may somewhat limit a politician's reach or ability to grow their support, given that filter bubbles make it unlikely that their posts will reach anyone who doesn't already support them. While partisan voters are unlikely to be swayed to change their vote by new information, undecided or independent voters can be influenced by a campaign. However, if those voters are not exposed to candidates' posts because their social networks are likely composed of people with similar views, candidates will not have an opportunity to sway their votes.

Of course, politicians are rarely able to completely circumvent journalists, who are at least partially influential in setting the news agenda through their selection, prioritization, and framing of stories (McCombs and Shaw 1972). While Trump and others may tweet or post updates to Facebook, only those posts that are judged to be newsworthy by journalists will get mainstream media coverage and influence the political news agenda. Journalists are likely to put those posts in context, to seek responses from opposition parties or constituents, and correct misinformation. If politicians are particularly savvy at posting updates about topics that are likely to get attention from journalists, they may have more success in influencing the news agenda.

Some efforts have been made to measure the extent to which social media popularity translates to offline political behavior and electoral success. Since candidates began using social media in 2006, research has shown some indication that political activity on Facebook "mirrors offline political action" (MacWilliams 2015). Barclay et al. (2015) found a strong positive correlation "between the number of 'likes' a party or its leader secured on their official Facebook fan page and their popular vote share" in a 2014 election in India. Another use of social media is to mobilize supporters to engage in political activities, to vote or promote campaign messages. At least one study has found an increase in voter turnout as a result of voter mobilization efforts (Jones et al. 2017).

There can also be downsides to engaging with the public directly through social media. People say they trust content from social media sites less than content from the professional news media (Mitchell et al. 2016). While trust in the news media is not high—around 22 percent of Americans trust information from news organizations a lot—only 4 percent of American adults who use the Internet have a lot of trust in the information they find on social media (Mitchell et al. 2016). Politicians can also make public mistakes on social media or engage with trolls, bots, or other accounts that can undermine their message or credibility. The ease of posting to social media, along with the lower expectation for formality, means that accidental posting is more likely than with press releases that usually go through an editing process before being sent. Social media use can also expose politicians to the possibility of losing control of messages in other ways. Constituents or journalists can respond to politicians or share messages with a counternarrative, disrupting the narrative the politician was attempting to put forward. There have been a few cases of politicians, including Donald Trump, retweeting or otherwise interacting with content from social media bots.

Social media sites can also expose politicians to hostility. The Committee on Standards for Public Life (2017) in the United Kingdom criticized Twitter, Facebook, and YouTube for aiding and abetting the harassment of politicians: "Although social media helps to promote widespread access to ideas and engagement in debate, it also creates an intensely hostile online environment. Some have felt the need to disengage entirely from social media because of the abuse they face, and it has put off others who may wish to stand for public office." The committee's report called intimidation in public life, which is primarily occurring through social media, "a threat to the very nature of representative democracy in the UK."

Increasingly, as social media sites become the places of public discourse, politicians may be obligated to engage with citizens through those media. The American Civil Liberties Union has challenged politicians in both political parties for blocking constituents on social media, claiming that it violates constitutional protections for free speech. The organization has already taken on the suit of a Georgia woman who filed a lawsuit against her representative, Paul Gosar, for blocking access to his Facebook page. The organization has also sent letters to three other Georgia politicians, Sen. Johnny Isakson and Reps. John Lewis and Barry Loudermilk, threatening similar legal action if they do not unblock constituents on social media or provide reasons for blocking them (Connolly 2018).

President Donald Trump has also faced legal challenges for his actions to block several users on Twitter. The Knight First Amendment Institute at Columbia University filed a lawsuit on behalf of seven people Trump blocked on Twitter, claiming their free speech rights were being violated, and a federal judge ruled in 2018 that Trump was violating users' First Amendment rights by blocking them from a public forum. The White House said that Trump's @RealDonaldTrump account is a personal account and not a government publication. The plaintiffs in the lawsuit pointed out that the president's press secretary had previously stated that tweets on the account should be understood as "official statements by the President of the United States." The outcome of this case may have repercussions for politicians using social media. An attorney for the Knight First Amendment Institute claims that the First Amendment creates an obligation for politicians on social media: "If the government opens up a space or hosts a kind of public forum where they allow the public to speak, they can't exclude someone from that forum based on their views" (Sydell 2017).

FURTHER READING

Anderson, Monica. 2015. "More Americans Are Using Social Media to Connect with Politicians." Pew Research Center. http://www .pewresearch.org/fact-tank/2015/05/19/more-americans-are-using-social-media-to-connect-with-politicians/.

Barclay, Francis P., C. Pichandy, Anusha Venkat, and Sreedevi Sudhakaran. 2015. "India 2014: Facebook 'Like' as a Predictor of Election Outcomes." *Asian Journal of Political Science* 23 (2): 134–160.

Committee on Standards in Public Life. 2017. "Intimidation in Public Life: A Review by the Committee on Standards in Public Life." https://www.gov.uk/government/publications/intimidation-in-public-life-a-review-by-the-committee-on-standards-in-public-life.

Connolly, Griffin. 2018. "ACLU Challenges Lawmakers Who Block People on Social Media." *Roll Call*, January 25. http://www.rollcall.com/news/politics/aclu-challenges-lawmakers-block-people-social-media.

Enli, Gunn. 2017. "Twitter as Arena for the Authentic Outsider: Exploring the Social Media Campaigns of Trump and Clinton in the 2016 US Presidential Election." *European Journal of Communication* 32 (1): 50–61.

Gerodimos, Roman, and Jakup Justinussen. 2015. "Obama's 2012 Facebook Campaign: Political Communication in the Age of the Like Button." *Journal of Information Technology & Politics* 12 (2): 113–132.

Jones, Jason J., Robert M. Bond, Eytan Bakshy, Dean Eckles, and James H. Fowler. 2017. "Social Influence and Political Mobilization: Further Evidence from a Randomized Experiment in the 2012 U.S. Presidential Election." *PLoS ONE* 12 (4).

MacWilliams, Matthew C. 2015. "Forecasting Congressional Elections Using Facebook Data." *PS: Political Science & Politics* 48 (4): 579–583.

McCombs, Maxwell E., and Donald L. Shaw. 1972. "The Agenda-Setting Function of Mass Media." *Public Opinion Quarterly* 36 (2): 176–187.

Mitchell, Amy, Jeffrey Gottfried, Michael Barthel, and Elisa Shearer. 2016. "The Modern News Consumer: News Attitudes and Practices in the Digital Era." Pew Research Center. http://www.journalism .org/2016/07/07/the-modern-news-consumer/.

Sydell, Laura. 2017. "First Amendment Advocates Charge Trump Can't Block Critics on Twitter." NPR, November 7. https://www.npr.org/ sections/alltechconsidered/2017/11/07/562619874/first-amendment-advocates-charge-trump-cant-block-critics-on-twitter.

Van Kessel, Patrick, Adam Hughes, and Solomon Messing. 2018. "Very Liberal or Conservative Legislators Most Likely to Share News on Facebook." Pew Research Center. http://www.pewresearch .org/fact-tank/2018/01/19/very-liberal-or-conservative-legislators-most-likely-to-share-news-on-facebook/.

Q24. DO NEWS MEDIA INCREASE POLITICAL POLARIZATION?

Answer: Yes and no. Highly partisan people tend to sit at the extremes of the political spectrum, and they are the ones who tend to be most influenced by partisan media, which only makes them more extreme and extends the reaches of the political spectrum. Those people also tend to have an outsized effect on politics, so their voices are louder, which helps them influence political outcomes. However, most Americans do not live at these extremes, and they do not appear to be heavily influenced by news media. More likely, nonpartisans are tuning out the news altogether thanks to a high-choice media environment where non-news options are endless (Prior 2013). And while social media often gets the blame for polarization, younger people who use social media are actually less polarized than older people who rely on cable news. While polarization has increased in the United States, many other factors also play a role, including education, race, religion, campaign spending, and election laws.

The Facts: Political polarization has been on the rise in the United States since the 1990s (Pew Research Center 2014). Much conventional wisdom suggests that a more polarized American citizenry is due to the rise of partisan media. While this is an attractive idea and is certainly true at some levels, the evidence that exists so far suggests this is an inaccurate or at best an incomplete picture of the way things are. Furthermore, while it's easy to target the "echo chambers" and "filter bubbles" of online and social media, researchers have found that individuals who consume information online (mainly younger people) see a wider array of media content and are less polarized than those who mainly consume cable television news (mainly older people). Much remains to be seen as the media environment continues to evolve, so this is an area ripe for further research, and in the meantime, scholars and other observers should be careful not to overstate the meaning or implications of emerging findings.

While many questions surround the causes of ideological differences, the feeling of growing political polarization that many Americans sense is real. A 2014 Pew Research survey of 10,000 American adults found that Americans are more divided along partisan lines than at any point in the previous two decades. Pew found that those who express "consistently" conservative or liberal opinions grew from 10 percent to 21 percent from 1994 to 2014. The split is strongest among those who are most active and engaged in political life, and the divisions often take on a hue of hostility and animosity toward people on the other side (Pew Research Center 2014). Where ideological overlap used to exist, virtually all Republicans are to the right of the median Democrat, and the same is true of Democrats regarding the median Republican. Partisan individuals now hold highly negative views of the opposing party to the point that 27 percent of Democrats and 36 percent of Republicans see the opposing party's policies as "so misguided that they threaten the nation's well-being" (Pew Research Center 2014, n.p.). Partisans, especially conservatives, also want to have friends and neighbors who share their political views.

This polarization among intense partisans mirrors an "activism gap," where those who hold consistently conservative and liberal positions are most likely to vote, especially conservatives, while those with more mixed positions are least likely. Partisans are also more likely to write letters to officials and give money to political candidates or groups, which means these uncompromising partisan voices are stronger and louder than those in the middle, where opinions are more moderate.

When it comes to news media, these partisans live in different worlds. Another Pew study on political polarization and media habits (Mitchell et al. 2014) found little overlap in the news sources consumed and trusted by liberals and conservatives, and they are most likely to interact with like-minded individuals, whether in person or online. Studies of the 2016 election have shown how divided the media environment is for conservatives and liberals. A Harvard University study concluded: "The structure of the overall media landscape shows media systems on the left and right operate differently. . . . Prominent media on the left are well distributed across the center, center-left, and left. On the right, prominent media are highly partisan" (Faris et al. 2017, 8).

According to the 2014 Pew study, regarding news sources, consistent liberals name a variety of preferred news sources at a rate of 10–15 percent each (Mitchell et al. 2014). These are mainly center or center-left sources, including CNN, MSNBC, NPR, and *The New York Times*. Consistent conservatives are tightly clustered around one source, Fox News, at a rate of 47 percent. When Pew asked about levels of trust regarding 36 widely known media sources, consistent conservatives reported trusting only 8, including *The Wall Street Journal*, The Blaze, Fox News, Breitbart, and Rush Limbaugh. On the other hand, liberals reported trusting 28 of the 36 sources, ranging from *The Economist* and BBC to *The Daily Show* and the Huffington Post. On social media, Facebook dominates among all Internet users as a source for information about politics, at 62 percent. Consistent liberals (49 percent) rely on Facebook slightly more than consistent conservatives (40 percent). Conservatives are more likely to see posts that match their own political views, and liberals are more likely to block or hide someone over a disagreeable political post. Both groups report paying a great deal of attention to news and politics, and they are most likely to talk politics and lead political discussions.

But just because partisans live in different information worlds, does that mean the information sources are making them partisan? Some scholars say yes, that consuming partisan media such as Fox and MSNBC does increase partisanship (Levendusky 2013). Others find that Americans who consume partisan news sources are already polarized and that consuming partisan news doesn't have much effect on their political positions. Rather, it is exposure to information that opposes their views that makes them dig in deeper and become more polarized (Arceneaux and Johnson 2013). Others suggest that increased media choice and polarization go hand in hand but only because a small handful of Americans were already highly polarized even before the digital age; when cable and the Internet gave birth to more partisan media options, it's no surprise that partisan citizens were eager to tune in (Prior 2013). There is a difficult chicken-and-egg question here: Do people watch Fox and become more conservative, or do they tune in to Fox because they are conservative? The best available evidence seems to support the latter idea, if only because scholars have yet to demonstrate a clear causal link between news consumption and polarization. This is partly due to weak measurement tools; relying on individuals to describe their media consumption patterns does not result in entirely reliable data for making causal claims.

While scholars might not agree on the chicken-and-egg question of news use and partisanship, there is one thing virtually all can conclude: the main problem with the modern media environment is not that partisan media increases polarization but rather the proliferation of non-news media options means more Americans than ever are tuning out of news altogether. These Americans make up the nonpartisan middle, and they are the majority. It might seem like a big deal that several million people tune in every night to hear Sean Hannity on Fox or Rachel Maddow on MSNBC, but that's still a small portion of the American electorate. The bulk of Americans are more likely to simply tune out, which leads to increased disengagement from the political process. As scholar Markus Prior has noted, "The main danger of this more partisan media environment is not the polarization of ordinary Americans but a growing disconnect between increasingly partisan activists and largely centrist and modestly involved masses" (Prior 2013, 123).

Partisan voices on the left and right are loud and influential, but they do not represent or speak for average Americans. And as partisan voices grow louder, critics fear that the moderate middle gets drowned out. All of this may contribute to an appearance of increased polarization when the reality is simply a failure to accurately represent the majority of Americans. As Pew (2014) concluded: "Because political participation and activism are so much higher among the more ideologically polarized elements of the population, these voices are over-represented in the political process. Even so, they do not make up the majority of voters, donors or campaign activists." Nonpartisan individuals, or those closer to the middle of the political spectrum, are not nearly as extreme in their uniformity of beliefs, their deep interest in news and politics, or their polarized news consumption. Learning and talking about politics are not nearly as important for nonpartisans, and when they do pay attention to news, their sources are varied or relatively centrist, including a mix of CNN, local TV news, and Fox News, as well as aggregators such as Yahoo! News and Google News, which gather material from a wide range of news outlets. When they use social media to pay attention to news, they see a wider representation of political viewpoints, and they are less likely to know about the political positions of their friends.

Social media and the rest of the Internet often get much of the blame for political partisanship from partisans and moderates alike. Conventional wisdom and lived experience tend to support the idea that through the process of "selective exposure," the web creates ideological bubbles where participants can carefully select what they want to see and can easily weed out anything that does not fit with their preexisting views. One of the first observers to make this point was Nicholas Negroponte (1995), who wrote in his book *Being Digital* about the idea of a "Daily Me," a virtual newspaper that reflected an individual's tastes and interests. This idea of "mass customization" now rules the Internet, where virtually every site and app are uniquely tailored to each individual user. This led scholars and tech experts to grow increasingly concerned about "filter bubbles" (Pariser 2011) and "echo chambers" (Sunstein 2017), where our personalized Internet experiences would drown out any voices unlike our own. This happens because the algorithms that decide what appears in our news feeds are created by for-profit companies such as Facebook, which want to deliver content that will keep users on the site rather than sending them clicking away in anger. In addition to algorithmic filtering, users can create their own bubbles by visiting only the sites they prefer and interacting and creating connections only with like-minded individuals.

While this filtering certainly takes place, research suggests it is not necessarily to blame for increasing polarization. One study found that polarization is increasing fastest among older Americans who don't use social media (Boxell, Gentzkow, and Shapiro 2017). This suggests that cable news and talk radio, which are preferred by older Americans, might be the main driving forces behind polarization, especially among highly partisan individuals. Social media users tend to see a wider array of content, and much of what appears in Americans' news feeds consists of baby photos and cat videos, not partisan polemics.

Finally, many observers have noted that media might not be the driving force behind polarization at all. There are plenty of cultural and demographic changes happening in the United States, such as widening gaps in education and wealth, and shifting views about race, religion, and social issues, such as gay marriage. Other structural factors, such as the gerrymandering of congressional districts and changing election laws, have also been cited as contributors to increased political polarization.

FURTHER READING

Arceneaux, Kevin, and Martin Johnson. 2013. *Changing Minds or Changing Channels? Partisan News in an Age of Choice*. Chicago Studies in American Politics. Chicago, IL; London: The University of Chicago Press.

Boxell, Levi, Matthew Gentzkow, and Jesse M. Shapiro. 2017. "Is the Internet Causing Political Polarization? Evidence from Demographics." Working Paper 23258. National Bureau of Economic Research. https://doi.org/10.3386/w23258.

Faris, Rob, Hal Roberts, Bruce Etling, Nikki Bourassa, Ethan Zuckerman, and Yochai Benkler. 2017. "Partisanship, Propaganda, and Disinformation: Online Media and the 2016 U.S. Presidential Election | Berkman Klein Center." Berkman Klein Center for Internet and Society at Harvard University. https://cyber.harvard.edu/publications/2017/08/mediacloud.

Levendusky, Matthew. 2013. *How Partisan Media Polarize America.* Chicago Studies in American Politics. Chicago, IL; London: The University of Chicago Press.

Levendusky, Matthew, and Neil Malhotra. 2016. "Does Media Coverage of Partisan Polarization Affect Political Attitudes?" *Political Communication* 33 (2): 283–301. https://doi.org/10.1080/10584609.2015.1038455.

Mitchell, Amy, Jeffrey Gottfried, Jocelyn Kiley, and Katerina E. Matsa. 2014. "Political Polarization & Media Habits | Pew Research Center." Pew Research Center. http://www.journalism.org/2014/10/21/political-polarization-media-habits/#.

Negroponte, Nicholas. 1995. *Being Digital.* 1st ed. New York: Knopf.

Pariser, Eli. 2011. *The Filter Bubble: How the New Personalized Web Is Changing What We Read and How We Think.* New York: Penguin Books.

Pew Research Center. 2014. "Political Polarization in the American Public."http://www.people-press.org/2014/06/12/political-polarization-in-the-american-public/.

Prior, Markus. 2013. "Media and Political Polarization." *Annual Review of Political Science* 16: 101–27.

Sunstein, Cass R. 2017. *#Republic: Divided Democracy in the Age of Social Media.* Princeton, NJ; Oxford: Princeton University Press.

5

"Fake News" and Misinformation

Though the phrase "fake news" has been used since at least the 19th century, its widespread use exploded during the 2016 U.S. presidential election season as then candidate and now president Donald Trump used it to refer to news organizations, especially those that published reports about him or his administration that challenged or otherwise cast doubt on their characterizations of various issues and events. In 2017, both the American Dialect Society and the *Collins English Dictionary* designated "fake news" as their "word of the year." But not all fake news is the same. The term has also been employed to describe propaganda, news fabrication, advertising, satire, and parody at different points. Understanding how these meanings differ and what is meant when people, especially public figures, use the term can help citizens avoid being misled and become more informed voters.

Q25. WHAT IS "FAKE NEWS"?

Answer: The term "fake news" is a bit of an oxymoron. News itself is generally defined as a truthful account of recent, interesting, or relevant events. That can seem at odds with the term "fake"—a word that is generally meant to describe something as untruthful or inauthentic. "Fake news" is material presented as real news—using similar design and style elements used in "real news"—but is generally produced for economic or ideological gain. It can include related concepts, such as satire, parody, and propaganda. It is different from journalism in that journalism is a profession and process focused on the production of truthful news, based on facts and a discipline of verification.

The Facts: The term "fake news" is ambiguous. Its meaning is vague and, in some respects, has changed over time—or at least the context in which it is used and its intended purpose has changed over time. Its meaning has included news satire, news parody, news fabrication, photo manipulation, advertising and public relations, and propaganda (Tandoc, Lim, and Ling 2017). In general, it refers to untruthful or inauthentic information presented in ways that resemble or mimic reports from news media. This misappropriation of news is often, though not always, done with the intent to confuse, trick, or persuade the intended audience, and it's often, though not always, done for economic or ideological benefit to those creating it.

Though there was significant use of the term shortly before and since the 2016 U.S. presidential election, the term "fake news" has been used for much longer. In the 19th century, the term usually referred to misinformation generally in contrast to a truthful account, and in the century's latter decades, the term often referred to the "yellow press" and "penny papers" that focused on sensationalism to sell newspapers.

In the early 20th century, the term was used often to refer to the fake stories offered by corporations and their press agents. A 1922 collection of journalistic codes of ethics published by the Ohio State University included a reference to the Kansas State Editorial Association's 1910 ethics code, which, among other things, condemned "fake illustrations," "fake interviews," and "the issuance of fake news dispatches" for the purposes of influencing stock prices, elections, or commercial activity (Myers 1922, 15). The group thought that such "fake news" was a particularly insidious form of advertising: "Some of the greatest advertising in the world has been stolen through the news columns in the form of dispatches from unscrupulous press agents" (Myers 1922, 15). A 1925 piece published in *Harper's Magazine* warned that new technology—the "news wires" that transmitted information over telegraph lines by news agencies like the Associated Press—could be used by "market riggers" to spread misinformation to affect stock prices; by "news fakers" to sell supposedly true, but made-up, localized stories to newspapers about their audience members; and by "professional propagandists" who attempt to influence press coverage for political or person gain" (McKernon 1925).

According to Google Ngram viewer, an online search engine that allows researchers to explore the relative usage of terms in printed books between 1800 and 2008, there was an increase in the use of "fake news" in the mid-1920s to the late 1930s. References in the latter years often made a contrast between war news from professional journalists and the propaganda aimed at pushing particular political causes. News organizations established practices and policies, such as using consistent news announcers on the radio, so that the public could distinguish between real and fake broadcasts. For much of the rest of the 20th century, the term was used relatively infrequently until the 1990s. During that decade, several books and periodicals used the term to discuss "video news releases" or TV packages meant to look like news stories and often played on newscasts but actually produced by public relations practitioners. In fact, the February 22, 1992, issue of *TV Guide* included a cover with "FAKE NEWS" as a banner headline and a special report on how "what we see isn't always news—it's public relations" (Lieberman 1992). Throughout the 1980s, 1990s, and 2000s, the term was also used to refer to work published by respected news organizations that was later found to be fabricated by journalists. *The Washington Post*, for example, won and had to return a Pulitzer Prize in 1982 for a story about a young boy addicted to drugs when it was discovered that the reporter, Janet Cooke, made up the character. In the late 1990s, *The New Republic* magazine fired a reporter, Stephen Glass, for fabricating parts of dozens of articles. The reporter, whose actions were later chronicled in the film *Shattered Glass*, went to great lengths to try to cover his tracks, including making fake websites and voice mail accounts for his sources.

Starting around 2000, the use of the term increased substantially, according to Google Ngram data. While past uses persisted, especially those related to the use of faked video, much of the use of the term was associated with news parody, especially Comedy Central's *The Daily Show*, which started in 1998, and *The Colbert Report*, which started in 2005. These types of shows focus on current events, including recent news, but present it in satirical ways to entertain the audience. The setup of the shows resembles a TV news set, with an anchor/host behind a desk, with short anchor-read segments and more highly produced "packages" that include "correspondents" and interviews. Though the primary purpose of these shows, according to creators and hosts, is entertainment and comedy, many argue that the impact of the shows on public discourse resembles journalism in some ways. Additionally, the work that some of these shows do in comparing current remarks by politicians to past remarks could arguably be similar to the traditional watchdog role of the press. Nonetheless, when pushed on the issue, personalities like Jon Stewart, who hosted *The Daily Show* from 1999 to 2015, said they were comedians first and foremost. He compared himself more to satirist and author Mark Twain than revered journalist Edward R. Murrow. Indeed, news satire has existed for many years, despite the increase in interest and scholarship focused on it in the 2000s. During the late 1990s and since the beginning of the 21st century, the term has also been used to refer to Internet sites offering false or misleading stories, including conspiracy theories.

While the development of fake news is nothing new, certainly in recent years, public awareness of the term has increased. For example, while individuals searched the Internet for the term throughout the 2000s and early 2010s, searches for the term "fake news" exploded in late 2016 and early 2017. According to Google Trends, which tracks the terms people search for on Google, the peak was February 2017. Between 2004, the earliest point at which Google makes trend data available, and September 2016, the search frequency averaged about one-twentieth of the February 2017 peak. In large part, this has to do with the increase of its use by then candidate and now president Donald Trump. During the campaign and since taking office, Trump has used the term to deride, criticize, and delegitimize the press. It's unclear what Trump means when he calls news "fake," though a May 2018 tweet from the president suggests that the way he uses the term is simply to refer to negative coverage: "The Fake News is working overtime. Just reported that, despite the tremendous success we are having with the economy & all things else, 91% of the Network News about me is negative (Fake). Why do we work so hard in working with the media when it is corrupt? Take away credentials?" (@realDonaldTrump, May 9, 2018).

The use of the term "fake news" has ebbed and flowed over the years, and its intended meaning has varied as well. Journalism scholars Edson Tandoc, Zheng Lim, and Richard Ling (2017) suggest that researchers have generally defined "fake news" in the following ways: news satire, news parody, news fabrication, photo manipulation, advertising and public relations, and propaganda. News satire's goal is to use humor and exaggeration to mock news shows. *The Daily Show* is a prime example. News parody is similar, though it doesn't use humor to comment on current events or media's coverage of them; rather, it makes up wildly exaggerated and absurdly fictitious stories that are funny in contrast to real news. An example is The Onion. Parody and satire operate on the assumption that there is an understanding between the writer and the audience that the material is, indeed, untrue or exaggerated.

News fabrication is material that is untrue or exaggerated but meant to trick audiences into believing it is true. It uses the style and form of journalism to misappropriate legitimacy. Though some material in the mainstream press has been fabricated on occasion, such as in the cases of Janet Cooke and Stephen Glass mentioned earlier, news fabrication as a type of fake news is different because the publishers deceive intentionally and take no action to ensure that audiences know the information is untrue. Often published on the Internet, these sites sound legitimate, such as abcnews.com.co (adding .co to the end of the ABC News URL) or the Denver Guardian (which sounds like it could be a legitimate publication and for a time used the tagline "Denver's oldest news source," a distinction belonging to *The Denver Post*). Such fake stories from the 2016 election included "Pope Francis shocks world, endorses Donald Trump for president" and "FBI agent suspected in Hillary email leaks found dead in apartment murder-suicide." Though the operators of these fake news sites sometimes refer to their work as satire and parody, some audience members still believe the information to be true (Allcott and Gentzkow 2017). Many creators are motivated by the economic gains achieved by audiences reading and sharing the stories on social media. The economic success of these sites in recent years has been facilitated by the structure of social media sites, which prioritize popular content and present it to more users.

Photo manipulation has also been identified as a type of "fake news" (Tandoc, Lim, and Ling 2017). This is when images or videos are altered to display a false story or narrative. This is a bit different from other types of "fake news" because this affects photos and videos, which audiences often see as more authentic—almost eyewitness—representations of news compared to text stories. With the advancement of digital editing technologies like Photoshop, these manipulations are more common. Well-known examples have included photos of planes in the Houston airport nearly completely submerged in water during 2017's Hurricane Harvey. Other examples are when authentic photos are shared but out of context or are used to sell false narratives. An example was a photo of Hillary Clinton leaning on aides as she stumbled up a few stairs during the campaign that was later used by partisan sites as evidence of Clinton's failing health. Though digital photo manipulation is more widespread than video manipulation, recent technological advances have made it much easier to fake video and audio.

Another definition for "fake news" is advertising material created to look like genuine news. Some have referred to video news releases as "fake news," as mentioned earlier, especially when used in news programming without the audience knowing. In print and online, so-called native advertising and advertorials (a portmanteau of advertising and editorial) both refer to advertising content presented as news stories, usually with small and sometimes barely noticeable disclaimers. The final type of "fake news" is propaganda (Tandoc, Lim, and Ling 2017). Unlike other kinds of fake news produced for economic gain, propaganda is produced for political purposes, to influence public opinion in support of or against a particular candidate, issue, or ideology. The authors note that much of propaganda is based on facts but presented in a biased way to promote a particular perspective.

Most fake news can be classified based on two factors: the level in which facts are used in its creation and the intent of the author to deceive the audience. For example, native advertising and propaganda are based on facts but intend to deceive the audience into wanting to buy something or adopting a particular viewpoint. News parody, on the other hand, is based in little fact but has little to no intention to deceive. News parody and satire, with their low intention to deceive, pose no threat to journalism. In fact, in some ways, they provide a value to the profession, with satire especially serving as a kind of watchdog of the watchdogs, pointing out when news organizations err, albeit in humorous ways (Tandoc, Lim, and Ling 2017).

The other types of "fake news," however, serve no productive role and only serve to damage the credibility of the institution of journalism and misinform a public with little time and resources available to separate the authentic news from the fake. Indeed, we live in an era of information abundance with increasingly sophisticated examples of "fake news" that challenge the mental shortcuts we've used in the past to assess credibility and truthfulness. Many scholars and educators have worked in recent years to develop news and media literacy programs that aim to stop the spread of fake news by empowering citizens to understand the difference between "fake news" and journalism. While fake news that is intended to deceive is created for political, ideological, or economic gain, journalism is created with the intent to inform the public. While there are sociological and market influences on the creation of news, most journalists abide by "the discipline of verification," whereby they work to verify facts with multiple sources and through multiple tests for accuracy before publishing (Kovach and Rosenstiel 2007).

FURTHER READING

Allcott, Hunt, and Matthew Gentzkow. 2017. "Social Media and Fake News in the 2016 Election." *Journal of Economic Perspectives* 31 (2): 211–236. doi:10.1257/jep.31.2.211.

Google. "Fake News." Google Ngram Viewer. Accessed June 29, 2018. https://books.google.com/ngrams/graph?content=fake+news& year_start=1800&year_end=2010&corpus=15&smoothing= 3&share=&direct_url=t1%3B%2Cfake%20news%3B%2CcO

Kovach, Bill, and Tom Rosenstiel. 2007. *The Elements of Journalism: What Newspeople Should Know and the Public Should Expect.* 1st revised ed. New York: Three Rivers Press.

Lieberman, David. 1992. "Fake News." *TV Guide* 40 (8): 10–11.

McKernon, Edward. 1925. "Fake News and the Public." *Harper's Monthly Magazine*, June 1, 528–536.

Myers, Joseph S. 1922. "The Journalistic Code of Ethics: A Collection of Codes, Creeds and Suggestions for the Guidance of Editors and Publishers." *The Ohio State University Bulletin* 27 (8): 1–85. https://books .google.com/books?hl=en&lr=&id=lucvAQAAMAAJ.

Tandoc, Edson C., Zheng W. Lim, and Richard Ling. 2017. "Defining 'Fake News.'" *Digital Journalism* 6 (2): 137–153. http://www.tandfonline .com/doi/abs/10.1080/21670811.2017.1360143?journalCode=rdij20.

Q26. DOES PRESIDENT TRUMP USE THE TERM "FAKE NEWS" TO TRY TO DISCREDIT ANY REPORTING THAT IS CRITICAL OF HIM OR HIS ADMINISTRATION?

Answer: Generally, President Donald Trump uses the term "fake news" in reference to news organizations that have published reports critical of him or that differ from claims he has made publicly, although in some instances he or his administration has later acknowledged the truth of those reports. He has sometimes used negative descriptions of entire news organizations—as biased, corrupt, dishonest, and bad—in these responses to specific news stories. He has called the press as a whole fake news and "the enemy of the American people," and he has also called specific reports and major news organizations fake news, including CNN, MSNBC, the major broadcast networks, *The New York Times*, and *The Washington Post*. He has never called the Fox News Channel fake news and on one occasion specifically excluded it when describing the other cable networks as fake news. This notable exception to the general hostility he displays for the press is usually attributed to the positive coverage he receives from many of Fox's on-air personalities, including Sean Hannity and the *Fox & Friends* morning show hosts. Trump's use of the phrase "fake news," which has a specific meaning referring to misinformation specifically created to look like credible news, confuses the issue for the public and dilutes the understanding of the term.

The Facts: The term "fake news" has been used for decades, most commonly to refer to satirical news, such as The Onion or *Saturday Night Live's* "Weekend Update" news parody segment. The term became more prominent during the 2016 U.S. presidential campaign and in the months following the election to describe stories that were wholly or mostly invented but made to look like news produced by professional journalists, for the purposes of swaying audiences or generating advertising revenue through clicks. Examples of these stories include the widely circulated fake story that Pope Francis had endorsed Donald Trump for president and the story that Hillary Clinton had an FBI agent killed.

Edson Tandoc, Zheng Lim, and Richard Ling (2017, 2) define fake news as "viral posts based on fictitious accounts made to look like news reports" and identified the two main motivations behind the production of fake news stories: financial and ideological. Fake news stories with an ideological motivation are of the kind created and promoted by social media accounts found to have connections with the Russian government. This strategic use of fake news stories to influence the American election was a concern for congressional investigators, the FBI, and other intelligence agencies, as well as for Facebook and other social media sites that have undertaken efforts to identify and remove fake news content. Other fake news stories are apparently created solely for the purpose of generating page views for boosting advertising revenue, due to the Google AdSense functions that charge advertisers and pay sites based on page views and clicks. These sites were created by users in both the United States and abroad, including a high number of fake news sites originating in Macedonia (Kirby 2016). While this second kind of fake news site does not have ideological goals, it can nonetheless capitalize on partisanship and confirmation bias to maximize its effectiveness.

Trump, however, has used the term differently from how it has been used by U.S. intelligence agencies, journalists, and other media observers. PolitiFact noted that "instead of fabricated content, Trump uses the term to describe news coverage that is unsympathetic to his administration and his performance, even when the news reports are accurate" (Holan 2017). An analysis by PolitiFact found that Trump used the term "fake news" 153 times from January to October 2017 in interviews and speeches and on Twitter (Holan 2017). His most frequent targets were "CNN (23 mentions in 2017) and NBC (19 mentions), followed by the New York Times (12 mentions) and the Washington Post (eight mentions)." One of the most notable tweets by Trump about fake news was on February 17, 2017: "The FAKE NEWS media (failing @nytimes, @NBCNews, @ABC, @CBS, @CNN) is not my enemy, it is the enemy of the American People!" He identified five specific news organizations, which included the three major broadcast networks, cable news network CNN, and *The New York Times*. More important, he called the media "the enemy of the American people," a statement that appears to be at odds with the traditional understanding of the important role a free and independent press plays in a democracy to hold public officials accountable. In a tweet on May 9, 2018, Trump equated "fake news" with any coverage of him of a negative or critical nature: "The Fake News is working overtime. Just reported that, despite the tremendous success we are having with the economy & all things else, 91% of the Network News about me is negative (Fake). Why do we work so hard in working with the media when it is corrupt? Take away credentials?"

Sometimes Trump has used the term to refer to the media generally, as in this tweet on October 1, 2017, about his administration's handling of the disaster relief response after Hurricane Maria: "We have done a great job with the almost impossible situation in Puerto Rico. Outside of the Fake News or politically motivated ingrates." In this case, it appears that Trump meant any news that was reporting his administration had not done a great job handling the disaster in Puerto Rico or perhaps just the news media in general. On December 13, 2017, Trump tweeted, "Wow, more than 90% of Fake News Media coverage of me is negative, with numerous forced retractions of untrue stories. Hence my use of Social Media, the only way to get the truth out. Much of Mainstream Meadia [*sic*] has become a joke! @foxandfriends." Again, the critical quality of the coverage seems to be his primary justification for employing the fake news label.

A January 14, 2018, tweet offers some insight into the basis for Trump's claims of fake news: "The Wall Street Journal stated falsely that I said to them 'I have a good relationship with Kim Jong Un' (of N. Korea). Obviously I didn't say that. I said 'I'd have a good relationship with Kim Jong Un,' a big difference. Fortunately we now record conversations with reporters . . . and they knew exactly what I said and meant. They just wanted a story. FAKE NEWS!" This tweet demonstrates a disagreement with a single word in a quotation from Trump in an interview. The newspaper released the recording, stating, "The Wall Street Journal stands by its transcript and is releasing the audio from this portion of the interview" (*Wall Street Journal* 2018).

Trump has singled out Fox News as an exception to the fake news label he applies to the rest of the media. On December 29, 2017, he tweeted,

"While the Fake News loves to talk about my so-called low approval rating, @foxandfriends just showed that my rating on Dec. 28, 2017, was approximately the same as President Obama on Dec. 28, 2009, which was 47%." He frequently mentions in tweets, with an @foxandfriends tag, the *Fox & Friends* morning program on the Fox News channel. He has also quoted the show's hosts and guests in tweets, indicating some level of endorsement of the views. He has retweeted @FoxNews and @FoxBusiness, the Twitter accounts of two Fox-owned programs. He has thanked Fox News and praised *Fox & Friends*: "Was @foxandfriends just named the most influential show in news? You deserve it—three great people! The many Fake News Hate Shows should study your formula for success!" (December 21, 2017).

In a sort of culminating event to his year of attacking the news media, at the end of his first year in office, Trump tweeted, "We should have a contest as to which of the Networks, plus CNN and not including Fox, is the most dishonest, corrupt and/or distorted in its political coverage of your favorite President (me). They are all bad. Winner to receive the FAKE NEWS TROPHY!" Trump later tweeted that he would announce the awards for "THE MOST DISHONEST & CORRUPT MEDIA AWARDS OF THE YEAR on Monday at 5:00 o'clock. Subjects will cover Dishonesty & Bad Reporting in various categories from the Fake News Media. Stay tuned!" Then, in early 2018, Trump said in a tweet that he would postpone the event: "The Fake News Awards, those going to the most corrupt & biased of the Mainstream Media, will be presented to the losers on Wednesday, January 17th, rather than this coming Monday."

Many scholars believe that this group of tweets offers some insight into what Trump means when he calls the news fake, corrupt, or otherwise untrustworthy. The recipients of the "awards" were CNN, with four mentions; *The New York Times*, with two mentions; and ABC, *The Washington Post*, *Time*, and *Newsweek*, receiving one mention each. The award page on GOP.com, titled "The Highly-Anticipated 2017 Fake News Awards," identified several stories, an op-ed, and a personal tweet that had been later corrected or retracted, and for which, in many cases, news organizations apologized. One organization was marked "fake news" for a photo tweeted by a reporter on his personal account, for which the reporter had apologized (Flegenheimer and Grynbaum 2018). While inaccuracy in news reports is a concern for journalists and may reduce public confidence in the press, the U.S. Supreme Court has held that the press should be allowed a degree of "breathing space" to make unintentional mistakes when reporting on public officials so "that debate on public issues is uninhibited, robust, and wide-open" (*New York Times Co. v. Sullivan* 1964).

Trump has used this criticism of the media to suggest limiting the press or punishing news organizations. For example, on October 11, 2017, he tweeted, "With all of the Fake News coming out of NBC and the Networks, at what point is it appropriate to challenge their License? Bad for country!" Later that same evening, he added, "Network news has become so partisan, distorted and fake that licenses must be challenged and, if appropriate, revoked. Not fair to public!" Perceived political bias, however, has never been sufficient basis for limiting freedom of speech or of the press—both of which are protected by the First Amendment to the U.S. Constitution—through the revocation of broadcast licenses by the Federal Communications Commission or other suppression efforts. The U.S. Supreme Court has been clear in limiting censorship of the press to very rare cases, those in which a clear and present danger to national security is evident. The Supreme Court ruled that the press must enjoy a great deal of freedom to report on public officials, to "avoid chilling the dissemination of truth and opinions." In that case, *New York Times Co. v. Sullivan* (1964), Justice William J. Brennan wrote, "We would, I think, more faithfully interpret the First Amendment by holding that at the very least it leaves the people and the press free to criticize officials and discuss public affairs with impunity," arguing further that "freedom to discuss public affairs and public officials is unquestionably, as the Court today holds, the kind of speech the First Amendment was primarily designed to keep within the area of free discussion." Criticism or negative coverage of a public official is an essential part of the role of journalists in a democracy. Even if Trump were able to provide evidence of political bias or partisanship, any attempt to censor the press or revoke broadcast licenses on that basis would be unconstitutional. Nonetheless, a recent poll shows that Trump's use of the term may be having an effect on Republican voters: "four in 10 Republicans consider accurate news stories that cast a politician or political group in a negative light to always be 'fake news'" (Gallup 2018).

FURTHER READING

Flegenheimer, Matt, and Michael M. Grynbaum. 2018. "Trump Hands Out 'Fake News Awards,' Sans the Red Carpet." *The New York Times*, January 17. https://www.nytimes.com/2018/01/17/business/media/fake-news-awards.html.

Gallup. 2018. "American Views: Trust, Media and Democracy. A Gallup/ Knight Foundation Survey." https://kf-site-production.s3.amazonaws

.com/publications/pdfs/000/000/242/original/KnightFoundation_
AmericansViews_Client_Report_010917_Final_Updated.pdf.

Holan, Angie D. 2017. "The Media's Definition of Fake News vs. Donald Trump's." PolitiFact, October 18. http://www.politifact .com/truth-o-meter/article/2017/oct/18/deciding-whats-fake-medias-definition-fake-news-vs/.

Kirby, Emma J. 2016. "The City Getting Rich from Fake News." *BBC Magazine*, December 5. http://www.bbc.com/news/magazine-38168281.

New York Times Co v. Sullivan. 1964. 376 U.S. 254.

Tandoc, Edson C., Zheng W. Lim, and Richard Ling. 2017. "Defining 'Fake News.'" *Digital Journalism* 6 (2): 137–153. http://www.tandfonline .com/doi/abs/10.1080/21670811.2017.1360143?journalCode=rdij20.

Team GOP. 2018. "The Highly-Anticipated 2017 Fake News Awards." GOP.com., January 17. https://www.gop.com/the-highly-anticipated-2017-fake-news-awards/.

Wall Street Journal. 2018. "Disputed Audio from Donald Trump Interview with WSJ." WSJ.com., January 13. http://www.wsj.com/video/ disputed-audio-from-donald-trump-interview-with-wsj/33003B4D-0DA4-4760-B913-0C2CDC903E74.html.

Q27. DID "FAKE NEWS" INFLUENCE THE OUTCOME OF THE 2016 PRESIDENTIAL ELECTION?

Answer: As of mid-2018 it is still not completely clear how much fake news influenced the 2016 election. News organizations, social media companies, and U.S. government agencies are still trying to determine the extent to which fake news stories reached American audiences in the run-up to the 2016 election and what impact those fake news stories might have had on voters. It is well established that many Americans across the political spectrum were exposed to fake news stories from both domestic and foreign sources and that many Americans may have believed those stories to be true or have been influenced in some way by their emotional impact. It is difficult to determine exactly how many people who saw fake news stories believed them and what influence, if any, those fake news stories had on voting decisions.

The Facts: The fake news stories that are thought to have played a role in influencing voters prior to the 2016 U.S. presidential election are fabricated stories created with no attempt to ascertain the facts but presented online in such a way that a reader might think they are real. The stories are posted at URLs that sound like real news organizations, such as denvernews.com, which is not a real newspaper, and feature headlines that are intended to bait viewers into clicking on the story or sharing it—often by appealing to partisan views or making sensationalistic claims. Edson Tandoc, Zheng Lim, and Richard Ling (2017, 2) defined this kind of fake news as "viral posts based on fictitious accounts made to look like news reports." The two main motivating factors behind the production of this kind of fake news story are financial and ideological. Financially motivated fake news stories were those produced purely to attract clicks and shares to generate advertising revenue through Google AdSense and similar advertisers. While those stories were not intended to promote a particular candidate or political ideology, they may have used divisive partisan issues to increase the virality of the stories. Ideologically motivated fake news stories were intended to appeal to partisan voters and confirm and exacerbate their existing biases, leading them to believe lies about the opposing candidate and/or party.

In order to understand the role fake news played in the 2016 presidential election, it is necessary to determine how many people saw fake news stories, how many people believed them, and what fake news stories said and then consider how fake news stories might have influenced voting decisions. There are two ways in which researchers have tried to measure how many people saw fake news stories prior to the 2016 election: surveys asking respondents which headlines they saw and internal data from social media companies such as Facebook.

Much of fake news spread on social media sites, where 67 percent of U.S. adults said they get news at least occasionally (Shearer and Gottfried 2017). A study by Andrew Guess, Brendan Nyhan, and Jason Reifler (2018) found that one in four Americans saw fake news stories and that Facebook was a "key vector of exposure to fake news," while "fact-checks of fake news almost never reached its consumers." Craig Silverman and Jeremy Singer-Vine (2016) also reported that the most popular fake news stories were more widely shared on Facebook than the most popular mainstream news stories during the 2016 campaign.

Facebook is the most popular social media site overall, and the most popular social media site for getting news, as 45 percent of Americans said the site was a source of news in 2016 (Shearer and Gottfried 2017). Senior executives from Facebook, Google, and Twitter testified in 2017 before the Senate Judiciary Subcommittee on Crime and Terrorism about the spread of information created by Russian-based accounts. Facebook acknowledged at the hearing that about 126 million Americans may have seen content from the Internet Research Agency (IRA), a Russian government–linked troll farm dedicated to creating fake accounts and spreading misinformation and partisan content, between June 2015 and August 2017 (Fiegerman and Byers 2017). Facebook reported that IRA-linked accounts had paid only about $100,000 to promote 3,000 ads or posts. Twitter told the committee that it had identified 2,752 accounts linked to the same agency and a total of 36,746 accounts that appeared to be associated with the Russian government (Fiegerman and Byers 2017). Twitter posted an update in January 2018 that it had identified 677,775 people in the United States who followed one of the IRA accounts, or had retweeted or liked a tweet from those accounts during the campaign, and "50,258 automated accounts that we identified as Russian-linked and Tweeting election-related content during the election period."

It is difficult to determine how many people believed specific fake news stories. Far fewer adults reported believing fake news stories than reported seeing them (Allcott and Gentzkow 2017), but a 2016 survey by BuzzFeed concluded that "fake news headlines fool American adults about 75 percent of the time" (Silverman and Singer-Vine 2016). A study of Stanford University students found that more than half were unable to correctly identify a reputable source of information (McGrew et al. 2017). Another study found that familiarity with a story can increase the perceived accuracy of a fake news headline, concluding that "a single exposure to fake news headlines was sufficient to measurably increase perceptions of their accuracy" (Pennycook, Cannon, and Rand 2017).

The fact that many users share stories online based on only the headline—before they have even read the story themselves—further increases the likelihood that Americans have been unwittingly passing on fake news stories. Fake news stories play into readers' confirmation bias—the tendency to seek out, recall, and give credence to information that confirms one's existing beliefs. Partisan voters were already feeling negative about the other candidate and were therefore more likely to believe stories that fit their existing views. They may have shared the stories without reading them or failed to fact-check them because of this tendency to believe information they agreed with. They wanted the stories to be true and so behaved as if they were.

Most analyses have indicated that "fake news was both widely shared and heavily tilted in favor of Donald Trump" (Allcott and Gentzkow 2017, 212). One study, for example, identified "115 pro-Trump fake stories that were shared on Facebook a total of 30 million times, and 41 pro-Clinton fake stories shared a total of 7.6 million times" (Allcott and Gentzkow 2017, 212). Silverman and Singer-Vine (2016) also found that the most discussed fake news stories favored Trump over Clinton. A 2018 Oxford University study of more than 13,000 politically active Twitter

users in the United States found that 55 percent of all "junk news"—
defined as sites that didn't follow basic journalistic practices and "deliberately publish misleading, deceptive or incorrect information purporting
to be real news"—was shared by those identified as Trump supporters,
while users identified with the Democratic Party and Progressive Movement groups combined to account for 1 percent of junk news traffic on
Twitter (Narayanan et al. 2018). Some of the sites included in this study,
however, would not have been considered fake news sites as many other
studies have defined them but rather something more like propaganda:
misleading information intended to promote a particular political agenda
but not completely fabricated.

Besides favoring Trump and casting Clinton in a negative light, these
IRA-linked accounts also tried to sow discord in the American political
landscape, posting content to inflame both sides of contentious issues.
Many of the fake accounts discovered and revealed by Facebook and Twitter were made to look like accounts supporting nationalist causes, with
names like "Being Patriotic" and "Securing Our Borders." They bought
ads on Facebook that attempted to stoke discord over the most controversial issues: abortion, gun rights, and lesbian, gay, bisexual, transgender,
and queer (LGBTQ) rights. Russian-linked accounts also posted content
in support of and against black activists. For example, "In the racially
charged national debate over mostly black NFL players protesting by
kneeling during the national anthem, Twitter accounts linked to the Russian 2016 influence campaign have tried to turn up the volume both on
pro-player and anti-player accounts" (Ewing 2017). These accounts even
organized rallies, in some cases urging protesters from both sides of a particular issue to attend. These techniques were not invented for the 2016
election but reflect a decades-long strategy by Russians to interfere in
the U.S. election process and the political operations of other countries.
What was new in 2016 is that they were able to gain access so easily to the
media through which many Americans were getting and sharing news.

Fake news was more popular among Trump supporters, either because
most of the stories favored Trump or because they were more likely
to visit fake news sites for another reason. Trump supporters "were
far more likely to visit fake news websites—especially those that are
pro-Trump—than Clinton supporters," reported one study, which found
that while one in four Americans visited a fake news site, fake news
consumption was "heavily concentrated among a small group—almost 6
in 10 visits to fake news websites came from the 10% of people with the
most conservative online information diets" (Guess, Nyhan, and Reifler
2018). Silverman and Singer-Vine (2016) also found that Republicans

were "more likely to view fake election news stories as very or somewhat accurate," about 84 percent of the time, compared to 71 percent of the time for Democrats. They found a similar gap between Trump and Clinton voters.

Following the election, Facebook published a report on "Information Operations," acknowledging the need to address what it called "false news": "We have had to expand our security focus from traditional abusive behavior . . . to include more subtle and insidious forms of misuse, including attempts to manipulate civic discourse and deceive people" (Weedon, Nuland, and Stamos 2017). The social media company identified additional issues such as false amplifiers, which it described as "coordinated activity by inauthentic accounts with the intent of manipulating political discussion (e.g., by discouraging specific parties from participating in discussion, or amplifying sensationalistic voices over others)." While social media companies conduct internal reviews, and congressional committees and U.S. security agencies continue to investigate the attempts of Russians to interfere in the election and identify ways to prevent it in the future, President Donald Trump has ignored or outright denied the existence of any such interference in the election.

FURTHER READING

Allcott, Hunt, and Matthew Gentzkow. 2017. "Social Media and Fake News in the 2016 Election." *Journal of Economic Perspectives* 31 (2): 211–236.

Ewing, Philip. 2017. "As Scrutiny of Social Networks Grows, Influence Attacks Continue in Real Time." NPR, September 28. https://www.npr.org/2017/09/28/554024047/as-scrutiny-of-social-networks-grows-influence-attacks-continue-in-real-time.

Fiegerman, Seth, and Dylan Byers. 2017. "Facebook, Twitter, Google Defend Their Role in Election." CNN Money, November 1. http://money.cnn.com/2017/10/31/media/facebook-twitter-google-congress/index.html.

Guess, Andrew, Brendan Nyhan, and Jason Reifler. 2018. "Selective Exposure to Misinformation: Evidence from the Consumption of Fake News during the 2016 U.S. Presidential Campaign." http://www.dartmouth.edu/~nyhan/fake-news-2016.pdf.

McGrew, Sarah, Teresa Ortega, Joel Breakstone, and Sam Wineburg. 2017. "The Challenge That's Bigger Than Fake News." *American Educator* 41 (3): 4–9.

Narayanan, Vidya, Vlad Barash, John Kelly, Bence Kollanyi, Lisa M. Neudert, and Philip N. Howard. 2018. "Polarization, Partisanship and Junk News Consumption over Social Media in the US." Data Memo. Oxford, UK: Computational Propaganda Research Project.

Pennycook, Gordon, Tyrone D. Cannon, and David G. Rand. 2017. "Implausibility and Illusory Truth: Prior Exposure Increases Perceived Accuracy of Fake News but Has No Effect on Entirely Implausible Statements." SSRN. https://papers.ssrn.com/sol3/papers.cfm?abstract_id=2958246.

Shearer, Elisa, and Jeffrey Gottfried. 2017. "News Use across Social Media Platforms 2017." Pew Research Center. http://www.journalism.org/2017/09/07/news-use-across-social-media-platforms-2017/.

Silverman, Craig. 2015. "Lies, Damn Lies, and Viral Content: How News Websites Spread (and Debunk) Online Rumors, Unverified Claims, and Misinformation." Tow Center for Digital Journalism. http://towcenter.org/wp-content/uploads/2015/02/LiesDamnLies_Silverman_TowCenter.pdf.

Silverman, Craig, and Jeremy Singer-Vine. 2016. "Most Americans Who See Fake News Believe It, New Survey Says." BuzzFeed, December 6. https://www.buzzfeed.com/craigsilverman/fake-news-survey.

Tandoc, Edson C., Zheng W. Lim, and Richard Ling. 2017. "Defining 'Fake News.'" *Digital Journalism* 6 (2): 137–153. http://www.tandfonline.com/doi/abs/10.1080/21670811.2017.1360143?journalCode=rdij20.

Twitter Public Policy. 2018. "Update on Twitter's Review of the 2016 U.S. Election." *Twitter Blog.* https://blog.twitter.com/official/en_us/topics/company/2018/2016-election-update.html.

Weedon, Jen, William Nuland, and Alex Stamos. 2017. "Information Operations and Facebook." Facebook, April 27. https://fbnewsroomus.files.wordpress.com/2017/04/facebook-and-information-operations-v1.pdf.

Q28. ARE "FAKE NEWS" AND OTHER TYPES OF MISINFORMATION MORE EASILY SPREAD BECAUSE OF SOCIAL MEDIA?

Answer: Yes. Social media is built to promote engagement with content through the acts of commenting on, liking, or sharing posts. Social media services then use that engagement data to decide which pieces of content to present to more users. And because fake news is often created to mimic real news—including its appeal to the elements of newsworthiness that real news uses to get attention, such as proximity, timeliness, or conflict—fake news tends to attract attention and engagement. Social media companies operate as both technology and media companies, though, unlike the latter, they generally do not employ human editors to assess the truthfulness of information. This difference—combined with the lightning speed with which information can be sent across the world via social media—"fake news" can spread more easily on a social platform than it would via traditional media.

The Facts: There is a famous saying that "a lie can travel halfway around the world before the truth has a chance to get its pants on." Misinformation has always been assumed to travel faster than truth, as that often-misattributed saying indicates, but in the age of social media, the pace can seem like superspeed. In one of the largest studies of its kind, researchers at the Massachusetts Institute of Technology (MIT) analyzed all Twitter data from 2006 to 2017, looking for stories that were verified true or false by six independent fact-checking organizations. The researchers looked for independent original tweets of these stories and then counted the number of times those stories were tweeted and retweeted. They found that false stories were spread more deeply (i.e., more retweets away from the original posting) and widely than the truthful ones (Vosoughi, Roy, and Aral 2018, 1148): "Whereas the truth rarely diffused to more than 1,000 people, the top 1 percent of false-news cascades routinely diffused to between 1,000 and 100,000 people." They found that falsehoods were 70 percent more likely to be retweeted than the truth. Truth took about six times as long to reach 1,500 people as falsehoods did. In particular, the researchers found that false political news traveled deeper and reached more people than other kinds of false information. Finally, though popular belief is that the spread of fake news is exacerbated by "bots" and other nonhuman actors, the MIT researchers found that such bots accelerated both fake and true news at the same rate. They suggested that such findings indicate that the greater spread of fake news is due to humans spreading it more than the truth.

Why might this be the case? Often falsehoods are intriguing, appealing to a human desire for novel information. Though the authors did not claim that falsehoods were more likely shared because of their novelty, they found that false news tended to have more novel information than the truth. They also found that individuals reacted to false news with words representing emotions like surprise and disgust compared to emotions of sadness, anticipation, and trust from factually accurate news. Indeed, the novel and strongly emotional topics of fake news in some ways tap into some of the same values of newsworthiness that genuine reporters use to guide their selection of stories.

Additionally, conflict or drama is often thought of as an element of newsworthiness. Audiences are used to seeing these values emphasized in legitimate reporting, so producers of false news are able to use the same values to entice audiences to consume, share, and react to the false narratives. Some scholars suggest that humans are "hardwired" for news—that we seek to monitor the world around us. Some suggest that instinct is biological, but others say the focus on bad and sensationalistic news, for example, is a product of cultural standards for newsworthiness that may go back as far as the yellow journalism days of the late 1800s. During that era, in an attempt to attract more readers, some newspapers started focusing on sensational stories and those involving prominent people. Researchers also suggest that vivid information—compelling stories about individuals—is more likely to be remembered. Finally, we tend to be biased news consumers, seeking out and being more accepting of information that aligns with our existing worldviews. However, these are factors that contribute to acceptance of fake news no matter the medium. What makes fake news particularly easy to spread on social media?

In an era of information abundance, people rely on others to determine which information to trust. A classic mass communication theory has tried to explain this; a two-step flow has posited that information, especially political ideas, tends to move from mass media outlets to opinion leaders in a community and then from those opinion leaders to less attentive members of the public. For much of the era of mass media in the latter half of the 20th century and early 21st century, this theory didn't quite work because many studies found that the public received much of its political information directly from mass media. However, in the era of social media, the theory may be more valid or at least may aid in audiences determining which mass media news sources to trust and consume. For example, research has shown that when political news is shared by Facebook friends, people tend to perceive the mass media news source as more trustworthy and are more likely to continue to follow news from that source (Turcotte et al. 2015). Moreover, the structure of news sites—both real and fake—is such that people are encouraged to share via social media, with buttons displayed prominently that allow sharing via various platforms with just a couple of clicks. The social media sites also make it easy to reshare or retweet material from friends and sources people follow. Though these features—and this psychology of believing information shared through interpersonal relationships—can be used for the spread of truthful news, they have the effect of allowing falsehoods to travel fast as well. More important, those features that allow engagement with others to be so easy are also the features that are easily manipulated by actors who wish to spread misinformation and false news.

The way in which social media sites present information to users serves primarily to elicit engagement, not filter truth from falsehoods. Data on what content is most engaging to users—in the form of reactions to the posts, behaviors such as likes, upvotes, comments, or shares—are fed into algorithms that determine which content to present to users. These algorithms are complex mathematical formulas that take into account many pieces of data to predict certain intended goals. For example, shopping sites like Amazon look at products we've purchased before, our search history, demographic information, the popularity of a product, and other data to make recommendations on products we would like. Social media sites use similar processes to determine what content we will be served. In an era when the Internet provides access to more information or products than we could consume, much less evaluate, these algorithms perform a vital role. However, when there is lack of an objective or easy measurement of quality, perhaps less important but more easily accessible measures are used.

With news, people want to have the most truthful information, but truth is a difficult construct to objectively measure by humans, let alone computers. So, more accessible measures like page views, likes, comments, and shares are used to approximate quality, on the assumption that individuals will choose the highest-quality information. High-quality information, therefore, rises to the top, and low-quality information sinks to the bottom. This is the basic theory of the marketplace of ideas. However, the marketplace assumes a market open to all potential information and free from nefarious influencers. What we're served on social media does not include all information. Through our own actions of filtering our friend and follower lists to include mostly those with whom we share interests and through our stronger engagement with those individuals, we are served more posts that align with our views and fewer that conflict with them. This creates an echo chamber where we're exposed more to ideologically friendly material (Bakshy, Messing, and Adamic 2015).

Additionally, social media popularity can be manipulated by bad actors who create and manage multiple fake accounts and use robots to artificially inflate the perceived quality of the content. As many as 15 percent of active Twitter accounts and as many of 60 million Facebook accounts may be robots, though pinpointing the exact prevalence is difficult (Lazer et al. 2018). Nonetheless, they are present, and those who employ them have aimed at spreading misinformation, including during election campaigns.

Some researchers have suggested the problem with social media sites is not only the spread of fake news but also the way the platforms have influenced institutional journalism (Bell and Owen 2017). For example, platforms like Facebook and Snapchat have partnered with news organizations to incentivize stories told on platform features like live video, which indirectly influence content. Also, the fact that social media systems use popularity and engagement as primary metrics means that journalism organizations are incentivized to create content that is scalable and shareable rather than seeking to report stories with high civic value. Finally, the lack of human editors—which is cost prohibitive and includes perceptions of introducing human bias in the filtering of content—inhibits platforms acting as de facto publishers from adhering to journalistic editorial standards. It should be noted, however, that given the overwhelming breadth of information, using some sort of algorithmic filtering might be required. Some researchers believe that refined measures might allow algorithmic filtering to truly assess quality of information and remove bias. For example, platforms could adjust their formulas to incorporate evaluations of source quality, and they could lessen the attempt to personalize the feeds to information from only like-minded friends (Lazer et al. 2018).

Social media has indeed changed news, and it has contributed to the widespread and easy dissemination of fake news. The platforms were built by technology companies to enable sharing of content, not media companies that produce and edit content. Though some say these social media platforms must act more like media companies now, most scholars and journalists agree that platforms like Facebook and Twitter must be more open and transparent about how their systems work to filter content and that they should partner with journalism and civic groups to ensure that their platforms are helping and not hindering the spread of high-quality, truthful information.

FURTHER READING

Bakshy, Eytan, Solomon Messing, and Lada A. Adamic. 2015. "Exposure to Ideologically Diverse News and Opinion on Facebook." *Science* 348 (6239): 1130–1132. doi:10.1126/science.aaa1160.

Bell, Emily J., and Taylor Owen. 2017. *The Platform Press: How Silicon Valley Reengineered Journalism.* New York: Tow Center for Digital Journalism. doi:10.7916/D8R216ZZ.

Lazer, David M. J., Matthew A. Baum, Yochai Benkler, Adam J. Berinsky, Kelly M. Greenhill, Filippo Menczer, Miriam J. Metzger, Brendan

Nyhan, Gordon Pennycook, David Rothschild, Michael Schudson, Steven A. Sloman, Cass R. Sunstein, Emily A. Thorson, Duncan J. Watts, and Jonathan L. Zittrain. 2018. "The Science of Fake News." *Science* 359 (6380): 1094–1096. doi:10.1126/science.aao2998.

Turcotte, Jason, Chance York, Jacob Irving, Rosanne M. Scholl, and Raymond J. Pingree. 2015. "News Recommendations from Social Media Opinion Leaders: Effects on Media Trust and Information Seeking." *Journal of Computer-Mediated Communication* 20 (5): 520–535. doi:10.1111/jcc4.12127.

Vosoughi, Soroush, Deb Roy, and Sinan Aral. 2018. "The Spread of True and False News Online." *Science* 359 (6380): 1146–1151. doi:10.1126/science.aap9559.

Q29. CAN ANYTHING BE DONE TO STOP THE SPREAD OF "FAKE NEWS"?

Answer: Yes. Social media users are the primary way fake news is spread and therefore hold the key to spotting it. Fact-checking by journalists or fact-checking sites can be useful in correcting misinformation but often do not have as great a reach as the fake news content they attempt to correct and in some cases may further contribute to the belief in misinformation. Social media sites, such as Facebook, can play a role in reducing the spread and visibility of fake news and reducing the mechanisms that reward sites for attracting attention. Advertising services such as Google AdSense that compensate sites when an ad posted on their page gets a view or click can create mechanisms to prevent fake news sites from profiting from the spread of false information, conspiracy theories, and other lies. Finally, American consumers of news can become more media literate and skilled at identifying and quashing fake news stories and identifying brazen lies and distortions from public figures that are passed along uncritically by mainstream news outlets.

The Facts: Misinformation in the form of conspiracy theories, hoaxes, rumors, and propaganda existed long before the creation of the Internet. However, the Internet, and social media sites in particular, created the conditions in which a particular kind of misinformation could quickly and easily spread to a large number of people. The term "fake news" is used by scholars to describe wholly or partly false content created to gain viral popularity for the purpose of ideological persuasion or financial gain (Tandoc, Lim, and Ling 2017). Creators of fake news do not seek truth but rather invent stories that appeal to the confirmation bias of partisans and post the stories in such a way that they resemble real news content in terms of format, URL, and other factors. Fake news stories can also be amplified by "bots." These are accounts that do not belong to or represent real people but rather are automated accounts created simply to share stories or respond to posts according to their scripts. The spread of fake news can lead to a misinformed public and even have real-world consequences when people take false information seriously. There are three factors contributing to the spread of fake news and therefore the prevention of fake news: social media users, online advertising services, and social media sites.

Often the impact of fake news stories is amplified through social media, where users may share or like content based only on the headline and excerpt, never visiting the original site where the story was posted. Since so much fake news spreads through social media sites, the individual users of these sites are instrumental to stopping fake news. Social media users need to be sufficiently news literate to identify fake news and fake accounts and respond appropriately. The most effective action is likely to simply ignore fake news stories, thus limiting their reach and starving them of any potential economic reward. Users can also counter fake news stories posted by social media connections or notify social media sites when they identify a fake news story or fake account, such as a bot. There is some evidence that this approach can be successful, such as the hashtag #yourslipisshowing used by feminist Twitter users to indicate accounts they suspected were bots or fake Russian accounts (Ganzer 2014). However, many social media users share stories without clicking on the links to the story; one study showed that nearly 60 percent of stories shared on Twitter were retweeted when the user had not clicked on the link (Gabielkov et al. 2016).

Media literacy is key to social media users recognizing possible fake news. Users must first be aware of confirmation bias and therefore be more suspicious of information that seems to confirm their existing views. Users also need to learn good strategies for checking information when they encounter it. A Stanford University study found many students were not capable of distinguishing between legitimate and dubious sources of information and struggled to evaluate tweets (Wineburg et al. 2016). This and other studies have observed that effective fact-checkers are more likely to move laterally—immediately clicking away to check other pages to research the site and its claims—rather than moving vertically—digging deeper into the site they're already on or clicking on links in social media posts to gauge the veracity of the claims being made and the trustworthiness of the source in general.

Dedicated fact-checking sites such as PolitiFact, FactCheck.org, and Snopes can play some role in countering misinformation by checking claims made in fake news stories. Fact-checking sites exist specifically to discover the truth of a claim that has been made in a story, verifying it through various means, including seeking multiple sources to respond to the claim, finding documents or reports that confirm or disconfirm the facts, and using other methods to determine the veracity of a claim. Journalists, meanwhile, do not have the resources to investigate every false news story that appears online. However, they might be well served to do a better job of communicating to the public the strategies they use in reporting and verifying stories and the requirements they have regarding verification prior to publication.

The Poynter Institute for Media Studies, a nonprofit school for journalism, created the International Fact-Checking Network in 2015 to monitor trends, surface common positions, promote standards, provide training, and advocate for fact-checking. The problem with relying on this method for correcting misinformation is that corrections or explainer stories often fail to keep up with the false information. Researchers report that "fact-checks of fake news almost never reached its consumers" (Guess, Nyhan, and Reifler 2018), and studies of corrections spread on Twitter found that the misinformation spread three times as widely as the follow-up corrective information. Fact-checking sites themselves can also come under attack for claims of bias by partisans who remain convinced of the truth of a story despite evidence to the contrary. Nonetheless, journalists and fact-checking sites can provide citizens with resources to combat misinformation, enabling individuals to inform themselves and others with accurate information to check the false stories they encounter online.

There is also some suggestion that correcting misinformation can have what researchers call a "backfire effect," causing people who believed the story in the first place to become further convinced of its veracity rather than accepting the correct information. A team of psychologists conducted a meta-analysis of corrective information and offered the following suggestions for correcting misinformation: avoid repeating the lie or rehashing its claims in detail, which can serve to reinforce it; encourage the audience to have a skeptical mind-set; and present new and credible information but keep expectations low (Chan et al. 2017). If users are provided with tools and strategies to do their own fact-checking, either through education in schools or libraries, or information provided by social media sites or other online sources, they may be more empowered to identify and counter fake news.

Finally, observers suggest that social media sites and advertising sites may have a role to play in stopping fake news from spreading online. The attention economy rewards sites for garnering more page views, incentivizing getting people's attention over providing high-quality, accurate, or verified information. The balance that news organizations have often sought to achieve between giving people information that they want and giving them information that they need has been somewhat upended in the social media landscape and by the advertising models that pay per page view. The algorithms of social media sites, which reward stories and promote them for gaining popularity in the form of "likes," comments, or shares, created the conditions that allowed fake news to spread so widely. Websites that promote news-like content to generate clicks, using "click-bait" headlines, were utilizing this same economic model before fake news sites came along. News organizations have been susceptible to similar urges, pursuing search-engine optimization strategies that sometimes focus on getting users to click on a story. A fundamental change in the way content competes for attention or is rewarded for getting attention could remove at least some of the motivation for fake news sites, especially those that are created solely for the purpose of generating revenue.

Meanwhile, social media sites, search engines, and advertising servers can also limit the spread of fake news by empowering users to identify fake accounts or pages and to take more robust monitoring measures themselves. Some sites have experimented with allowing users to mark, flag, or rate stories as a way to stem the spread of fake news. Google launched a "knowledge panel" in November 2017, a feature that displayed information about publishers in its search results. The feature included a "Reviewed Claims column that matched outlets' disputed claims with fact checks contributed by independent fact-checking organizations to the Schema.org ClaimReview markup" (Funke 2018), but that element was suspended after criticism from conservative news outlets caused Google to announce that the feature was not working as intended and they would continue to experiment. Facebook introduced a new strategy in 2018 to combat fake news, by reducing the amount of news that shows up in user feeds, showing more posts from family and friends and "local news sources," and surveying users about which news sources they trust to create a ranking of trustworthiness. There are clear issues with this system given that audiences are so strongly divided along partisan lines in terms of which news sources they trust. While Facebook CEO Mark Zuckerberg said that he hoped that these changes would provide users with more "trusted" sources of information, family and friends may be the source of partisan and misguided information, and may further contribute to the creation of filter bubbles. Facebook was also experimenting with transparency in ad services, requiring advertisers to have Facebook pages, and placing all ads in a section that can be viewed, even if they aren't part of the intended audience. Meanwhile, private, closed messaging services such as WhatsApp may create conditions for the spread of fake news that cannot be prevented by crowdsourcing efforts or features and will leave most of the responsibility on individual users. This has already become an issue in Brazil, where WhatsApp is more popular than Facebook (Kulwin 2018).

FURTHER READING

Chan, Man-pui S., Christopher R. Jones, Kathleen H. Jamieson, and Dolores Albarracín. 2017. "Debunking: A Meta-Analysis of the Psychological Efficacy of Messages Countering Misinformation." *Psychological Science* 28 (11): 1531–1546. http://journals.sagepub.com/doi/full/10.1177/0956797617714579.

Funke, Daniel. 2018. "Google Suspends Fact-Checking Feature over Quality Concerns." Poynter, January 19. https://www.poynter.org/news/google-suspends-fact-checking-feature-over-quality-concerns.

Gabielkov, Maksym, Arthi Ramachandran, Augustin Chaintreau, and Arnaud Legout. 2016. "Social Clicks: What and Who Gets Read on Twitter?" ACM SIGMETRICS/IFIP Performance, Antibes, Juan-les-Pins, France.

Ganzer, Miranda. 2014. "In Bed with the Trolls." *Feminist Media Studies* 14 (6): 1098–1100.

Guess, Andrew, Brendan Nyhan, and Jason Reifler. 2018. "Selective Exposure to Misinformation: Evidence from the Consumption of Fake News during the 2016 U.S. Presidential Campaign." http://www.dartmouth.edu/~nyhan/fake-news-2016.pdf.

Kulwin, Noah. 2018. "WhatsApp Is Causing a Serious Fake News Problem in Brazil." VICE News, January 17. https://news.vice.com/en_us/article/mbpkyv/whatsapp-is-causing-a-serious-fake-news-problem-in-brazil.

Lee, Michelle. 2017. "Fighting Falsehoods around the World: A Dispatch on the Growing Global Fact-Checking Movement." *The Washington Post*, July 14. https://www.washingtonpost.com/news/fact-checker/wp/2017/07/14/fighting-falsehoods-around-the-world-a-dispatch-on-the-global-fact-checking-movement/.

Madrigal, Alexis. 2018. "5 Questions about Facebook's Plan to Rate Media by 'Trustworthiness': What Could Go Wrong?" *The Atlantic*, January 19. https://www.theatlantic.com/technology/archive/2018/01/facebook-media-trustworthiness/551045/.

Poynter. (n.d.). "Fact-Checking." https://www.poynter.org/channels/ fact-checking.

Tandoc, Edson C., Zheng W. Lim, and Richard Ling. 2017. "Defining 'Fake News.'" *Digital Journalism* 6 (2): 137–153. http://www.tandfonline .com/doi/abs/10.1080/21670811.2017.1360143?journalCode=rdij20.

Wineburg, Sam, Sarah McGrew, Joel Breakstone, and Teresa Ortega. 2016. "Evaluating Information: The Cornerstone of Civic Online Reasoning." Stanford Digital Repository. http://purl.stanford.edu/fv 751yt5934.

Zuckerberg, Mark. 2018. "Facebook Post." Facebook, January 19. https:// www.facebook.com/zuck/posts/10104445245963251.

6

❖❖❖

Representation and Reality in News Coverage

Philosophers and scholars have long grappled with questions of epistemology—how humans come to know the world around them. We learn a great deal of what we know from the signs and symbols in our environments, and this includes the news media. But how accurate are those signs and symbols? What gaps exist between reality and the representations that are conveyed by news media? This chapter examines news coverage of five different content areas in order to compare news representations with actual empirical reality. Generally, gaps exist between representations and reality, and news consumers should know where these exist and how to adjust their own perceptions accordingly. Good journalists work to narrow these gaps and make their news coverage as accurate as possible.

Q30. IS THE WORLD REALLY AS DANGEROUS AS NEWS MEDIA SEEM TO SUGGEST?

Answer: No, the world is not as dangerous as it appears to be in news media. Dramatic, negative events are reported more frequently in the news than they occur in the world. The media's tendency to cover bad news has been tied to audience preferences for disaster, scandal, and conflict, which, some have suggested, is related to a basic human evolutionary need to identify danger in the world. Other explanations include the media's structural biases that lead journalists to cover bad news more than positive news.

The Facts: Media scholars have long focused on the disconnect between reality and representations of reality in news media. Negative and scary news is one area where the distortion of reality is particularly concerning. While all news media have a tendency to cover negative news, television news may be the worst. Cultivation theory studies dating back to the 1970s have demonstrated that there is a large disparity between the reality of the world and the way it is portrayed on television drama and in TV news (Gerbner and Gross 1976). These studies not only found a significant disparity between reality and the world portrayed on television, but they also concluded that the more television people watched, the more they believed that social reality aligned with the television reality. The high incidence of violence on television led researchers to identify the "mean world index" and the "mean world syndrome"—the idea that consuming violent content led viewers to believe the world was more dangerous than it was. Studies found a relationship between heavy television viewing and fears of becoming a victim of a crime; light viewers predicted their weekly odds of being a victim of crime to be 1 out of 100, while heavy viewers estimated the risk to be 1 out of 10. Crime statistics from that era indicated that the weekly odds of being a victim of crime were actually closer to 1 out of 10,000 (Gerbner and Gross 1976). Heavier viewers also overestimate how many people are involved in law enforcement and are more suspicious of others' motives. Cultivation theory studies have pointed to a special role for local television news in influencing viewers' perceptions of criminal activity, which causes heavy viewers to develop a heightened fear of crime due to the frequency of reporting and sensationalized reporting about violence and crime. A large volume of research since the 1970s has measured cultivation effects on various issues, and a 1999 meta-analysis reviewed these studies, confirming a significant relationship (Shanahan and Morgan 1999).

There are several possible reasons for this disparity in coverage, but structural biases are one likely explanation (Shoemaker and Reese 2014). Structural biases are the ways of seeing, gathering, and presenting information that are embedded in journalists' practices and skew coverage. These include a so-called bad news bias as well as temporal and visual biases that privilege recent information and stories with visual elements.

Bad news bias is the tendency to report on scandals, disasters, crime, and other negative events. This predilection dates back to the days of so-called yellow journalism, which emphasized scandal and salacious news as a way to draw in readers of the late 19th century. To some extent, covering negative news is an almost inevitable result of seeking new and interesting information. Reporting that most everything is fine and most people are having relatively successful lives, following laws, and avoiding disaster and scandal would not make for a very interesting news day. News values emphasize coverage of exceptions to the normal state of affairs, creating the circumstances for surprising events to take over the news cycle. Surprising events are generally things that have gone wrong, such as natural disasters or accidents and crime or violence. Adding to this is the fact that traditional journalistic ethics includes a commitment to hold elected officials and other powerful institutions accountable, and sometimes the simplest way to appear to hold power accountable is to report on wrongdoing or violations of norms or laws.

Temporal bias is the bias in favor of recent and new information. Journalists have a tendency to cover the most recent news, often a single random event that draws attention, rather than to cover trends and pervasive issues. Scholar Shanto Iyengar (1996) describes this as episodic versus thematic framing. Episodic frames focus on specific individuals and events, and this can cause audiences to perceive social issues as the result of individual failings instead of seeing the larger social, political, or economic contexts in which they take place. Thematic frames focus on those larger contexts and can lead audiences to see issues as the result of social, political, or economic factors beyond the control of individuals.

The overemphasis of episodic framing may make it more difficult for audiences to understand the broader contexts and larger forces that influence their daily lives. The timeliness of a news story will often earn it coverage, both because it attracts attention from viewers and because of pressures on journalists. A recent event provides easy content that may require less time to report than a longer trend story, and it may have what journalists call a "news peg"—something that makes it a timely story on a particular day—which may not be as easy to identify in stories about broader issues. This tendency may be exacerbated by cuts to newsrooms and investigative teams, which leaves fewer journalists with less time to produce content.

Journalists tend to use episodic framing, in part because pressures to publish or air new content constantly allow coverage to be driven by single events, rather than broader perspectives of ongoing issues. Jenny Kitzinger (2009, 4) has suggested that "the news media will tend to focus on risks which kill, injure, or threaten many people at one time, rather than have a cumulative effect over the years. Threats to 'people like us' gain more attention, as will attractive or famous victims or unattractive sources of threat."

For example, child abductions, while terrible and traumatic, are relatively uncommon—about 250,000 children in the United States are abducted each year, the vast majority by family members (Sedlak et al. 2002). However, child abductions receive a great deal of media coverage. Moreover, "the media was more likely to report on incidents in which children were abducted by nonfamily members (nonfamily abductions) and strangers (stereotypical kidnappings) than would be expected given their actual frequency of occurrence" (Taylor et al. 2011, 26). Meanwhile, childhood obesity is a far more common problem, affecting 12.7 million young Americans (Ogden et al. 2015)—50 times as many children as are abducted. But the issue of childhood obesity receives far fewer headlines. Childhood obesity lacks an obvious news peg without a precipitating event that would draw national attention to the issue.

Meanwhile, a 2004 Kaiser Family Foundation report has pointed out that media may in fact be part of the problem, as time children spend consuming media may displace time spent on physical activities, and media are full of ads promoting unhealthy foods. Similarly, school shootings and mass shootings receive a great deal of news coverage, but far more people are killed by self-inflicted gun wounds each year, and overall violent crime has been declining for the past three decades. Studies have demonstrated that while violent crime has been declining and represents an extremely small percent of crimes, coverage of violent crime is disproportionately high (see, e.g., Tiegreen and Newman 2009). For example, in 1981, half of crime news in New Orleans was about homicides, which represented only 0.4 percent of the crimes committed (Sheley and Ashkins 1981). In *The Chicago Tribune* in the 1980s, 26 percent of crime stories were about murder, while only 0.2 percent of crimes committed were murder (Howitt 1998). *The Los Angeles Times* reported 80 percent of local murders but only 2 percent of local physical and sexual assaults, misrepresenting the relative frequency with which these crimes occur (Dorfman, Thorson, and Stevens 2001). This reporting has a clear impact on public perceptions. One 2001 study, for example, noted that 68 percent of Americans in 1998 said violent crime in the United States was on the increase, despite the fact that violent crime had been decreasing steadily since 1993 (Dorfman, Thorson, and Stevens 2001). In 2016, a majority of voters said crime had gotten worse in the United States since 2008, even though violent crime and property crime rates had fallen by 19 and 23 percent, respectively (Gramlich 2016).

Critics have also argued that television news especially tends to frame events episodically and contributes to an understanding of events as unrelated and random rather than part of a larger context (Iyengar 2015). This may be attributed to the fact that television is such a visual medium, and television journalists are drawn to cover stories with strong visual elements. Natural disasters, violent attacks, protests, and the like provide more visual materials for television coverage.

Some research suggests that the responsibility for bad news lies with the consumers, who respond more strongly to negative information. Jill McCluskey, Johan Swinnen, and Thijs Vandemoortele (2015) created a model that found news consumers showed a preference for bad news, perceiving it to have more value and provide a greater advantage for them, even if it also made them more depressed. The authors concluded that their model demonstrated a societal preference for bad news, one which caused newspapers to report more negative news to attract more readers and thus more advertisers. One reason for the preference news audiences show for negative information is the human tendency to search for and remember negative news, which psychologists call negativity bias. Studies have found evidence of negativity bias in measuring the influence of comparable positive and negative information on evaluations (Ito et al. 1998).

The interaction of the structural biases of journalists and the negativity bias of news audiences may create a kind of negativity feedback loop that encourages negative coverage because it is rewarded by the audience. The economic model of most news organizations is reliant on advertisers, to whom news organizations sell their audience—this is known as the "audience as product"—thereby creating the demand for news organizations to grow their audience as much as possible in order to attract more advertisers and increase their profit margins. Since journalists now have constant and immediate detailed information about users' interactions with news content online, they may be even more responsive to the behaviors of users. Folker Hanusch and Edson Tandoc (2017) have suggested that the availability of information about how readers respond to content is increasingly shaping the work of the journalists who have access to that information and that journalists are becoming more open to taking into account audience feedback.

In the face of the persistent negativity of the news, some scholars point to the generally positive direction of world events and history. Cognitive psychologist and popular science writer Steven Pinker (2018b) is well known for his insistence on focusing on the positive view of our present day. He has emphasized such things as the worldwide increase in life expectancy, ongoing improvements to education and access to information, and increasing expansion of civil rights and equality to women and sexual minorities. Perhaps more important than noting these general trends of improving quality of life around the world is Pinker's argument that apocalyptic thinking is dangerous. Pinker has warned that an overly negative perspective can lead to consequential reactions to false alarms, uses mental energy that should better be spent dealing with real issues, and can lead to a defeatist attitude: "Sowing fear about hypothetical disasters, far from safeguarding the future of humanity, can endanger it" (Pinker 2018a).

FURTHER READING

Dorfman, Lori, Esther Thorson, and Jane E. Stevens. 2001. "Reporting on Violence: Bringing a Public Health Perspective into the Newsroom." *Health Education and Behavior* 28 (4): 402–419.

Gerbner, George, and Larry Gross. 1976. "Living with Television: The Violence Profile." *Journal of Communication* 26 (2): 172–199.

Gramlich, John. 2016. "Voters' Perceptions of Crime Continue to Conflict with Reality." Pew Research Center. http://www.pewresearch .org/fact-tank/2016/11/16/voters-perceptions-of-crime-continue-to-conflict-with-reality/.

Hanusch, Folker, and Edson C. Tandoc. 2017. "Comments, Analytics, and Social Media: The Impact of Audience Feedback on Journalists' Market Orientation." *Journalism*: 1–19.

Howitt, Dennis. 1998. *Crime, the Media and the Law.* West Sussex, England: John Wiley and Sons Ltd.

Ito, Tiffany A., Jeff T. Larsen, N. Kyle Smith, and John T. Cacioppo. 1998. "Negative Information Weighs More Heavily on the Brain: The Negativity Bias in Evaluative Categorizations." *Journal of Personal Social Psychology* 75 (4): 887–900.

Iyengar, Shanto. 1996. "Framing Responsibility for Political Issues." *Annals of the American Academy* 546 (July): 59–70, 62.

Iyengar, Shanto. 2015. *Media Politics: A Citizen's Guide.* 3rd ed. New York: W. W. Norton & Company.

Kaiser Family Foundation. 2004. "The Role of Media in Childhood Obesity." Washington, DC: Henry J. Kaiser Family Foundation. https://kaiserfamilyfoundation.files.wordpress.com/2013/01/the-role-of-media-in-childhood-obesity.pdf.

Kitzinger, Jenny. 2009. "The Media and Public Risk." [Project Report]. URN 09/14, Cardiff University.

McCluskey, Jill J., Johan Swinnen, and Thijs Vandemoortele. 2015. "You Get What You Want: A Note on the Economics of Bad News." *Information Economics and Policy* 30 (1): 1–5.

Ogden, Cynthia L., Margaret D. Carroll, Cheryl D. Fryar, and Katherine M. Flegal. 2015. "Prevalence of Obesity among Adults and Youth: United States, 2011–2014." CDC. https://www.cdc.gov/nchs/data/databriefs/db219.pdf.

Pinker, Steven. 2018a. "The Dangers of Worrying about Doomsday." *The Globe and Mail*, February 24. https://www.theglobeandmail.com/opinion/the-dangers-of-worrying-about-doomsday/article38062215/.

Pinker, Steven. 2018b. *Enlightenment Now: The Case for Reason, Science, Humanism, and Progress.* New York: Penguin.

Sedlak, Andrea J., David Finkelhor, Heather Hammer, and Dana J. Schultz. 2002. "National Estimates of Missing Children: An Overview." NISMART. https://www.ncjrs.gov/pdffiles1/ojjdp/196465.pdf.

Shanahan, James, and Michael Morgan. 1999. *Television and Its Viewers: Cultivation Theory and Research.* Cambridge: Cambridge University Press.

Sheley, Joseph F., and Cindy D. Ashkins. 1981. "Crime, Crime News, and Crime Views." *Public Opinion Quarterly* 45 (4): 492–506.

Shoemaker, Pamela J., and Stephen D. Reese. 2014. *Mediating the Message in the 21st Century: A Media Sociology Perspective.* 3rd ed. New York: Routledge/Taylor & Francis Group.

Taylor, Justine, Danielle Boisvert, Barbara Sims, and Carl Garver. 2011. "An Examination of Media Accounts of Child Abductions in the United States." *Justice Policy Journal* 8 (2): 4–28.

Tiegreen, Sara, and Elana Newman. 2009. "Violence: Comparing Reporting and Reality." Dart Center for Journalism & Trauma. https://dartcenter.org/content/violence-comparing-reporting-and-reality.

Q31. DO NEWS MEDIA ACCURATELY REPRESENT SCIENTIFIC KNOWLEDGE AND CONSENSUS?

Answer: Sometimes yes, but mostly no. News media are a chief source of information on scientific issues, as most Americans have little direct knowledge of or experience with scientific advances in understanding climate change, environmental issues, medicine, health care, and other topics. Public perceptions about the state of scientific research on these and other issues, however, often are wildly inaccurate, which suggests that news outlets could do a better job of providing comprehensive and contextual information on scientific topics. Because scientific research is complex, it often can be challenging for news organizations to cover, particularly in a media environment motivated by popularity and profitability. The best science reporting appears in specialty outlets and programs such as National Geographic and Nova and in major newspapers with dedicated science sections such as *The New York Times.*

The Facts: Scientific issues are notoriously difficult to communicate. Even excellent journalists with time, resources, and relevant knowledge often struggle to distill and explain complex scientific topics in ways that can be readily grasped and understood by the general public. For journalists who lack time and expertise, the task becomes far more challenging. Furthermore, scientists themselves often are not much help. Because of their deep expertise, they can have a hard time making it clear why their work matters and explaining to reporters what the public needs to know. Even when scientists do communicate clearly, it's still possible for a reporter to misunderstand the topic at hand and botch the story, which can make scientists wary of the press and reluctant to talk to reporters in the first place. Finally, for mainstream commercial news media outlets that already are constrained by resources or are in a race to maximize profits, it can be difficult to provide nuanced reporting on difficult scientific topics.

Critics say that American news media's failure to accurately communicate about science is a serious problem. Because much of modern human civilization is made possible by science and technology, it is tremendously important that humans understand how science works and gain a sense of the implications of scientific advances in understanding. These range widely, from individual-level issues, such as the safety and efficacy of medical treatment or the effects of smoking on human health, to global issues, such as the effects of chemicals on the environment or the consequences of human-caused climate change. The implications also range widely. Knowledge about the safety and efficacy of vaccines is vital in order to protect public health from easily preventable diseases such as measles. Broad understanding of the scientific consensus around human-caused climate change will be necessary to prevent parts of the planet from becoming uninhabitable and creating widespread devastation.

Perhaps the most obvious example of these challenges can be seen in news coverage of climate change. The scientific consensus that anthropogenic (human-caused) climate change is a reality has been clear for some time. Virtually all scientists and scientific organizations agree that human activity is the primary cause of global warming (Cook et al. 2016). For example, the Intergovernmental Panel on Climate Change, a group of 1,300 independent scientific experts from all over the world, concluded in

2014 that "human influence has been the dominant cause of the observed warming since the mid-20th century." But media representations of the issue have often painted a more muddled picture of scientific uncertainty. As a result, public perceptions of the issue do not correspond with scientific realities. According to the Yale Project on Climate Change Communication, in 2016, a national total of 63 percent of Americans believed global warming is happening, but percentages from one county to the next varied widely (from 43 to 80 percent) (Marlon et al. 2016). Nationally, the Yale project found that only 52 percent of Americans believed global warming is mostly caused by human activities. It also reported that only 48 percent of Americans say most scientists believe global warming is happening at all. At the same time, 70 percent of Americans say they trust climate scientists about global warming. A disconnect clearly exists between the scientific consensus and public perceptions. And to make matters worse, the issue is highly partisan. Overall, 82 percent of Democrats think global warming is happening compared to only 50 percent of Republicans. Those numbers drop when individuals are asked whether human activity plays a role: only 65 percent of Democrats and 31 percent of Republicans say yes, according to one study (Mildenberger et al. 2016).

Disconnects between representation, reality, and perception are not a new concern. In his 1922 book *Public Opinion*, the journalist Walter Lippmann described how news media provides the basis for social reality. "The world outside and the picture in our heads" is the phrase he used to distinguish the real world from the one constructed through the news media. Ultimately, Lippmann saw this disconnect as a fatal flaw of democracy; without an accurate understanding of reality, self-governing citizens would be unable to effectively exercise their democratic voice. Of course, media sources constitute only one of many influences on our perceptions of reality, along with other institutions of society: family, religion, school, government, and so on. But today more than ever, we come to know our world through mediated representations. Since the advent of the Internet, advocates have hoped that access to a wide variety of perspectives and news sources would lead to the democratization of media production and consumption. In many ways, that has happened, but the results are not always ideal. Misinformation, propaganda, and conspiracy theories gain easy traction online, and even some mainstream news outlets have found success by peddling falsehoods.

An analysis of cable news coverage of climate science by the Union of Concerned Scientists (UCS) in 2014 found a mixed amount of inaccuracies among prominent sources (Huertas and Kriegsman 2014). According to the UCS report, CNN was accurate about 70 percent of the time and misleading about 30 percent of the time. CNN's misleading coverage could be attributed to "debate" segments that attempt to convey balance by pitting a believer in climate change against a denier. This type of "false balance," which is common across news media, gives the false impression that the science on global warming is a subject of continued heated debate among scientists. The UCS report concluded that the "biggest step that CNN could take to increase accuracy is to stop hosting debates about established climate science and instead focus debates on whether and how to respond to climate change through climate policy." The UCS analysis found that Fox News was misleading most of the time, with only 28 percent of coverage deemed accurate. The UCS report recommended that "the most productive step Fox News could take would be for hosts and guests to better differentiate between scientific facts about climate change and political opinions about climate policy." MSNBC fared best with an accuracy rating of 92 percent. Misleading coverage on MSNBC tended to overstate the effects of climate change. These findings and conclusions are consistent with other research examining television news coverage of climate change research (Boykoff 2008; Feldman 2016).

Online and social media environments offer an equally mixed bag. Research has found positive effects of social media use on climate change opinion, knowledge, and behavior. While social media can encourage climate change skepticism, it also can increase factual knowledge about the topic and can provide a useful space for discussion with others (Anderson 2017). Other research, however, suggests the multitude of voices online does not lead to robust scientific information or quality discussion. Climate scientists tend not to be major players in online discussions, and the information that does exist remains oriented around specialized audiences rather than the broader public (Schäfer 2012). Furthermore, a Pew Research Center survey found that millions of people encounter science-related information on social media. However, this content tends to include promotions for programs and events as well as practical tips for personal improvement but little in the way of robust science news (Hitlin and Olmstead 2018).

Another science news topic of concern is the supposed link between vaccines and autism. In actuality, there is no scientific validity to this alleged link. The idea of a link was based on a single scientific study that was later found fraudulent due to a conflict of interest and eventually retracted (Godlee, Smith, and Marcovitch 2011). One hallmark of sound science is the replication process, where patterns of evidence are necessary for making causal connections. Science (like good journalism) is also based on accountability and transparency, where errors are corrected and explained in an open manner. Nevertheless, despite the lack of support-ing evidence, the vaccine-autism myth exploded, particularly in fact-free corners of the online environment but also in mainstream news cover-age. Similar to coverage of climate change, news coverage throughout the early 2000s offered a "balanced" view of the issue even when no evi-dence of a link existed and any suggestion of the idea had been thoroughly debunked by the scientific community (Dixon and Clarke 2013). This type of false balance can sow confusion and mislead viewers, which has resulted in an increase in parents who seek "personal belief" exemptions to avoid vaccinating their children. Regions with lower vaccination rates also have reduced their "herd immunity," which protects communities from contagious diseases, and have seen increases in disease outbreaks (Mooney and Raja 2014).

The waters are further muddied by the amount of propaganda and mis-information being intentionally infused into the public sphere by those who want to advance their own interests on science-related topics. As science historians Naomi Oreskes and Erik M. Conway detail in their book, *Merchants of Doubt*, special interests have long sought to sow confu-sion by suggesting there is a lack of settled science on a number of issues where scientific consensus actually is well established (Oreskes and Con-way 2011). These topics have ranged from earlier controversies regarding tobacco smoking, acid rain, the pesticide DDT, and the hole in the ozone layer to aforementioned "controversies" surrounding vaccines and climate change. For example, tobacco companies evaded regulation for decades by insisting that nicotine was not addictive and that smoking did not pose a major health risk despite settled science to the contrary. In general, a failure to accurately depict the scientific process and its findings leads to gross misperceptions on the part of the American public about the reality of important issues, as well as the pros and cons of options to mitigate or otherwise address those issues.

FURTHER READING

Anderson, Ashley A. 2017. "Effects of Social Media Use on Climate Change Opinion, Knowledge, and Behavior." In *Oxford Research Encyclopedia of Climate Science*. Oxford University Press. https://doi .org/10.1093/acrefore/9780190228620.013.369.

Boykoff, Maxwell T. 2008. "Lost in Translation? United States Televi-sion News Coverage of Anthropogenic Climate Change, 1995–2004." *Climatic Change* 86 (1–2): 1–11. https://doi.org/10.1007/s10584-007-9299-3.

Burkeman, Oliver. 2003. "Memo Exposes Bush's New Green Strategy." *The Guardian*, March 4. http://www.theguardian.com/environment/2003/mar/04/usnews.climatechange.

Cook, John, Naomi Oreskes, Peter T. Doran, William R.L. Anderegg, Bart Verheggen, Ed W. Maibach, J. Stuart Carlton, et al. 2016. "Consensus on Consensus: A Synthesis of Consensus Estimates on Human-Caused Global Warming." *Environmental Research Letters* 11 (4): 048002. https://doi.org/10.1088/1748-9326/11/4/048002.

Dixon, Graham N., and Christopher E. Clarke. 2013. "Heightening Uncertainty around Certain Science: Media Coverage, False Balance, and the Autism-Vaccine Controversy." *Science Communication* 35 (3): 358–382. https://doi.org/10.1177/1075547012458290.

Feldman, Lauren. 2016. "Effects of TV and Cable News Viewing on Climate Change Opinion, Knowledge, and Behavior." *Oxford Research Encyclopedia of Climate Science.* November. https://doi.org/10.1093/acrefore/9780190228620.013.367.

Godlee, Fiona, Jane Smith, and Harvey Marcovitch. 2011. "Wakefield's Article Linking MMR Vaccine and Autism Was Fraudulent." *BMJ* 342 (January): c7452. https://doi.org/10.1136/bmj.c7452.

Hitlin, Paul, and Kenneth Olmstead. 2018. "The Science People See on Social Media." Pew Research Center. http://www.pewinternet.org/2018/03/21/the-science-people-see-on-social-media/.

Huertas, Aaron, and Rachel Kriegsman. 2014. "Science or Spin? Assessing the Accuracy of Cable News Coverage of Climate Science." Union of Concerned Scientists. https://www.ucsusa.org/global-warming/solutions/fight-misinformation/cable-news-coverage-climate-change-science.html.

Jang, S. Mo, Brooke W. Mckeever, Robert Mckeever, and Joon Kyoung Kim. 2017. "From Social Media to Mainstream News: The Information Flow of the Vaccine-Autism Controversy in the US, Canada, and the UK." *Health Communication.* https://doi.org/10.1080/10410236.2017.1384433.

Lippmann, Walter. 1922. *Public Opinion.* New York: Harcourt.

Marlon, Jennifer, Peter Howe, Matto Mildenberger, and Anthony Leiserowitz. 2016. "Yale Climate Opinion Maps—U.S. 2016." Yale Program on Climate Change Communication. http://climatecommunication.yale.edu/visualizations-data/ycom-us-2016/.

Mildenberger, Matto, Jennifer Marlon, Peter Howe, Xinran Wang, and Anthony Leiserowitz. 2016. "Partisan Climate Opinion Maps 2016." Yale Program on Climate Change Communication. http://climatecommunication.yale.edu/visualizations-data/partisan-maps-2016/.

Mooney, Chris, and Tasneem Raja. 2014. "How Many People Aren't Vac-cinating Their Kids in Your State?" *Mother Jones*, February 17. https://www.motherjones.com/environment/2014/02/vaccine-exemptions-states-pertussis-map/.

Oreskes, Naomi, and Erik M. Conway. 2011. *Merchants of Doubt: How a Handful of Scientists Obscured the Truth on Issues from Tobacco Smoke to Global Warming*. Paperback ed. New York: Bloomsbury Press.

Schäfer, Mike S. 2012. "Online Communication on Climate Change and Climate Politics: A Literature Review." *Wiley Interdisciplinary Reviews: Climate Change* 3 (6): 527–543. https://doi.org/10.1002/wcc.191.

Q32. ARE MINORITIES AND WOMEN ACCURATELY REPRESENTED IN NEWS MEDIA?

Answer: As with most media representations, some distortion happens with the frequency and manner in which women and minorities are por-trayed. Generally, women and minorities appear less frequently in the news media than the real world, and many representations emphasize or rely on stereotypes. Female politicians and other prominent women have long been subject to very different scrutiny from the kind faced by their male counterparts, with perceptions of their appearance and sexuality often given levels of attention not found in coverage of men. Represen-tations of racial minorities are often tied to crime or terrorism out of pro-portion with reality. Religious minorities and sexual minorities suffer from many of the same issues of omission and stereotyping.

The Facts: Before addressing whether any groups are accurately or proportionately represented in the media, it may be useful to review the arguments that journalists have an obligation to present a representative picture of the world to their audiences. These arguments have their basis in the 1947 Hutchins Commission Report on Freedom of the Press and the social responsibility theory of the press laid out in that report. The Hutchins Commission was tasked with evaluating the role of media in a democratic society and its performance in that role. Among the respon-sibilities of the media that the commission identified was "the projection of a representative picture of the constituent groups of society" (Commis-sion on Freedom of the Press 1947). Similarly, the Knight Commission's 2009 report on the Information Needs of Communities in a Democracy stated that one hallmark of healthy democratic communities was the presence of "local media—including print, broadcast, and new media—[that] reflect the full reality of the communities they represent." Implicit in these ideas is the expectation that media has some responsibility to accurately present members of the public to each other. Specifically, the Hutchins Commission report stated, "The Commission holds to the faith that if people are exposed to the inner truth of the life of a particular group, they will gradually build up respect for and understanding of it" (Commission on Freedom of the Press 1947). Reflecting this priority, the Society of Professional Journalists' code of ethics includes a provision to "boldly tell the story of the diversity and magnitude of the human experience. Seek sources whose voices we seldom hear." This assumption about the importance of representation in media underlies a consideration of whether the news media accurately represents women and minorities. The ways in which race, gender, religion, sexuality, and other identity markers intersect are complicated, and these are affected by a range of various issues related to structural inequality in society. It's important to note that media representations are a significant but narrow part of this equation.

Questions about representation have to do with both the presence of women and racial minorities (how often they appear in news media) and the way in which they are represented when they do appear. It may be helpful to first consider what portion of the population is female, as well as what portion is made up of racial and ethnic, religious and sexual minorities. Women made up 50.8 percent of the U.S. population in the 2016 Census data. In terms of race/ethnicity, in a 2015 survey, 17.3 percent of the population identified as Latino, 14.6 percent as black or African American, and 5.2 percent as Asian. Regarding religion, 30 percent of the population identified themselves as non-Christian: 22.8 percent unaffiliated or no religion, 1.9 percent Jewish, 0.9 percent Muslim, 0.7 percent each Hindu and Buddhist, and 1.8 percent other religions (Pew Research Center 2015). Regarding sexuality, there are complications in finding accurate numbers, but a Gallup poll in 2017 found that about 4 percent of Americans identify as lesbian, gay, bisexual, or transgender (Gates 2017).

As noted by Adrienne Lafrance (2016) in *The Atlantic*, "Male dominance in global media is well documented, and has been for many decades. . . . [Men] make more money, get more bylines, spend more time on-camera, and are quoted far more often than women." One of the earliest volumes to problematize the representation of women in the media was *Hearth and Home* by Gaye Tuchman, Arlene Kaplan Daniels, and James Benet (1978). This text pointed out the absence of women from mass media, which Tuchman called "symbolic annihilation" (Gerbner's 1972 term), and the stereotyped ways women were presented when they did appear in the media. The authors identified issues with advertising, television, film, and news. A Media Watch (1995) global analysis found that 19 percent of people featured in news stories on the day of the international study were women and that they were most commonly portrayed as victims, mothers, and wives. "If news media fail to report the views of women judges, women parliamentarians, or women business leaders," wrote scholars Carolyn Byerly and Karen Ross (2006, 40), "but always report on violent crimes against women, then it is hardly surprising that the public fail to realize that women do in fact occupy significant roles in society or, equally, that men are much more likely to be victims of serious crime than women." This perspective echoed the findings of Karen Ross, who had previously examined content issues and argued that women parliamentarians are treated very differently by media than their male counterparts. Women are "persistently trivialized by media speculation over their private lives, domestic arrangements, and sartorial style: they might be allowed to speak about policy, but their potency as change agents or even as serious politicians is casually undermined by the media's use of extraneous detail such as their age, their shoes, or their latest haircut" (Ross 2013, 98).

Women are less frequently quoted as sources in news stories, as exemplified in a 2013 analysis of 352 front-page *New York Times* stories, in which reporters quoted 3.4 times as many male sources as female sources (Layton and Shepard 2013). Other studies have found that the disparity is not simply in numbers: an analysis of 889 newspaper stories found that "male sources and subjects received more mentions and were placed more prominently in the stories" (Armstrong 2004) and that stories written by women were more likely to include females in the news story.

The concept of symbolic annihilation has also been used to discuss the absence of racial and ethnic minorities. Again, minorities do not appear in news media with a frequency that corresponds with their representation in society, and when they do appear in news media, they are often stereotyped or limited to certain genres or roles. Cultivation theory studies have been conducted on television content for years and generally found a disproportionate number of people of color appearing in crime stories. Travis Dixon and Daniel Linz's (2000) study of television news reports found that white people are more likely to be portrayed as victims of crimes, while blacks and Latinos are more likely to be portrayed as lawbreakers. In both cases the racial groups were overrepresented in terms of actual likelihood to be a victim or perpetrator of a crime. More recently, a 2015 study found that "Blacks were actually 'invisible' on network news, being underrepresented as both violent perpetrators and victims of crime" (Dixon and Williams 2015). However, whites were accurately represented as criminals. Moreover, Latinos were greatly overrepresented as undocumented immigrants, while Muslims were greatly overrepresented as terrorists on network and cable news programs. Travis Dixon's 2017 study of news coverage in Los Angeles again found that whites were significantly overrepresented as victims and officers but showed some progress in that blacks and Latinos were accurately depicted in terms of rates of perpetrating crimes. Megan Pacely and Karen Flynn's 2012 study of media coverage of bullying of queer youth found a discrepancy in representation, with white males being disproportionately portrayed as victims of bullying in media stories about the bullying of queer youth, despite the fact that the majority of young queer bullying victims are not white males.

Issues with the lack of presence and limited representation of women and minorities in news media are often traced to the historically limited presence of women and minorities in newsrooms. Print and online newsrooms in the country are certainly not in line with the national population, as women made up 39 percent of newsroom employees in the 2017 American Society of News Editors survey, and minorities made up 11 percent overall, although 24.3 percent of online newsroom staff were racial or ethnic minorities. One analysis indicated that stories by women also are frequently relegated to particular sections; women's bylines appeared on the majority of stories in five sections: fashion, dining, home, travel, and health, while men's bylines were the majority of stories in the seven largest sections, including U.S. news, world news, opinion, and business (Cohen 2014). A 2014 Radio Television Digital News Association survey found that 31 percent of TV news directors and 20 percent of general managers were women, and women made up 40 percent of the overall TV workforce. Minorities made up 22 percent of the overall workforce on television and radio (Papper 2014). However, the author noted, "In the last 24 years, the minority population in the U.S. has risen 11 points; but the minority workforce in TV news is up less than half that (4.6), and the minority workforce in radio is up 2.2" (Papper 2014). Meanwhile, pay gaps related to gender and race persist among reporters. Lars Willnat and David Weaver (2014) found that the median income for male journalists in 2012 was $53,600, while the median income for female journalists was $44,342. A 2018 report by the Los Angeles Times Guild found that the average salary for female reporters at *The Los Angeles Times* was $87,564, while the average for men was $101,898. A similar gap existed around race: the average salary for people of color at the *Times* was $85,622, compared to an average of $100,398 for white reporters.

FURTHER READING

American Society of News Editors. 2017. "ASNE, Google News Lab Release 2017 Diversity Survey Results with Interactive Website." ASNE.org. http://asne.org/diversity-survey-2017.

Armstrong, Cory L. 2004. "The Influence of Reporter Gender on Source Selection in Newspaper Stories." *Journalism & Mass Communication Quarterly* 81 (1): 139–154.

Byerly, Carolyn M., and Karen Ross. 2006. *Women and Media: A Critical Introduction*. Malden, MA: Blackwell.

Cohen, Philip N. 2014. "The Most Comprehensive Analysis Ever of the Gender of New York Times Writers." *Family Inequality*. https://family inequality.wordpress.com/2014/04/29/gender-nytimes/.

The Commission on Freedom of the Press. 1947. *A Free and Responsible Press*. Chicago, IL: University of Chicago Press.

Dixon, Travis L. 2017. "Good Guys Are Still Always in White? Positive Change and Continued Misrepresentation of Race and Crime on Local Television News." *Communication Research* 44 (6): 775–792.

Dixon, Travis L., and Daniel Linz. 2000. "Race and the Misrepresentation of Victimization on Local Television News." *Communication Research* 27 (5): 547–573.

Dixon, Travis L., and Charlotte L. Williams. 2015. "The Changing Misrepresentation of Race and Crime on Network and Cable News." *Journal of Communication* 65 (1): 24–39.

Gates, Gary J. 2017. "In U.S., More Adults Identifying as LGBT." Gallup, January 11. http://news.gallup.com/poll/201731/lgbt-identification-rises.aspx.

Knight Commission (on the Information Needs of Communities in a Democracy). 2009. "Informing Communities: Sustaining Democracy in the Digital Age." Washington, DC: The Aspen Institute.

Lafrance, Adrienne. 2016. "I Analyzed a Year of My Reporting for Gender Bias (Again)." *The Atlantic*, February 17. https://www.theatlantic.com/technology/archive/2016/02/gender-diversity-journalism/463023/.

Layton, Alexi, and Alicia Shepard. 2013. "Lack of Female Sources in NY Times Front-Page Stories Highlights Need for Change." *Poynter*, July 16. https://www.poynter.org/news/lack-female-sources-ny-times-front-page-stories-highlights-need-change.

Los Angeles Times Guild. 2018. "It's in the Data: Tronc Underpays Women and People of Color at the L.A. Times." April 11. https://latguild.com/news/2018/4/11/its-in-the-data-tronc-underpays-women-and-people-of-color-at-the-la-times.

Media Watch. 1995. "Global Media Monitoring Project: Women's Participation in the News." Ontario, Canada: National Watch on Images of Women/Media Watch.

Paceley, Megan S., and Karen Flynn. 2012. "Media Representations of Bullying toward Queer Youth: Gender, Race, and Age Discrepancies." *Journal of LGBT Youth* 9 (4): 340–356.

Papper, Bob. 2014. "Women, Minorities Make Newsroom Gains." Radio Television News Directors Association. July 28. http://www.rtdna.org/article/women_minorities_make_newsroom_gains#.VBHE9i5dXv8.

Pew Research Center. 2015. "America's Changing Religious Landscape." May 12. http://www.pewforum.org/2015/05/12/americas-changing-religious-landscape/.

Ross, Karen. 2013. *Gendered Media: Women, Men, and Identity Politics.* Lanham: Rowman and Littlefield Publishers, Inc.

Society of Professional Journalists. 2014. "SPJ Code of Ethics." SPJ.org. https://www.spj.org/ethicscode.asp.

Tuchman, Gaye, Arlene K. Daniels, and James Benet (Eds.). 1978. *Hearth and Home: Images of Women in the Mass Media.* New York: Oxford University Press.

U.S. Census Bureau. "2012–2016 American Community Survey 5-Year Estimates." https://factfinder.census.gov/faces/tableservices/jsf/pages/productview.xhtml?src=bkmk

Willnat, Lars, and David Weaver. 2014. *The American Journalist in the Digital Age: Key Findings.* Bloomington, IN: School of Journalism, Indiana University.

Women's Media Center. 2014. "The Status of Women in the U.S. Media 2014." http://wmc.3cdn.net/2e85f9517dc2bf164e_htm62xgan.pdf.

Q33. DOES NEWS COVERAGE OF THE ECONOMY REFLECT THE AVERAGE AMERICAN'S REALITY?

Answer: Essentially, no. Most news coverage about the economy is not inaccurate, but it tends to focus on superficial measures and issues that do not have an effect on many Americans' lives. News coverage of the U.S. economy tends to emphasize the health of the U.S. stock market and other indicators that are not relevant to the economic reality of the average American. It also rarely addresses labor issues or the problem of economic inequality or its root causes. However, the relationship between news coverage of the economy and the health of the economy may be complicated somewhat by the influence of consumer attitudes on economic trends.

The Facts: Some media critics assert that a disconnect exists between news about the economy and the lived reality of most Americans. They charge that the limitations of news coverage about the economy are similar to those that plague most news coverage about politics and other issues: "horse-race coverage"; stories dictated by government reports; a few major stories originating in New York and Washington, D.C., that dominate coverage; episodic framing; and structural biases. These factors result in an overemphasis on coverage of topics that don't affect most Americans and a lack of coverage of issues like labor issues, working conditions, fair wages, economic inequality, or the lives of the poor in the United States. Additionally, critics contend that coverage of market news can affect public opinion, which is a crucial factor influencing consumer confidence and ultimately the health of markets, so there may be a somewhat self-reinforcing effect of news coverage about the economy.

Coverage of economic news generally accounts for a small percentage of most general news organizations' content. Besides the business-focused trade publications that tend to emphasize information that traders would find useful, most daily newspapers have a business section, and broadcast and cable news programs cover economic news as part of their daily programs. However, unless there is a major milestone in the Dow Jones Industrial Average, a big gain or loss in the stock market, or sustained recessionary conditions, economic news receives relatively little attention. During the first few months of the economic recovery in 2009, for example, news about the economic crisis accounted for about 46 percent of overall news coverage, according to a study by the Pew Research Center (2009). By July of that year, coverage of the crisis was down to 16 percent of all news. There were marked differences among the different media, however, as newspapers devoted "the most attention to the economy, offering more localized coverage, giving voice to a more diverse range of sources and producing a higher level of enterprise reporting than other media sectors" (Pew Research Center 2009), while network television news aired regular features about the impact of the recession on average Americans, and cable television and talk radio focused on political aspects of the economic stimulus package championed by the Obama administration as a vehicle to pull the nation out of recession.

Coverage of economic news is often simple and limited to a single item on the gains or losses of market indicators that day. Similar to political coverage that is often focused on the "horse race" aspect of elections and reporting who is ahead and who is behind rather than why and what their policies are, economic coverage tends to emphasize the rise or fall of certain numbers without providing a great deal of context and explanation. The daily rise or fall of certain economic indicators (the Dow Jones, the Nasdaq Composite index, etc.) is reported as if they are markers for the overall economy, despite criticism from many economists that suggests the stock market indicators are not useful. An analysis by Pew (2009) found that in reporting about the economic recovery in 2009, "the mainstream press focused on a relatively small number of major storylines, mostly generated from two cities, the country's political and financial capitals" and that "phrases and ideas that reverberated most in the coverage came early on, mostly from government, particularly from the president and the chairman of the Federal Reserve." However, only about 54 percent of Americans are invested in the stock market, and the richest 10 percent of Americans own 84 percent of stocks (Wile 2017), meaning that the health of the market has little or no direct bearing on the financial health of nearly half the country. Other numbers, such as monthly government reports on the unemployment rate, jobs (lost or created), and average wages, are often reported in the news but similarly lacking in context or explanation, simply as a matter of comparison to previous months or a trend.

Newspapers historically provided greater coverage to labor issues, with most major newspapers assigning a reporter to cover labor. With cuts to newsroom budgets resulting in layoffs and buyouts and a drastic reduction in the overall newsroom workforce, there are few labor reporters left. Steve Greenhouse, former labor reporter for *The New York Times*, said in 2018 that at one time he was the only labor reporter working for a major daily newspaper in the United States (Fraser et al. 2018). Of course, reporters on other beats can still cover labor issues, but it is a marked decline. Union membership has also declined from a peak of 35 percent of workers to 11 percent in 2013 (DeSilver 2014), so the need for a beat reporter to cover labor-management relations may be perceived to be much less than in the past.

The relationship between economic and political interests undoubtedly has an effect on news coverage of the economy. The same forces and work routines and structural biases that result in political voices having a great deal of influence on the tone and perspectives that appear in news stories about politics result in those same voices being overrepresented in coverage of the economy. In the case of the economy, politicians can use that same influence to push an agenda that will disproportionately benefit their donors rather than working for the good of the general public. A 2014 study by political scientists Martin Gilens and Benjamin Page concluded that when the economic elite support a particular policy change, it has about a 45 percent chance of becoming law, and that when the economic elite oppose a policy, it has an 18 percent chance of becoming law. While the authors acknowledge that sometimes those same laws are also supported by the middle class and poor, the numbers indicate an outsized influence by those with more financial resources.

There are two chief opposing views of the tone of economic news. On one side are those who argue that news about the economy is overly negative and too critical of institutions, a state of affairs attributed to overzealous journalists who adopt a "watchdog" role. On the other side are those arguing that due to the corporate ownership of the vast majority of news media organizations, the reliance on advertising dollars for revenue, and ingrained journalistic practices that depend on elite sources connected to financial institutions and the wealthiest individuals and corporations, journalists are constrained from really critiquing the economic system. In an effort to determine which side is correct, Christopher Kollmeyer (2004, 432) conducted a content analysis of economic news covered by *The Los Angeles Times* and compared it to the performance of the California economy and found that "despite growth patterns that overwhelmingly favored economic elites, the negative news about the economy disproportionately depicted events and problems affecting corporations and investors instead of the general workforce." Based on these findings, Kollmeyer concluded that "the news media, when reporting on the economy, tend to privilege the interests of corporations and investors over the interests of the general workforce" (433).

Another concern of economists and media scholars studying economic news is that news coverage of the economy may have a great deal of influence on citizens' perceptions of the economy, which can then influence the economy. When news media convey economic data to citizens, they send signals about the health of the economy through the tone and frequency of economic reporting and influence public opinion. Public attitudes about the economy, such as public confidence, can have a strong effect on the growth and health of the economy. Stuart Soroka, Dominik Stecula, and Christopher Wlezien (2015, 457) claimed that news coverage "reflects change in the future economy, and that this both influences and is influenced by public evaluations." A 2003 study by Joe Bob Hester and Rhonda Gibson concluded, "Media coverage, particularly the media's emphasis on negative news, may have serious consequences for both expectations of and performance of the economy" (73).

Their 2003 study about public understanding of the U.S. economy demonstrated that Americans are affected by the generally negative tone of coverage. Hester and Gibson (2003, 85) concluded, "As second-level agenda-setting theory suggests, the media may go further than telling people what to think about; they may actually tell people how to think about a subject." There also remains a great divide between reality and perception of the economy. As with many issues, ideology plays a strong role in public opinion about the economy and can guide the way audiences seek and interact with information. Alan Blinder and Alan Krueger concluded in a 2004 paper, "Ideology seems to play a stronger role in shaping opinion on economic policy issues than either self-interest or knowledge, although specific (as opposed to general) knowledge does influence opinion on a number of matters" (386).

Economic news is subject to the same structural biases that affect all news, especially status quo bias. The status quo bias in the media is the tendency to assume that the current state of affairs is preferable. The status quo bias in media is related to the psychological or emotional bias of the same name that describes the tendency to consider the current baseline as a reference point and perceive any change from that as a loss. In the case of economic news, that means there is little debate in the media about the merits of capitalism. Reporters rarely report on the growing economic inequality in the country or the issues that contribute to its continuing growth. News about the economy may mention wage growth or wage stagnation but rarely addresses the fairness of wages or whether people are earning a living wage or doing meaningful work. As with much reporting, news about the economy tends to use what Shanto Iyengar (2015) called episodic framing rather than thematic framing, meaning that it emphasizes single events out of context rather than explaining broader trends and patterns. Few stories cover the large number of Americans living in poverty or the working poor (Sanders 2018).

Since most news media rely on the "audience as product" model that requires selling their audiences to advertisers and running ads alongside (or before and after) news content, reports about the economy are often bookended by messages designed to encourage more consumption and promote consumerism in general. Any criticism of or questioning the economic system or the capitalistic model demanding constant growth may be drowned out by the frequent messages promoting the very behaviors that drive that system. As Kollmeyer (2004, 449) put it bluntly, "In a democracy, the news media should help expose weaknesses in society's major institutions and facilitate rational debates on appropriate policy solutions to the identified problems. Scholars and media critics, however, overwhelmingly agree that the news media in the United States fall far short of this ideal."

FURTHER READING

Blinder, Alan S., and Alan B. Krueger. 2004. "What Does the Public Know about Economic Policy, and How Does It Know It?" Brookings Papers on Economic Activity. https://www.brookings.edu/wp-content/uploads/2004/01/2004a_bpea_blinder.pdf

DeSilver, Drew. 2014. "American Unions Membership Declines as Public Support Fluctuates." Pew Research Center. http://www.pewresearch.org/fact-tank/2014/02/20/for-american-unions-membership-trails-far-behind-public-support/.

Fraser, Max, Steven Greenhouse, Jane Slaughter, and Sarah Jaffe. 2018. "Labor Journalism Today: Three Interviews." *Labor: Studies in Working-Class History of the Americas* 15 (1): 81–91. https://muse.jhu.edu/article/687273/summary.

Gilens, Martin, and Benjamin I. Page. 2014. "Testing Theories of American Politics: Elites, Interest Groups, and Average Citizens." *Perspectives on Politics* 12 (3): 564–581.

Hester, Joe Bob, and Rhonda Gibson. 2003, Spring. "The Economy and Second-Level Agenda Setting: A Time-Series Analysis of Economic News and Public Opinion about the Economy." *Journalism and Mass Communication Quarterly* 80 (1): 73–90.

Iyengar, Shanto. 2015. *Media Politics: A Citizen's Guide.* 3rd ed. New York: W. W. Norton & Company.

Kollmeyer, Christopher J. 2004. "Corporate Interests: How the News Media Portray the Economy." *Social Problems* 51 (3): 432–452.

Pew Research Center. 2009. "Covering the Great Recession: How the Media Have Depicted the Economic Crisis during Obama's Presidency." Pew Research Center. http://www.journalism.org/2009/10/05/how-economic-coverage-varied-media-sector/.

Sanders, Bernie. 2018. "The Corporate Media Ignores the Rise of Oligarchy. The Rest of Us Shouldn't." *The Guardian*, March 16. https://www.theguardian.com/commentisfree/2018/mar/16/corporate-media-oligarchy-bernie-sanders.

Soroka, Stuart N., Dominik A. Stecula, and Christopher Wlezien. 2015, April. "It's (Change in) the (Future) Economy, Stupid: Economic Indicators, the Media, and Public Opinion." *American Journal of Political Science* 59 (2): 457–474.

Wile, Rob. 2017. "The Richest 10% of Americans Now Own 84% of All Stocks." *Time*, December 19. http://time.com/money/5054009/stock-ownership-10-percent-richest/.

Wright, Erik O., and Joel Rogers. 2011. *American Society: How It Really Works.* New York: W. W. Norton & Company.

Q34. DO NEWS MEDIA ACCURATELY REPRESENT THE REALITIES OF WAR?

Answer: Yes and no. Whether Americans are accurately informed about issues of war and peace depends largely on what news sources they consume, as is the case with most newsworthy topics. Journalists play a major role in relaying information about foreign policy and international events, as most Americans have no direct experience with such matters. Some journalists and news organizations have the knowledge, experience, time, and resources to provide excellent information to the public. Others provide flawed reports that rely too heavily on official sources and are reluctant to be critical of government policy and action due to cultural and commercial pressures. Official government sources from the White House, Pentagon, and Central Intelligence Agency (CIA) often try to exert considerable control of the images and stories gathered by news organizations in combat zones and other theaters of military action.

The Facts: News media play a significant mediating role regarding the American public's understanding of foreign policy in general and military actions in particular. Because few Americans have any firsthand knowledge of international affairs or American actions overseas, news media provide the primary source of information, and having quality information is the only way Americans can knowledgeably support or reject the actions of their government.

Covering foreign affairs well presents a major challenge for several reasons. First, to really get the story right, reporters need to be informed themselves on a given situation, including what are often complex intricacies regarding regional geopolitics. For example, reporters who know little about the history of the Middle East are not well equipped to understand the implications and consequences of military action there, no matter how well intentioned it might be. Second, at least some information must come from firsthand observation, which often means putting journalists in dangerous situations. It also requires money. Sending correspondents overseas and maintaining regional news bureaus are expensive. When news budgets are tight, these providers of firsthand accounts are among the first things to be cut. Third, when covering military conflict, American journalists in a war zone often depend on the protection of the U.S. military at the same time they are supposed to maintain a critical distance in their reporting. This has the potential to create an uncomfortable conflict of interest. Fourth, the military employs media specialists to help control what gets reported and to limit journalist access in some cases. This can make it hard for journalists to get the real story.

As a result of budget constraints and limited access, war reporting often ends up relying heavily on the proclamations of official sources such as presidents, military officials, legislators, and foreign policy leaders. When these voices offer relatively uniform opinions, reporters are less likely to seek out and convey alternative points of view. Scholars sometimes describe this situation in terms of "indexing theory," which suggests that the press serves primarily to represent only the perspectives of dominant voices of power (Bennett 1990, 2016). In other words, the news is an "index" of elite opinion. If there is a great deal of debate about a topic among elites, news will reflect this. Often, debate is more limited, as with the 2003 decision to invade Iraq by the administration of President George W. Bush. In such cases, news coverage will tend to reflect this. As W. Lance Bennett notes, "The overriding norm of contemporary journalism seems to involve compressing public opinion (at least law-abiding, legitimate opinion) to fit into the range of debate between decisive institutional power blocs" (Bennett 1990, 124–125). Public opinion is then constructed based on news media representations of elite perspectives. This is particularly apparent with military-related stories, since information is closely guarded and many Americans have little personal knowledge about foreign affairs in general.

Other scholars and practitioners have offered similar criticisms. As scholar and journalist J. Herbert Altschull (1995, 68) has written, "When the United States is in collision with another nation, it is not necessary to give equal attention to both sides to the dispute; to do so is to be unpatriotic." In other words, coverage of international conflict is likely to reflect an American, or even xenophobic, point of view and to neglect other perspectives. In their book *Manufacturing Consent*, Edward Herman and Noam Chomsky (2002) detail a "propaganda model," which suggests that public consent for political and economic policy is "manufactured" through news media propaganda. Based on their analysis of news coverage of several foreign conflicts, the authors propose five "filters" through which all information must pass before it can reach the public: owners, advertisers, sources, flak (or negative reactions from powerful influencers), and an ideology of fear of other cultures. Critics of the propaganda model say it oversimplifies the news-making process and fails to consider the amount of debate and disagreement that is present in various news media outlets. Herman and Chomsky counter that such disagreement only exists to the extent that it is tolerated by powerful interests.

It is an unfortunate irony that at times when the American public is most in need of critical, objective, nuanced reporting, they are often less likely to get it. This is problematic because when it comes to matters of war and peace, the stakes could not be higher. As Knight Ridder newspaper editor John Wolcott noted about the 2003 Iraq war, the question of whether to go to war is the most important decision a country must make (Buying the War 2007). It is incumbent upon journalists to ask the hard question: Is this really necessary?

The 2003 Iraq War provides strong evidence of the mediating influence of news media on public understanding and perception and illustrates the consequences of news media's failure to ask critical questions and seek verification of claims. Instead, many mainstream outlets supported the George W. Bush administration and its case for war without examining the evidence at hand (Bennett, Lawrence, and Livingston 2008). The effect was striking. Even as support for the war grew, nearly two-thirds of Americans held significant factual misperceptions regarding the case for war. One major survey (Kull, Clay, and Evan 2003) asked Americans about claims being made by Bush administration officials, including the assertions that (1) clear evidence existed that Saddam Hussein was working closely with Al Qaeda, (2) weapons of mass destruction had been found in Iraq, and (3) world public opinion favored the United States going to war with Iraq. All three of these claims were false, but 60 percent of Americans held at least one of these misperceptions. Not surprisingly, people who held these misperceptions were more likely to support the war effort.

The study also asked individuals about their preferred news source and found significant differences. At one end of the spectrum, only 23 percent of consumers of PBS and NPR held one or more misperceptions; 77 percent held none. One or more misperceptions were held by 47 percent of consumers of print media, 55 percent of NBC and CNN viewers, 61 percent of ABC viewers, 71 percent of CBS viewers, and 80 percent of Fox News viewers. This is only one study, and many variables affect public opinion. However, this study and others like it provide evidence that news can have a significant influence on accuracy of perceptions and the public consensus that emerges from those perceptions.

Since the 2003 Iraq War, many news outlets have acknowledged their failure to adequately scrutinize the administration's claims in support of the war. Notably, *The New York Times* second-guessed some of its own coverage in a 2004 editorial. While the *Times* defended much of its reporting as accurate and complete, it acknowledged that "we have found a number of instances of coverage that was not as rigorous as it should have been. In some cases, information that was controversial then, and seems questionable now, was insufficiently qualified or allowed to stand unchallenged. Looking back, we wish we had been more aggressive in re-examining the claims as new evidence emerged—or failed to emerge" (*The New York Times* 2004). The editorial went on to detail many of the claims that were not sufficiently challenged. The *Times* was not alone, as many major journalists and outlets have since admitted that their reporting on Iraq fell short.

It's good to see journalists holding themselves accountable, as this is one hallmark of quality journalism. It's also easy to be sympathetic considering the high levels of nationalism and desire for retaliation in the wake of the September 11, 2001, terrorist attack. At the same time, the challenging climate and high stakes are exactly why Americans require a strong, autonomous journalism that can ask difficult questions even in tough times. Consider that more than 4,000 American soldiers have died in Iraq since 2003, and more than 100,000 Iraqis are dead as a result of the conflict. The removal of Saddam Hussein created a vacuum of power that destabilized the region, led to a refugee crisis, and created conditions for the rise of the Islamic State. All of this could still have happened even with the toughest journalism imaginable, but perhaps a better informed American citizenry would have been better equipped to more carefully assess the case for war.

The challenges of war reporting go back many decades. News coverage of World War II is often thought of as a high-water mark as journalists faced few restrictions and had relatively open access to battlefields and sources. "In the handling of the press," recalled World War II general (and later president) Dwight Eisenhower, "the American practice was to provide every facility that would permit an individual to go wherever he wanted, whenever he wanted. While this imposed upon us some additional administrative burdens, it paid off in big dividends because of the conviction in the minds of all that there was no attempt to conceal error and stupidity" (Eisenhower 1997, 300–301). When it came to the Vietnam War in the 1960s, American reporters continued to have widespread access to the battlefield without direct military control. According to some, because reporters were free to cover the war as they saw fit, they ultimately were able to paint a picture of the futility of American involvement in the conflict, which helped to turn public opinion against the war effort and led to American withdrawal and defeat. On the other hand, in his book *The Uncensored War*, scholar Daniel Hallin (1989) details how the professional routines of journalism actually led reporters to paint a highly idealized and generally favorable picture of the war effort. Rather than operating from an "objective" viewpoint, reporters often presented themselves as patriots and described the war in terms of "our peace effort." Reporting only turned critical after elite opinion became divided and public opinion had already begun to sour. Hallin describes this period in terms of the "sphere of legitimate controversy," which, like indexing theory, suggests that journalism need only pay attention to the competing perspectives of elite opinion.

War reporting changed significantly after the Vietnam War. Regardless of its accuracy, the idea that the press "lost" the war for the United States led the military to change many of its policies toward the press. Reporters faced more stringent controls and more limited access. As a result, reporting relied much more heavily on official statements and became even less inclined to cover conflict from a neutral point of view. When the United States invaded the Caribbean island nation of Grenada in 1983, press access was restricted for days, until after the operation was over, and then a small group of reporters was given a tour by military officials. This "press pool" approach came to be the model for future conflicts, particularly the 1991 U.S. Persian Gulf War. Press access was severely restricted, and members of the press pool were taken to preapproved sites on tours controlled by the military. A similar approach was employed in the invasions of Afghanistan and Iraq in the early 2000s, and the practice of "embedding" reporters with certain troops became standard operating procedure as a way to control and limit press access.

It's important to note that military strategy must always account for the role of the press and must find a balance between the need to control information and support press freedom. Military strategists have a compelling need to limit information about troop movements and battlefield secrets. Traditionally, journalists have respected these needs, even working cooperatively with government officials to suppress or embargo reporting on sensitive information until it will no longer compromise the safety of American troops. At the same time, the American public requires a vibrant and critical journalism if they are to make informed decisions about the actions carried out in their name by their government. Finding the correct balance is tricky but vital.

FURTHER READING

Altschull, J. Herbert. 1995. *Agents of Power: The Media and Public Policy.* 2nd ed. White Plains, NY: Longman USA.

Bennett, W. Lance. 1990. "Toward a Theory of Press-State Relations in the United States." *Journal of Communication* 40 (2): 103–127. https://doi.org/10.1111/j.1460-2466.1990.tb02265.x.

Bennett, W. Lance. 2016. *News: The Politics of Illusion.* 10th ed. Chicago, IL; London: University of Chicago Press.

Bennett, W. Lance, Regina G. Lawrence, and Steven Livingston. 2008. *When the Press Fails: Political Power and the News Media from Iraq to Katrina.* Studies in Communication, Media, and Public Opinion. Chicago, IL: University of Chicago Press.

Buying the War: How Big Media Failed Us. 2007. *Bill Moyers Journal.* Accessed April 5, 2018. Video, 1:22. http://billmoyers.com/content/buying-the-war/.

Eisenhower, Dwight D. 1997. *Crusade in Europe.* Baltimore, MD: Johns Hopkins University Press.

Entman, Robert M. 2004. *Projections of Power: Framing News, Public Opinion, and U.S. Foreign Policy.* Studies in Communication, Media, and Public Opinion. Chicago, IL: University of Chicago Press.

Hallin, Daniel C. 1989. *The Uncensored War: The Media and Vietnam.* Berkeley: University of California Press.

Herman, Edward S., and Noam Chomsky. 2002. *Manufacturing Consent: The Political Economy of the Mass Media.* New York: Pantheon Books.

Kull, Steven, Ramsay Clay, and Lewis Evan. 2003. "Misperceptions, the Media, and the Iraq War." *Political Science Quarterly* 118 (4): 569–598. https://doi.org/10.1002/j.1538-165X.2003.tb00406.x.

The New York Times. 2004. "FROM THE EDITORS; The Times and Iraq." May 26, sec. World. https://www.nytimes.com/2004/05/26/world/from-the-editors-the-times-and-iraq.html.

7

The Future of Journalism

Journalism has faced incredible challenges in the first two decades of the 21st century, including lost revenue and declining public trust, forcing newsgathering organizations and journalists to reexamine their business models and their relationships with the public. Many of these challenges have been spurred or at least exacerbated by technology. Even in this time of change, however, journalism has persevered and provided individuals with vital news and information about issues and events of importance. Though journalism likely will continue to have a strong role in sustaining democracy, its future depends on responding to technology and other changes with both a willingness to adapt and a commitment to the public service mission of the profession. It will depend on the ability of citizens to become more savvy consumers of news and information, which will require widespread news and media literacy. It will also depend on future developments in communication law and policy, which will have indirect effects on the quality and quantity of journalism going forward.

Q35. IS AMERICAN JOURNALISM DYING?

Answer: No, it is not dying, although modern American journalism is suffering from a variety of ills and challenges that need to be addressed. Traditional journalism certainly has struggled in the 21st century due to economic, technological, and political transformations, but many excellent practitioners and news outlets continue to provide citizens with high-quality reporting. At the same time, the number of journalists doing this work has declined dramatically, and new challenges from the Internet demonstrate the need for support. New and emerging business models as well as public policy solutions can provide the support journalism needs to survive and thrive in democratic society. News and media literacy education also have a vital role to play in K–12 and higher education.

The Facts: American journalism has never been perfect, but it has played a major role in maintaining a viable democracy for more than two centuries. Today, Americans have never needed journalism more. As the world and daily life grow more complex, and as humanity faces growing challenges related to the stability of the planet, people need reliable information on which to base their individual decisions and to engage in successful policy making. Today, however, the press is weakened, embattled, and undermined by technological, economic, and political changes that have transformed how Americans communicate and learn about important events and issues. Many have asked whether journalism will survive this revolution. No one knows for sure, but many promising opportunities exist as temporary and permanent solutions to the crisis. These include new and emerging business models, nonprofit and philanthropic efforts, public policy solutions related to news subsidies and public and community media, and educational efforts in news and media literacy.

Nonprofits such as the Center for Investigative Reporting and *Mother Jones* have been producing investigative journalism for decades, but a variety of new nonprofit news outlets have emerged more recently, ranging from those with a national focus such as ProPublica and the Center for Public Integrity to those with a local or regional focus such as *MinnPost*, *The Texas Tribune*, and Voice of San Diego. Still others focus on specific issue areas such as The Marshall Project on criminal justice, Stateline on state policy, and InsideClimate News on environmental issues. Some of these outlets have also partnered with more traditional news media, as ProPublica has done with some 90 outlets, including *The New York Times* and NPR. These nonprofit outlets often rely on a mix of small individual contributions, private donors, foundations, and grants. These alternative funding sources can help insulate nonprofit news organizations from market pressures and profit motives, allowing them to provide valuable public service journalism that's freely available to all (Lewis 2007).

ProPublica, for example, has won several Pulitzer Prizes, including, in 2010, the first prize to go to an online-only publication, for an investigative story about a hospital's decision-making in the wake of Hurricane Katrina. ProPublica is based in New York City and is run by the former managing editor of *The Wall Street Journal*. It has a staff of 75 reporters who often receive quite generous salaries compared to pay at other major news outlets, which helps attract and retain talented journalists. Pro-Publica was started and is funded by billionaires at the Sandler Foundation and has also received contributions from the Knight Foundation, MacArthur Foundation, Pew Charitable Trusts, Ford Foundation, and the Carnegie Corporation. ProPublica's stated mission is to "expose abuses of power and betrayals of the public trust by government, business, and other institutions, using the moral force of investigative journalism to spur reform through the sustained spotlighting of wrongdoing" (ProPublica n.d.). Similar to other nonprofits, ProPublica is explicitly aimed at the kind of reporting that is quickly disappearing from many mainstream and for-profit news outlets as market pressures force cuts to in-depth reporting.

While nonprofit journalism offers a promising solution, some observers suggest caution. The main downsides are that these funding sources can be tenuous, unreliable, and difficult to acquire, and these outlets sometimes have a narrow focus with limited reach and impact (Pickard 2017). Media scholar Rodney Benson (2018) has studied nonprofits and found that, because foundations often require economic sustainability as well as civic impact, these outlets face market-oriented pressures that lead them to replicate traditional commercial news content or limit their reach to small, elite audiences. Benson suggests long-term funding with no strings attached will be necessary to reduce limitations currently faced by nonprofits.

Another approach puts a single (often billionaire) owner at the helm of a privately held news organization. Recent examples include the purchase of *The Washington Post* by Amazon owner Jeff Bezos, *The Boston Globe* by Boston Red Sox owner John Henry, and *The Las Vegas Review-Journal* by casino magnate Sheldon Adelson. There are definite pros to private ownership in the hands of wealthy, well-meaning "benevolent billionaires" who want to give back to society and can afford the kinds of losses that often accompany public service journalism. On the other hand, observers have expressed concerns about an "oligarchy media model" that puts enormous power in the hands of a few unaccountable owners who might not be as benevolent as consumers might hope and might allow their own political and economic interests to influence the operations and content of the news organizations they control (Benson and Pickard 2017).

Yet another new approach to energizing the field of journalism centers on the venture capitalists of Silicon Valley and their cash infusions into digital media start-up companies, such as Vox Media and BuzzFeed, which have received several hundred million dollars. This also applies to new

platforms such as Medium and Storyful. Often rooted in the latest technological innovations, these new enterprises are potentially well situated
to support journalism in new and existing forms. So far, venture-backed
news start-ups have generally preserved traditional journalistic practices,
although they do offer potential innovations ranging from algorithmic
personalization to technology-based news production (Usher 2017). As
usual, these new approaches require caution. Funding sources can influence news products in positive and negative ways, and the expectations of
returns on investment can replicate the same market pressures that have
limited the potential of journalism in the past.

A different approach to "saving" journalism can be found in public
policy solutions that rely on taxpayer funding, such as support for public and community media, and subsidies for existing news outlets. Public
funding for media is relatively paltry in the United States, with about
$1.35 per person each year, or 0.01 percent of the federal budget, going
to the Corporation for Public Broadcasting, which disseminates funds to
PBS and NPR. Virtually all other developed nations outspend the United
States by large amounts in this area. Some argue that media of any kind
deserves no special treatment or funding and that it is best left to markets to produce what Americans want and need. On the other hand, not
only does the press specifically receive constitutional protection under
the First Amendment, but news media is also instrumental in maintaining
a citizenry capable of self-governance. Proponents of public funding for
journalism also argue that the United States actually has a long history
of subsidizing the press, including printing contracts and postal subsidies
dating back to the early 1800s, due to the important role it plays in democratic society (McChesney and Nichols 2010). "Market failure" is the
term used by scholars to describe any situation where private business
is unable to produce a sufficient quality or quantity of a good or service
humans need. Products that can't be adequately produced by markets are
often thought of as "public goods," such as national defense, fire and police
services, postal delivery, and environmental goods such as clean air and
water. In these cases, the government intervenes and creates policies and
subsidies to ensure the delivery of these goods. Many journalism scholars
and other supporters believe news and information should be considered
a public good because of the inability of markets to meet the needs of the
public in this area. Thus, government funding for public and community
media can play a role in strengthening the news media landscape.

Some argue in response that the First Amendment prevents the government from playing such a role in journalism and that government
interference—even if designed to provide support for news—violates

the notion of a free press. However, the case is often made that the First Amendment does not prohibit positive or affirmative involvement by government. For example, in the 1945 case *Associated Press v. United States*, the Court ruled against the Associated Press due to restrictions placed on access to the news wire service that the Court deemed in violation of the Sherman Anti-Trust Act. This precedent not only supports the idea that the government is empowered to break up media monopolies, but it also suggests a role for government in encouraging a greater flow of diverse information through policies and subsidies. In the Court's opinion, Justice Black wrote that it "would be strange indeed however if the grave concern for freedom of the press which prompted adoption of the First Amendment should be read as a command that the government was without power to protect that freedom. . . . That Amendment rests on the assumption that the widest possible dissemination of information from diverse and antagonistic sources is essential to the welfare of the public, that a free press is a condition of a free society" (*Associated Press v. United States* 1945).

Another important point is that any nation's media system is not an inevitable or immutable thing; rather, it is constructed through elaborate laws and policies ranging from the assignment of broadcast licenses to terms of copyright. That is to say, the government is always involved. As legal scholar Cass Sunstein (2007, 219) writes: "The question is not whether we will regulate speech, but how—and in particular how we can do so while promoting the values associated with a system of free expression, emphatically including democratic self-government." A number of potential policy solutions have been proposed, ranging from increased funding for public and community media to a public tax credit that citizens could assign to the nonprofit news outlet of their choice (McChesney and Pickard 2011). Such solutions will always be controversial, and it's unlikely that major public funding for any kind of American journalism will become a reality in the near future. However, Americans maintain that public media is a good investment; as the information landscape grows ever messier, a public policy solution could have greater appeal.

One more way to boost quality journalism deals with the demand side rather than the supply side: the education of news audiences through news and media literacy education. "Media literacy" is the umbrella term used for a range of educational interventions that promote critical analysis of media content, industries, and effects (Potter 2016). News literacy is a subfield that focuses more narrowly on news and information content but can also include learning about news production, distribution, and consumption, including the cognitive biases that humans bring to their reading and viewing of news. Some form of media education has been around for at least a century, beginning with the emergence of film in the 1920s as some educators became concerned that viewers would have difficulty separating representations from reality. Today, media literacy is taught around the world and is better established in other developed nations, many of which have instituted media education as part of required K–12 curriculum. The United States lags behind these nations and has yet to formalize media literacy in any concrete way. Instead, media literacy receives a smattering of inconsistent attention in American schools. A few states have introduced and passed legislation to incorporate media literacy education into their K–12 curriculum, but these cases remain the exceptions. Instead, media literacy makes its way to students through less formal channels offered by teachers, librarians, administrators, community leaders, scholars, and journalists.

Since the rise of the misinformation age, and especially in the wake of the 2016 presidential election, many stakeholders have expressed growing concerns that American citizens are not equipped with the skills they need to tell the difference between accurate, reliable information and misinformation; fake news; conspiracy theories; and lies. Educating students and citizens is a promising way to help them analyze news content as well as the contexts in which it is produced and distributed, including the market forces that constrain news content and the technologies and algorithms that customize a web user's information bubble. This is no simple or quick fix, but many recommendations have been made to help spread these important educational interventions. These include support for community-level digital and media literacy initiatives, partnerships for teacher education, development of assessment measures, and increasing visibility of media literacy through public service announcements and conferences (Hobbs 2010). While American journalism faces an uncertain future, American citizens certainly will need to be well educated to navigate the increasingly murky waters of the media landscape.

FURTHER READING

Anderson, C. W., Leonard Downie, and Michael Schudson. 2016. *The News Media: What Everyone Needs to Know.* New York: Oxford University Press.

Associated Press v. United States. 1945. 326 U.S. 1.

Benson, Rodney. 2018. "Can Foundations Solve the Journalism Crisis?" *Journalism* 19 (8): 1059–1077. https://doi.org/10.1177/1464884917724612.

Benson, Rodney, and Victor Pickard. 2017. "The Slippery Slope of the Oligarchy Media Model." *The Conversation*. http://theconversation .com/the-slippery-slope-of-the-oligarchy-media-model-81931.

Hobbs, Renee. 2010. "Digital and Media Literacy: A Plan of Action." The Aspen Institute. https://knightfoundation.org/reports/digital-and-media-literacy-plan-action.

Lewis, Charles. 2007. "The Nonprofit Road." *Columbia Journalism Review*. https://www.cjr.org/feature/the_nonprofit_road.php.

McChesney, Robert, and John Nichols. 2010. *The Death and Life of American Journalism: The Media Revolution That Will Begin the World Again*. Philadelphia, PA: Nation Books.

McChesney, Robert W., and Victor W. Pickard (Eds.). 2011. *Will the Last Reporter Please Turn Out the Lights: The Collapse of Journalism and What Can Be Done to Fix It*. New York: New Press.

Pickard, Victor. 2017. "Can Charity Save Journalism from Market Failure?" *The Conversation*. http://theconversation.com/can-charity-save-journalism-from-market-failure-75833.

Potter, W. James. 2016. *Media Literacy*. 8th ed. Los Angeles: SAGE.

ProPublica. n.d. "About Us." Accessed April 13, 2018. https://www .propublica.org/about/.

Shafer, Jack, and Ben Mathis-Lilley. 2007. "What Do Herbert and Marion Sandler Want?" *Slate*, October 15. http://www.slate.com/articles/ news_and_politics/press_box/2007/10/what_do_herbert_and_marion_ sandler_want.html.

Sunstein, Cass R. 2007. *Republic.Com 2.0*. Princeton, NJ: Princeton University Press.

Usher, Nikki. 2017. "Venture-Backed News Startups and the Field of Journalism." *Digital Journalism* 5 (9): 1116–1133. https://doi.org/10.1080/ 21670811.2016.1272064.

Q36. WILL TECHNOLOGICAL CHANGES CONTINUE TO INFLUENCE HOW JOURNALISM IS PRACTICED?

Answer: Yes. Technology will continue to affect journalism as it has in the digital age, disrupting news habits and commercial news business models. Technology has provided significant benefits to both journalists and consumers, who have greater, easier, and more instantaneous access to more news and public information than ever before. Nonetheless, news media organizations will continue to face challenges, such as increased competition, decreased control over distribution mechanisms, and new technologies such as automation that threaten to radically change the nature of newsgathering and reporting. These issues, along with those pertaining to how technology and media content industries will intersect in the future, will inform how each industry performs and what consumers and citizens come to expect from journalism.

The Facts: Though technology's influence on journalism seems especially challenging today, technological innovation and invention have for much of the history of mass communication actually aided journalists' ability to report the news and distribute it for public consumption. The invention of the printing press led to the invention of newspapers. The telegraph and telephone allowed reporting from far-off places to be shared more easily and quickly. The development of radio and television allowed for breaking news to be reported and shared with audiences in real time. Each of these technologies influenced journalism in significant ways, just as the Internet and digital technology are doing today. Journalism scholar John Pavlik (2000, 2001) suggests that technology shapes journalism in at least four areas: (1) the routines and work practices of journalists, (2) the news content itself, (3) the structure of news organizations and newsrooms, and (4) the relationship between and among news organizations and the various institutions they interact with and the audiences they serve. This provides a useful framework for charting recent changes and considering other developments that may continue to influence journalism.

Many scholars suggest that journalistic work routines are one of the most consequential sources of influence on journalistic work product (Schudson 2011). In other words, the day-to-day habits of journalists—the sources they call, the structure in which a story is constructed and told, the increasingly compressed time in which they have to complete the stories, and so on—often unintentionally shape stories. Technology has indeed changed the nature of journalistic work. Since the development and widespread use of the Internet in the middle to late 1990s, journalists have increasingly relied on new innovations for both reporting and storytelling. Many news organizations actually mandate more use of such technologies. Social media has had a tremendous impact on journalistic routines. Many journalists say that social media has enhanced the ability for them to do their jobs, for example, by having more and sometimes better access to sources and greater ability to interact with audiences. According to a 2013 survey of American journalists, about 75 percent said they use social media in their daily work, with about 80 percent of those who use it saying it's at least somewhat important to their jobs (Willnat, Weaver, and Wilhoit 2017). According to the survey, most journalists used it, however, to consume news ("check for breaking news," 78.5 percent; "check what others are reporting," 73.1 percent), while fewer used it for original reporting purposes ("find sources," 54.1 percent; "verify information," 24.7 percent; "find additional information," 56.2 percent). About 60 percent said they use it to keep in contact with their audiences, and 47 percent said they use it to "monitor discussions." While 80 percent agreed that social media allows them to promote their work more and 69 percent agreed that it helps them engage with audiences more, less than half (48.9 percent) said that it has helped them "communicate better with people relevant" to their work. Even fewer agreed that social media increased their credibility as a journalist (29.7 percent) and made them more productive (25 percent). These findings suggest that while social media has had positive influences on individual journalists' routines and practices, there are some challenges that remain in how journalists see the value of such technology. Many journalism scholars and professional journalism leaders (e.g., Singer 2011; Spyridou et al. 2013) have suggested that journalism needs to embrace social media, especially in making journalistic practice more like a conversation among journalists and various stakeholders and audiences.

Other technological innovations, such as smartphones and computer applications that allow for easy multimedia production, have contributed to changes in journalistic routines that focus on not just reporting a story but also producing content across platforms and formats. The research, writing, communication, video shooting and editing, and photography work that can be done on a smartphone today would have taken thousands of dollars' worth of equipment in the 1990s and 2000s but can now be replaced with one device that costs hundreds. One 2012 survey of American newspaper reporters found that 76 percent owned and used a smartphone; about half of journalists (48 percent) said their employers required or strongly encouraged having smartphones (Molyneux 2014). Most (72 percent) said smartphones improved their work, but many (35 percent) said it helped make them feel like they are "always on call or never free from work."

Social and mobile media has significantly influenced, and certainly will continue to influence, the jobs and routines of journalists. Just as automation and artificial technology have influenced other fields, it's likely that these technologies will impact journalism. In fact, they already have. For example, *The Los Angeles Times* uses computer programs to write basic news stories about earthquakes and homicides, and the Associated Press has used them to write data-driven sports and corporate earnings report stories. Some futurists and artificial intelligence (AI) researchers conceive of a time when AI has the ability to be creative, essentially mirroring human mental processes to reason, think abstractly, and even invent. But even the most advanced algorithms today constitute what researchers call "narrow AI" or "weak AI," which are able to perform specific tasks within a limited context, such as predicting weather, looking for insights and patterns in databases, and recognizing faces in an image.

Scholar Noam Lemelshtrich Latar (2018) suggests that some of these AI limitations present opportunities for journalists. For example, AI has a hard time understanding or expressing human emotion. It also lacks the ability to be as creative as humans and to make connections not previously experienced. Also, even though AI has made advancements in understanding human natural language, it's limited in its ability to understand metaphors and humor, for example, making writing stories with depth, richness, and empathy difficult. Latar and other scholars suggest that human journalists must "think different," looking for new ways to tell stories and using AI as a tool to improve the more complex journalism only humans can produce. Journalists seem to understand this. One study analyzed journalists' blog posts and newspapers articles about the development of AI technologies and found that they saw AI tools as aiding journalists and providing potential opportunity, such as by allowing AI to do routine stories and other tasks, thereby freeing up journalists to focus on nonroutine and in-depth stories (van Dalen 2012). It can also help journalists do their jobs by sorting through large sets of data to find trends or to help journalists with better research and easier fact-checking. For instance, BuzzFeed News used machine learning to find spy planes by analyzing flight tracking data, and ProPublica used it to analyze what topics are most important to members of Congress by analyzing hundreds of thousands of press releases. *The New York Times* and Reuters are developing tools that will provide journalists with real-time research and contextual information about topics as they type stories. In a report written partially by AI technology discussing how newsrooms should respond in the age of "augmented journalism," the Associated Press said, "Streamlining workflows, taking out grunt work, crunching more data, digging out insights and generating additional outputs are just a few of the mega-wins that have resulted from putting smart machines to work in the service of AP's journalism" (Marconi, Siegman, and Machine Journalist 2017, 1). Though AI is limited, scholars suggest that journalists should continue to monitor and adapt to the use of AI in newsrooms (Latar 2018) and that citizens and journalists alike should consider how "automated journalism" may influence the very definition of newswork and journalistic authority (Carlson 2015).

In addition to journalistic work routines, technology has and will continue to have an impact on the content of journalism. The idea that technology is a driver of the content is reminiscent of the ideas of scholars like Marshall McLuhan, who coined the phrase "the medium is the message," and Neil Postman, who argued that the way cultures process and prioritize ideas and information is largely a function of the medium that carries those messages. Though this theory of "technological determinism" has been criticized by other scholars for its simplicity and overvaluation of the role of technology in cultural development, the way social media technologies, in particular, have developed in the past decade have had tremendous impact on journalism.

Though platforms rarely exert direct editorial control over what a publisher chooses to publish, platforms do build the closed platforms that increasingly host the content, and they build the algorithms that serve that content to users. With newspapers and TV, for example, media companies controlled both the creation and dissemination of content. Now, either the news content lives on a media company's website but gets a significant amount of traffic from social media and search engines, or the news content is published "natively" to a social media platform like Facebook Instant Articles, Facebook Live Video, and Snapchat Stories, to name a few. According to a report from the Tow Center for Digital Journalism, about 48 percent of all social media posts published by 14 large publishers in a sample week in February 2017 were native to the social media platform. That means that a reader could interact with a *Washington Post* article without ever leaving Facebook or going to *The Washington Post* website because of the platform's Instant Articles tool. Social media platforms controlling the form of the content can dictate certain aspects of the content itself. For instance, Facebook's Mark Zuckerberg has said that by 2020, a majority of content on the platform will be video. Such a plan puts pressure on news organizations that use the service to produce more video, a costly endeavor and one that can lead to a "visual bias," or an unintended focus on content that makes good video over other important stories that might be less visually appealing or harder to tell via the medium. "Publishers are making micro-adjustments on every story to achieve a better fit or better performance on each social outlet," said scholars Emily Bell and Taylor Owen (2017, 39) in their Tow Center report. They note the importance of audience strategists and social media editors in shaping content, reporting that one editor told them that "if their audience team doesn't think a story will perform, it may not be assigned."

Finally, technology influences both journalism organizations themselves and the way they interact with other organizations. According to

Bell and Owen, journalism has gone through two waves of recent technological change, the first being the move to simply replicate traditional storytelling online in the late 1990s and early 2000s, and the second being the move toward widespread multimedia storytelling and Web 2.0 interactive technologies in the mid-2000s to the early 2010s (Bell and Owen 2017). Many journalists were skeptical of early moves online, but the second wave brought exciting new storytelling tools and widespread experimentation in newsrooms across the industry. It led to the creation of new roles in newsrooms that converged media across typical newspaper, television, and radio lines—web writers were employed at TV stations and video producers were employed by newspapers, for example. However, that time also brought significant structural changes that came about in part because of financial challenges. Newspapers especially, and to a lesser extent television, have been challenged by more competition for advertisers' dollars. Newspapers were uniquely affected by the steep decline in classified advertising as a result of sites like Craigslist and because of poorly timed debt acquisitions. The financial challenges, in large part, have pushed many newsrooms to significantly reduce reporting staffs while at the same time continuing to push those journalists who remain to do more with fewer resources. It has also pushed newsrooms to adjust staffing in other ways, refocusing on positions and reporting beats that are more likely to attract online audiences. Individual reporters sometimes have the ability and expectation to produce and publish content quickly, sometimes with more limited editorial oversight. In both exciting and challenging ways, technology has and will continue to push newsrooms to change their own organizational structures and workflows.

These first two "waves" of recent technological innovation were major shifts to the news industry to be sure, especially the second, but some saw the breakdown of traditional media organizations' tight control over both content creation and distribution to be positive, especially given the open nature of the Internet. However, in this "third wave," which started in the early 2010s and continues today, the promises of openness and transparency in journalism are challenged by the increasing use of and reliance on a small set of companies, especially social media companies, that create relatively closed platforms where citizens spend most of their online lives. "The principles of the open web, which held promise for citizens and journalists alike, have given way to an ecosystem dominated by a small number of platform companies who hold tremendous influence over what we see and know," said scholars Bell and Owen (2017). Indeed, now and in the foreseeable future, the relationship between newsgathering organizations and the large platforms that control access to audiences will continue to be of special importance in understanding the role of technology in journalism and journalism in society.

Scholars and journalism experts have posed a number of important questions that journalism and technology industries as well as the general public will have to struggle with. Chief among them are the questions, what is a media company and what is a tech company? Traditionally, technology companies, even those that house content such as Facebook, have clearly asserted that they are not media companies or publishers. They've done this for good reasons, such as the benefits of being more appealing to investors as a tech company as opposed to a media company and because tech companies are afforded special legal protections, such as Section 230 of the Communications Decency Act of 1996, which gives platforms broad immunity from liability for what their users post (Napoli and Caplan 2017).

Supporters argue that this distinction is appropriate for many tech companies, in part because without protections like Section 230, platforms would be forced to be more heavy-handed in censoring user content. However, many scholars and analysts have criticized social media platforms in particular, because while they claim to be technology companies, they increasingly function like media companies or publishers. There's starting to be some recognition of this fact. Facebook, for example, has traditionally defined itself as a technology company, with Zuckerberg saying in congressional testimony in April 2018 that "I consider us to be a technology company, because the primary thing that we do is have engineers who write code and build products and services for other people." However, in the same hearing, which focused in part on the role Facebook played in spreading misinformation during the 2016 U.S. presidential election, Zuckerberg went on to say that the company does bear some responsibility for the content its users share. What does that mean for the future? Certainly it means that the roles and expectations of media companies and publishers and technology companies and platforms will continue to be debated as policy makers look at potential regulations and as those within and outside media and technology organizations work out what they believe the expectations are for each. Wherever the debate leads will have implications for journalism and its role in society.

FURTHER READING

Bell, Emily, and Taylor Owen. 2017. *The Platform Press: How Silicon Valley Reengineered Journalism*. New York: Tow Center for Digital Journalism. https://towcenter.org/research/the-platform-press-how-silicon-valley-reengineered-journalism/.

Carlson, Matt. 2015. "The Robotic Reporter: Automated Journalism and the Redefinition of Labor, Compositional Forms, and Journalistic Authority." *Digital Journalism* 3 (3): 416–431. doi:10.1080/21670811 .2014.976412.

Latar, Noam Lemelshtrich. 2018. *Robot Journalism: Can Human Journalism Survive?* Hackensack, NJ: World Scientific Publishing Co. Pte. Ltd.

Marconi, Francesco, Alex Siegman, and Machine Journalist. 2017. *The Future of Augmented Journalism: A Guide for Newsrooms in the Age of Smart Machines*. New York: The Associated Press. https://insights.ap.org/ uploads/images/the-future-of-augmented-journalism_ap-report.pdf.

Molyneux, Logan. 2014. "Reporters' Smartphone Use Improved Quality of Work." *Newspaper Research Journal* 35 (4): 83–97. doi:10.1177/ 073953291403500407.

Napoli, Philip, and Robyn Caplan. 2017. "Why Media Companies Insist They're Not Media Companies, Why They're Wrong, and Why It Matters." *First Monday* 22 (5). http://firstmonday.org/ojs/index.php/fm/ article/view/7051/6124.

Pavlik, John. 2000. "The Impact of Technology on Journalism." *Journalism Studies* 1 (2): 229–237. doi:10.1080/14616700050028226.

Pavlik, John. 2001. *Journalism and New Media*. New York: Columbia University Press.

Schudson, Michael. 2011. *The Sociology of News*. New York: W. W. Norton & Company.

Singer, Jane. 2011. "Journalism and Digital Technologies." In *Changing the News: The Forces Shaping Journalism in Uncertain Times*, edited by Wilson Lowrey and Peter J. Gade, 213–229. New York: Routledge.

Spyridou, Lia-Paschalia, Maria Matsiola, Andreas Veglis, George Kalliris, and Charalambos Dimoulas. 2013. "Journalism in a State of Flux: Journalists as Agents of Technology Innovation and Emerging News Practices." *International Communication Gazette* 75 (1): 76–98. doi:10.1177/1748048512461763.

van Dalen, Arjen. 2012. "The Algorithms behind the Headlines: How Machine-Written News Redefines the Core Skills of Human Journalists." *Journalism Practice* 6 (5–6): 648–658. doi:10.1080/17512786.201 2.667268.

Willnat, Lars, David H. Weaver, and G. Cleveland Wilhoit. 2017. *The American Journalist in the Digital Age: A Half-Century Perspective*. New York: Peter Lang Publishing.

Q37. WILL JOURNALISM PLAY A SIGNIFICANT ROLE IN THE FUTURE OF AMERICAN DEMOCRACY?

Answer: Yes, but the extent of its influence will depend on how the broader information ecosystem is structured, how citizens view the role of the news media, and how journalism itself is practiced. Since the founding of the United States, journalism has been a primary vehicle for the production of accurate, verifiable information that citizens need, and this is not likely to change. But this is a time of information abundance, where overwhelming amounts of information—true and false—can be spread quickly, widely, and easily. Journalism and many other social and democratic institutions currently suffer from low public trust and confidence, and citizens often feel so overwhelmed by the prospect of having to fact-check and question everything they see or hear that they simply disengage from participatory democracy. Though that's a challenging backdrop for journalism to survive, much less thrive, it is possible so long as news organizations and related information professions don't ignore this context and instead adapt to it by reimagining underlying structures.

The Facts: Since even the early days of the American colonies, journalism has played a role in informing citizens and holding people and institutions accountable, from relaying news about unsuccessful military expeditions in 1690 in the colonies' first newspaper, *Publick Occurrences*; to Nellie Bly's exposé in 1887 of the conditions of New York mental hospitals; to the publication in 1971 of the Pentagon Papers, which documented government deceptions about the Vietnam War; to *The Washington Post's* work in 2018 in revealing past sexual harassment allegations against Roy Moore, a U.S. Senate candidate in Alabama. But during all these periods, journalism has faced challenges. *Publick Occurrences* was published only once because the colonial government shut it down. Newspapers were able to publish the Pentagon Papers but not before weathering an unsuccessful attempt by the Nixon administration to suppress the release of the information. Journalism continues to face challenges. Some scholars and journalists say the most recent challenges are indeed existential; they question whether journalism will survive. Many also question what role journalism will play in democracy and civil society as America moves deeper into the 21st century. More broadly, many question what role truthful, verifiable information and facts will play in a democracy when citizens find it increasingly difficult to differentiate accurate, fact-based sources of news information, which they need to fully engage in democracy, from sources that traffic in falsehoods, distortions, or sensationalistic content.

This begs the question, then: Can the broken information ecosystem adapt to meet positive, prodemocracy, prosocial goals? Experts are split on the prospects. The Pew Research Center in 2017 (Anderson and Rainie 2017) asked more than 1,100 Internet research scientists; business leaders; journalists; policy makers; and other information, communication, and technology experts the following question: "In the next 10 years, will trusted methods emerge to block false narratives and allow the most accurate information to prevail in the overall information ecosystem? Or will the quality and veracity of information online deteriorate due to the spread of unreliable, sometimes even dangerous, socially destabilizing ideas?" Just over half (51 percent) of respondents said that things will not improve. Some indicated that the mere fact that the new ecosystem allows for vastly more people to be involved means more problems, allowing humans as well as artificial intelligence to spread false narratives easily. Others said it's a problem with human nature—that people are selfish and tribal by nature and saddled with brains that are not wired to contend with the current pace of technological change. A major theme highlighted the economic drivers of the media ecosystem, with one expert saying that "when there is value in misinformation, it will rule" (11). Many believe that there will be quality information from reliable sources, and a small segment of the population will use it and even pay for it, but everywhere else, "chaos will reign" (14).

The other half of the experts that Pew surveyed on the future of the media ecosystem were hopeful. Some suggested technology helped create the problems, but it can also be the source of many solutions. For example, a professor of informatics and computing who focuses on creating technology to detect false narratives suggested that social media algorithms can be developed that incorporate journalistic ethics, in ways similar to how e-mail spam filters are made. Others have suggested that social media companies will be a part of the solution because they have not only ethical but also some economic and market pressure to provide trusted, verified information. That economic pressure may be increasing with additional recent scrutiny over the prevalence of fake news on social media platforms.

Others suggested regulatory remedies to address the proliferation of "fake news." For example, if social media companies are more legally liable for the content on their platforms, they may be more mindful of its veracity and effects. Some suggest regulatory remedies will come because of a growing skepticism that private technology companies can be trusted with the important public role of safeguarding our media and digital ecosystems. Other hopefuls suggest that human nature—a source of the problem rather than solution for many of those who are less optimistic about the information ecosystem's future—will play a role in pushing us together to solve the problem. Some suggest consumers who become "fed up with false narratives" (25) will demand more trusted sources and ways to more easily assess the veracity of information and the credibility of a source. "We were in this position before, when printing presses broke the existing system of information management," noted one researcher at a large U.S.-based technology company. "A new system emerged and I believe we have the motivation and capability to do it again" (27).

Still others say that technology alone will not be able to solve the problem. They point to a need to redesign how our news media ecosystem is funded. Right now, the U.S. system is mostly commercial, often with large, corporate interests far removed from community and journalistic missions that influence the fate of newsrooms and their ability to produce quality journalism. A retired Harvard social policy professor told the Pew survey that advertising money, the primary source of revenue for newspapers and other news media companies for more than a century, is "drying up" and will be unlikely to find an easy replacement (31). Another expert said the current state of media should be "a wake up call to the news industry, policy makers, and journalists to refine the system of news production" (31). Many call for significant increases in public funding of news media, viewing commercial revenue sources like advertising as likely to produce economic and not necessarily democratic ends. Experts also indicate that a key strategy for the future of American journalism is to place a greater societal focus on information and media literacy. In fact, one Pew survey participant said the current information ecosystem is made worse by tech but actually is caused by a "perfect storm of poor civics knowledge and poor information literacy skills" (33). A public policy and digital government scholar surveyed said the spread of fake news is in large part due to "whether or not people exercise critical thinking and information-literacy skills," (33) suggesting that these skills need to become fundamental competencies in our educational systems. Together with technological innovation, it may be that these public funding and educational solutions "tip the balance toward a better information environment," as one scholar surveyed by Pew suggested (27).

Whether through technology or policy innovation in the way media is funded and citizens are educated, some thought leaders believe there is a path forward. Journalism can and should be involved in and encourage the development of these solutions that could improve the overall information ecosystem in which journalism operates. More important, the profession must also reexamine some of its practices and routines to ensure it is continually operating in the public interest and is strong enough to play the role it needs to play in democratic civil society. To examine what it needs to do, it's useful to understand the underlying reasons journalism is in its current weakened position.

Scholars Ed Madison and Ben DeJarnette (2018) say that "journalism has become a dirty word" for six primary reasons. First, journalism has a diminished gatekeeping role. Before the Internet, newsgathering organizations had very little competition, especially during most of the 20th century, which meant that journalists played a large role in determining the information that proceeded through the gates and was reported to the public. But the Internet has torn down those gates, and new mechanisms for controlling the information, such as social media sites, don't share the same values of news organizations in their commitment to informing the public. Second, they say journalism has "lost its teeth" and its willingness to publish important yet controversial material, especially in those newsrooms that face economic challenges, intense competition, and corporate owners that focus more on profits than mission. They cite as examples the largely uncritical lead-up to the Iraq War in the early 2000s and the unedited, non-fact-checked speeches by Donald Trump that TV and cable news aired throughout the 2016 Republican primaries. About the latter example, Madison and DeJarnette quoted Les Moonves, CEO of CBS, who said of such coverage that it "may not be good for America, but it's damn good for CBS." Third, they cite the lost momentum of the journalism reform movement of the late 1980s and most of the 1990s. This "public journalism" movement emphasized journalism as an active part of the democratic process that was meant to provide explanation and analysis of the effect of public policy proposals, doing so not in a neutral way but as a fully invested member of the community who wants it to succeed. Fourth, traditional media has had trouble attracting younger audiences. Though some critics say that younger generations are disengaged, others suggest that younger generations simply consume news in ways that are different from older generations. Fifth, local journalism has less power than it once did. In the days of family ownership of local newspapers, for example, publishers were members of their communities and therefore were invested in them, sometimes making decisions with negative, short-term economic consequences but positive, longer-term benefits for the state of the community, the credibility of the paper, and audience loyalty. Increasingly, however, local news organizations are owned and operated by conglomerates that prioritize shareholders who expect quarter-over-quarter profits. Madison and DeJarnette's sixth and final reason for journalism's decline is its relationship with politics. Though contentious and adversarial relationships have always existed between journalists and those in power, they contend that the relationship has become downright disrespectful and vitriolic, including politicians sidestepping journalists completely, claiming they report "fake news," and vilifying them by claiming, as President Trump has done, that most journalists are "dishonest" and "enemies of the people."

Some of these ailments could be addressed by implementing some of the overarching technological and public policy suggestions made by the scholars surveyed by Pew, mentioned earlier. For example, algorithms and other technology may provide some ability to reconstruct torn-down gates, though it will need to be developed with a clear goal of weeding out false narratives and not promoting viral yet untrue information. Additionally, a reliance on public funding rather than advertising as a primary source of operating revenue might relieve the pressure on publishers and media leaders to show large profits, which has had the effect of developing fiercely partisan (and often popular and inexpensive) content at the expense of in-depth coverage of important public issues. Media and information literacy might help develop news media consumption habits among young people who may continue those habits throughout their lives.

Of course, these solutions could help journalism survive and thrive, and certainly journalism should play a major role in developing them. But there are some changes journalism can make itself. For example, digital media has pushed journalists to try new storytelling tools, but most content is still published in the same old story forms, using the same routines that the industry used before the Internet. As one analysis pointed out, "Rather than disengaging from civic life, it appears millennials may actually be turning off David Muir to start watching John Oliver, Trevor Noah, and Samantha Bee; ditching the Sunday sports section for *The Ringer*, *The Undefeated*, and *Bleacher Report*; trading in newspaper opinion columns for essays on *Salon* and *Slate*; and replacing 1,500-word business stories from the *Wall Street Journal* with a series of 20-word bursts texted to their phones by *Quartz*" (Madison and DeJarnette 2018, 19). Simply put, journalists can rethink how they engage with their audiences, keeping in mind that one method of content delivery does not necessarily serve or reach all audiences.

Journalism can also continue to engage with the public in ways that are supportive of democracy. Some observers assert that journalists should see themselves as part of the communities they serve rather than fiercely independent individuals who only cover others' stories. Though this organized strategy originated in the late 1980s and throughout the 1990s under the banners of "public journalism" and "civic journalism," it lost its momentum in part because of the digital media transition pulling away the profession's attention. It also lost momentum because few newsroom leaders endorsed its principles, which required a reconceptualization of traditional principles like journalistic independence. Up until the last decade or so, newsroom leaders were able to ignore calls for reimagining the relationships between journalists and the public. The pre-social media, pre-mobile publishing, pre-Internet days meant that traditional news organizations had little competition and therefore little external pressure to change. Scholars Pablo J. Boczkowski and Seth C. Lewis (2018, 177) suggest this caused a "self-centeredness" among journalism leaders and journalists, "a decades-long conviction about the inherent value of journalism in society and an assumption that exploring new relationships was unnecessary if not even detrimental." They suggest the solution is a "relational journalism" that moves away from a one-way, journalist-to-audience transfer of information to a networked environment where journalists work together across news organizations to collaborate for the public good; where journalists work "in the open" and involve various stakeholders, including the audience, in the reporting and storytelling process; and where journalists engage in initiatives created explicitly for the purpose of listening to the public to ensure journalism is serving its communities. Indeed, this is an evolution of "public journalism" and similar movements, and continuing in that evolution may prove valuable to journalism going forward.

Finally, journalists can do a better job explaining to people what it is they do and showing the public the value of their work. News literacy tools delivered in educational settings could help in this regard—especially lessons that focus on explaining what journalists do, how and why they do it, and how broader news and information ecosystems work. But journalists themselves can also play a role in educating the broader public and explaining their work. The Trusting News Project, an initiative of the Reynolds Journalism Institute, works with individual newsrooms to develop strategies to help them build and maintain audience trust and credibility. In 2016, they asked local newsroom partners to interview community members about the relationship the local newspaper had with the community, but many of those interviewed would quickly jump to evaluations of national news media's coverage, especially about politics. "They wanted to talk about 'the media,'" wrote Joy Mayer (2018), director of the project. "They weren't thinking about the person they were eyeball to eyeball with." Mayer wrote that newsrooms, especially local ones, must tell "a consistent, repetitive story about what motivates our work, the range of information and stories we offer, who we are, how we operate, and how people can reach us." Others have suggested that journalists should show the public when their reporting efforts, especially the investigative ones, result in positive social effects, like reducing government waste (e.g., Newton 2013).

Indeed, journalism's role in the future of American democracy is not a given; it will take work on the part of journalists; the public; and political, business, education, technology, and other leaders to adapt and change our information ecosystem to address myriad concerns. But it's possible that responding to these challenges will help reinvent and sustain American journalism—and thereby help ensure the survival of American democracy.

FURTHER READING

Anderson, Janna, and Lee Rainie. 2017. *The Future of Truth and Misinformation Online*. Washington, DC: Pew Research Center. http://www.pewinternet.org/2017/10/19/the-future-of-truth-and-misinformation-online/.

Boczkowski, Pablo J., and Seth C. Lewis. 2018. "The Center of the Universe No More: From the Self-Centered Stance of the Past to the Relational Mindset of the Future." In *Trump and the Media*, edited by Pablo J. Boczkowski and Zizi Papacharissi, 177–185. Cambridge, MA: MIT Press.

Madison, Ed, and Ben DeJarnette. 2018. *Reimagining Journalism in a Post-Truth World: How Late-Night Comedians, Internet Trolls, and Savvy Reporters Are Transforming News*. Santa Barbara, CA: Praeger.

Mayer, Joy. 2018. "A More Nuanced Understanding of 'Journalism' Is Desperately Needed—and We Need Our Communities' Help." *Poynter* (blog). June 29, 2018. https://www.poynter.org/news/more-nuanced-understanding-journalism-desperately-needed-and-we-need-our-communities-help.

Newton, Eric. 2013. "If Investigative Journalists Don't Explain Why Their Work Matters, Who Will?" *Searchlights and Sunglasses: Field Notes from the Digital Age of Journalism*. Accessed June 30, 2018. http://www.searchlightsandsunglasses.org/if-investigative-journalists-dont-explain-why-their-work-matters-who-will/.

Index

About the Authors

Seth Ashley, PhD, is an associate professor of journalism and media studies at Boise State University. His research on media literacy, media sociology, and communication policy has been published in a range of peer-reviewed outlets, including the *Journal of Media Literacy Education; Communication Law and Policy; Journalism & Mass Communication Educator; Communication and the Public; Media, War & Conflict*; and the *Journal of Broadcasting & Electronic Media*. Ashley earned his PhD and MA at the University of Missouri School of Journalism. He has worked as a writer and editor for newspapers and magazines as well as a designer and technician for film, theater, and music.

Jessica Roberts, PhD, is an assistant professor of communication studies at Universidade Católica Portuguesa in Lisbon, Portugal. Her recent research on citizen journalism and social media has been published in *Journalism* and the *International Journal of Communication*. Roberts earned her PhD at the University of Maryland, her MA at the University of Southern California, and her BA at the University of Michigan.

Adam Maksl, PhD, is an associate professor of journalism and media at Indiana University Southeast, where he teaches digital journalism and social media classes, advises the multiplatform student news laboratory, and researches news and media literacy. Maksl's research has been published in top-rated journals in his field, including *Journalism & Mass Communication Quarterly; Journalism & Mass Communication Educator*; the *Journal of Media Literacy Education; Electronic News*; and *Cyberpsychology, Behavior & Social Networking*. His teaching focuses on multimedia storytelling, reporting, and communications law. Maksl has a PhD in journalism from the University of Missouri, an MA in journalism from Ball State University, and a BS in secondary journalism education from Indiana University–Bloomington.